Prais

"*SHOT* inspires through its , gritty honesty. It's a testament that hope and reconciliation can pierce through even the most tragic circumstances. What an adventure!"

— Jeremy Parsons, TV host

"Doubt can be a loud part of our lives. *SHOT* reminds me that even despite deep struggles, tribulation and questioning, God and His love will always be there. In following the story of the DeSotos, I am reminded of the importance of listening and following God's nudges. I now feel even more empowered to continue using my voice and my influence to serve and to encourage."

— Justin Rudd, Chief Inspiration Officer at JustinRudd.com, founder of Long Beach Community Action Team (CAT)

"I've known the generalities of Pete and Dara's story for a long time. But this revealing description of their impossible situation shows how almost anything in life—no matter how dire—can be endured with two simple components: faith and love."

— Gary Hoffman, host of *Gary and Shannon*, KFI AM 640

"A profound book. Incredible vulnerability, hard life lessons learned, and a beautiful story of a couple giving their life to help others. It deeply impacted me."

— Michael Goldstone, Chief Operating Officer for Regency Lighting

"I will never forget the moment I first heard that Peter had been shot. The next few days and month were full of anxiety, doubt, and anger for Peter, Dara, and everyone closest to them. This book does an excellent job recounting those difficult moments of crisis, while asking the hard question: How do you trust God again after something bad happens while obeying Him? *SHOT* captures the struggle of both Peter and Dara to understand why God called them to El Salvador, process the shooting, and ultimately rebuild trust and find rest in God."

— Ron Bueno, founder and Executive Director of ENLACE

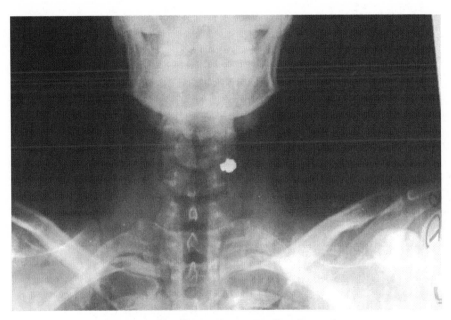

X-ray of bullet in Peter DeSoto's neck.
Taken January 18, 2007 at Ciudad Barrios medical clinic.

To the changemakers in El Salvador—both Salvadorans and foreign missionaries from around the world. Those that live each day striving to make Jesus a reality in a country wrestling with intense violence and pervasive poverty, who daily serve others without much recognition or reward, trusting that God will bless their efforts and use them to build His Kingdom.

And to all those in El Salvador whom we have heard countless times say "para servirle" *(in order to serve you), or* "Dios le bendiga" *(God bless you), this book is for you.*

AUTHOR'S NOTE

This is a work of creative nonfiction. The story spans the course of nearly four decades. To weave it all together as accurately and faithfully as possible, I relied upon hours of personal interviews and journal and blog entries from Dara and Peter DeSoto, as well as extensive research about the history and culture of El Salvador. Some time lines have been collapsed, and names of certain people have been either changed or omitted entirely to preserve their safety.

Psalm 64 & Psalm 116: A Mashup

"They shoot from ambush at the innocent;
they shoot suddenly, without fear . . .
Surely, the human mind and heart are cunning.

I love the Lord for he heard my voice;
he heard my cry for mercy . . .

I trusted in the Lord when I said,
'I am greatly afflicted';

The Lord is gracious and righteous;
our God is full of compassion . . .

All people will fear;
they will proclaim the works of God,
and ponder what He has done."

(New Living Translation)

Table of Contents

INTRODUCTION

The first time I heard Peter DeSoto speak was in the spring of 2013. I was sitting in the audience of my church and in truth, I wasn't listening. I was too busy sizing him up. He was a young man, late thirties, forty at the most. He had tan skin and dark hair and he looked healthy. *So why the voice?*

I kept pondering that question as Pete continued to speak. His words a forced whisper. They were raspy, haunting. I kept waiting for someone to explain why. *He was a chronic smoker. He was sick. He was playing a practical joke.*

And then it came. Pete said it: He had been shot in the neck. By a masked gunman.

The room went silent.

He probably should have died, except the bullet lodged in his esophagus, missing his trachea and spinal cord by one centimeter and permanently damaging his vocal cords.

I was humbled and intrigued—not just by the shooting—but by all of it. The fact that Pete had a wife and four children when it happened. That they had been missionaries in El Salvador, and that years after the incident, this man I saw standing in front of me had a rock solid faith seemingly born out of his tragic experience.

For the next two years, Pete and his wife Dara worked on staff at my church. All four of their children would help on Sunday mornings, waking up early to make coffee and set up chairs. Dara ran the children's ministry and Pete ran everything else. He gave sermons, organized community outreach events, trained volunteers, and nearly always had a smile on his face.

The more I volunteered alongside the DeSotos on Sunday mornings, the more I sensed something growing inside me. A longing of sorts.

The day Pete approached me to see if I would be interested in writing this book, he also emailed me a collection of files. One of them was a copy of Dara's journal that she kept while in El Salvador. A PDF document spanning twenty-two pages, all single spaced. No paragraph breaks.

Through reading it, a fuller version of their story began to emerge. I realized Pete and Dara weren't just the glowing, spiritual superheroes I had made them out to be in my mind. They were something better than that. They were average people with doubts and fears and messy pasts. In fact, there was a time in their lives when they were similar to me: insecure in their faith, but hoping and wishing for something stronger and more solid. Unsure how to get there, but fumbling toward that goal all the same.

It was then I became interested in telling their story. My ability to relate to them came into focus and I had what I like to call an "Amy Poehler Moment." In her memoir, *Yes Please,* Amy Poehler longs to be a successful comedian one day. She writes:

> A lot of people ask me if I always knew I was going to be on *Saturday Night Live.* I think the simple answer is: yes. I don't mean to sound cocky. I didn't know if I had the talent or drive, I just had a tiny little voice whispering inside of me . . . We all have a tiny whispery voice inside of us, but the bad ones are usually at a lower register and come through a little clearer. I don't know where the good voice came from . . . But ever since I was a small child, I would look at places where I wanted to be and believe I would eventually be on the other side of the glass.

Something about Pete and Dara's story opened me up to that whispery voice inside. It told me to keep going. Keep praying and seeking and pressing into my desire to be on the other side of the glass. With God, as opposed to peeking in from a distance and observing other people whose faith was more developed than my own.

Not an easy task. And the gnawing question at the heart of it all was whether or not it would be worth it. Is seeking God worth it if I'm not sure that I can trust Him?

Like most other things people long for in this life, it's a risk. But if you want something bad enough, you'll make the wager.

The first risk all three of us took together—Pete, Dara, and me— was doing a Kickstarter campaign to raise money for this book. If I was going to tell a story that wasn't my own, set in a country I had never stepped foot on, I was going to need a lot of information. And the best place to get it would be El Salvador. I would need to travel there, take time off of work, conduct over a dozen interviews, gain firsthand experience in Central America, and learn the art of storytelling on a much larger scale than I had done before as a freelance journalist.

Who was going to pay for all this?

Kickstarter seemed the best option, so we went for it knowing we might fail. We filmed a book trailer, created a website, and used our connections on Facebook to launch a five week campaign. Not only did we meet our goal, but we exceeded it by several thousand dollars.

In November of 2015, my husband and I flew to El Salvador with Pete and Dara, right as the country's murder rate was starting to make international headlines. While there, I was given a crash course introduction to El Salvador's two rival gangs, MS-13 and Barrio 18. I retraced Pete's steps on the day he was shot, stayed in one of the houses where he used to live, and interviewed many of his Salvadoran friends and coworkers. I got to meet Dara's former Spanish teacher Marlena, and hear about her father getting kidnapped by a death squad during El Salvador's civil war.

I had no idea what death squads were, so I started researching. I read Joan Didion's account of being a war reporter in El Salvador back in 1982. I read historical novels and anthropological studies on the country. I watched documentaries. I continued to interview eyewitnesses of Pete's shooting. The more I learned, the more I realized the depth and breadth of what this story contained.

This wasn't just a narrative about a couple, this was a narrative about a country, too.

I began to see ways that the stories overlapped—how the people of El Salvador were in a fierce process of longing and searching all their own. How they were pressed up against dread, day after day. Violence and fear surrounding them on all sides. In a country plagued by natural disasters, intense poverty, and gang violence, every day felt more volatile than the last.

In the face of it all, the question of hope kept emerging. How do we capture it? How do we find it? How do we continue to long for something when there is zero evidence we may ever get it?

I don't know what it is you long for. But my hope, *our hope*, is that this book would spur you toward it as you wrestle and seek and question and search. If there's one thing Pete and Dara have taught me and that I have found throughout my own faith walk, it's the art of perseverance. The art of continuing even when it seems you cannot do it anymore because that moment you most want to quit might be the very thing that propels you forward—to the other side of the glass.

PROLOGUE

January 18, 2007

Los Abelines, El Salvador

The steering wheel vibrated, sending a series of tingling sensations through Peter DeSoto's fingertips. He tightened his grip and began the sharp, slow turn required to guide his Nissan Patrol through the bumpy contours of the Salvadoran jungle. He had driven this road several times now—the road from Abelines to San Salvador—and the magic of it was that every trip had been different. The muddy pathways forever morphing in unpredictable ways.

Pete glanced in the rearview mirror and caught the blurry reflection of his passengers in the backseat. His friend and co-worker Absalon had closed his eyes and leaned his head against the seat. The white cords of his headphones dangled from his ears. Next to him Dr. Mireia was staring out the window, perhaps recalling the many people she had treated that afternoon at the clinic Pete and his colleagues were helping to build.

A stray branch scratched across the front windshield and as the Nissan Patrol inched itself around yet another blind corner, Pete was startled by a shrill scream, like a wounded animal gone mad.

The noise was coming from a male whose frame and height were small, like that of a teenager. His entire face was covered by a black mask and he was holding a .22 caliber rifle. He was close enough for Pete to see his muddy brown eyes. They bore into him from behind the mask and told a story Peter knew not how to translate.

"*Bájate!*" someone yelled from the backseat. "Get down!"

POP! POP! POP! POP! POP! A barrage of bullets pierced the door and blew through the car window. Pete heard the ping of metal on metal and felt a sharp burning sensation in his neck, like a glowing orange cattle prong had seared his flesh and was getting hotter with every second.

The door behind Pete shook with the force of another bullet landing right below the window pane, forcing the glass to crack in one loud break.

"Get out!" Absalon yelled. "Open the door and get on the ground."

Pete scrambled over the front seat, droplets of blood sprinkling across the gray interior. Clouds of dust rose up as he fell to his knees next to the Nissan.

The blood gushed from his neck in a warm and steady trickle. Without even thinking, his hand went straight for the wound. *Must stop the bleeding. Must stop the bleeding.* Yet, even that Pete couldn't control. The blood seeped past any barrier he tried to create. His eyes widened as he opened his mouth to inhale, but the air around him wasn't cooperating. His mind told him to breath deeper, suck in more oxygen, as if he were on a treadmill at the gym. But still the air evaded him. His chest tightened and he could feel his head growing dizzy.

Pete closed his eyes and managed a raspy gulp of air. *Please help me*, he prayed. A calmness began to wash over him. The gut wrenching scream of that man, the brown eyes, the ski mask, the sound of the bullets blasting through the glass—all of it grew dim, giving way to total and complete silence.

PART ONE

LONGING

In youth, longing can feel romantic.
As years go by, it loses its luster when our desires both magnify in importance, yet decrease in likelihood.

The shape of longing shifts again in old age, as we long less for things we haven't experienced, than for things we have. We long for lost relationships, for beautiful moments in time.

But longing is never something we finish. It forever and always is.
The only question is what to do with it.

CHAPTER 1

The Road to Abelines

El Salvador, 2003

The village of Los Abelines cannot be found on any maps. There are no highway signs detailing how many miles it will take to reach it, nor will there be any welcome signs announcing your arrival. You would be lucky, in fact, if you didn't miss the turn off for the unpaved road leading deep into the volcanic hillsides where Abelines towers over the lush valleys of El Salvador that border Honduras.

Of all the thousands of people living in the Abelines region, not one of them will say that it is an easy journey to get in and out. One must climb a narrow winding road "paved" with uneven rocks. The road's dips and curves are ever surprising, ever evolving, depending upon how the rain molds and shapes them over time. The path is surrounded by tropical plants reaching to the sky, by mossy boulders and strands of ivy, hanging freely. Yellow butterflies dance along the green walls and the soil below is a dusty rose, marred and tinted by the continuous rain of blood that's been shed on it over the past century. Blood that runs deep in an intricate web of veins.

The road to Abelines requires crossing two shallow rivers, neither of which have bridges. At times, the road hugs the encroaching cliff side where drivers dare not let their eyes peer downwards into the echoing jungle below. The reward will come later though, at the top of the hill when that first glimpse of the panorama unfolds.

Imagine the greenest mountains ever seen and multiply them by infinity. Like a child standing on top of the world and marveling at how great and wide and perfect it all is.

And then the rain will come.

For an American man named Peter DeSoto, this was rain like he had never experienced before. It arrived in thunderous bursts, creating an orchestra all its own, clapping against terracotta rooftops and turning the ground to mush. It splattered and danced and roared across the endless green valleys that began in El Salvador and continued on into the neighboring countries of Nicaragua and Honduras.

Pete stood alone in an adobe church and listened as the storm continued its thunderous song. He closed his eyes, and as the sound pored over him, he felt something moving deep inside. It was welling up in his chest and gaining strength like a crescendo. In a moment, he felt as though he was going to burst from the insides, his desire was so strong.

He didn't want to go home.

Pete blinked and noted a small brown scorpion scurrying across the edge of the concrete floor. *Apparently I'll be praying with my eyes open today,* he thought. The scorpion population was unnerving, as were many things he had experienced so far: The children's bellies swollen from malnutrition. The man at the clinic with a tumor the size of a boulder attached to his abdomen and wrapping around his back. Like the others Peter had encountered in this community of Abelines, the man's head hung low, eyes focused downward.

It was hard to stomach a place so devoid of hope.

Large drops of water formed at the crack inside the ceiling of the windowless church and plopped into the wooden bucket placed underneath it. The plopping grew more consistent as the rain picked up speed.

He didn't want to go home. *Was that it?*

No, not exactly. His wife Dara was at home in the United States and Pete had been missing her every minute of the last week in El Salvador. He couldn't wait to get back to her and all three of their kids, PJ, Isaac, and Hannah. PJ was their oldest and he was five already, as hard as that was to believe. Hannah, their youngest, was less than a year old, and Isaac was three. It was a house full of chaos, but it was beautiful, nonetheless. A cottage home in the suburbs outside of Los Angeles. It was nestled in a cul-de-sac in the city of Valencia, a city that had recently adopted the tagline "Just another day in Awesometown."

Each street perfectly manicured, lined with emerald lawns and chaparral landscaping. Not a bad place to return to, indeed.

But, yet.

Pete watched as the scorpion continued its trajectory from the makeshift wooden pulpit to the patch of daylight flooding in through the doorway. The leaking ceiling continued to drip, and his attention shifted from the scorpion to the leak and back again. The absurdity of this scene made Pete laugh. *How was it even possible?* After a week of being in El Salvador and building latrines—hauling cement up steep hillsides, digging muddy ditches, wiping sweat from his forehead in the thick, humid air, swatting mosquitoes, and fighting the pain that began to spread across his lower back and shoulders, as his body was more accustomed to sitting at a desk than performing manual labor—how was it possible this had been one of the best weeks of his life?

The rain continued in its intensity. As Pete looked around the dark, adobe church, he thought of Pastor Victorio Paz who preached here every Sunday. Pastor Victorio who stood all of five feet tall, with a gray cowboy hat and a square chunk of a mustache decorating the top of his lip. The mustache was something Pete just couldn't get over. As inappropriate as it sounded, the guy looked like a mini-Latin Hitler with that thing. Except his eyes were much kinder, of course, and his smile more sincere. But that mustache.

Pete wanted to joke with Victorio about it. The joke was on the tip of his tongue one day as they were working side-by-side, but he knew he couldn't yet. Maybe one day when they knew each other better. One day when Pete and his family lived and worked in El Salvador as missionaries . . .

That was really what he was after, wasn't it? That's what the desire welling inside his chest was calling him to right now, like a whisper of an invitation.

"Church is about serving," Pete's father, John DeSoto had said. As a pastor of a small church outside San Diego, John's action echoed the sentiment.

Throughout his childhood, Pete and his younger brother Matt had awoken with the sun every Sunday. They climbed into John's pickup truck to be shuttled to the school where Mira Mesa First Assembly held their weekly worship gatherings. Pete unlocked the closet doors behind the stage and began unloading the requisite coffee shuttles and signs pointing parents to the children's ministry. They set up row after row of heavy metal chairs arranged into less than perfect lines. A few bars of piano flooded the room and the worship team belted out the opening verses to whatever songs they planned to sing once services began.

When all was set into place—the weekly bulletins folded, the grape juice poured into tiny plastic cups for communion, the offering baskets lined up and ready to be passed—it was time to hop back in the pickup truck and make the rounds. They stopped at the houses of people who didn't have cars or adequate transportation to church because they were unemployed, had recently gotten out of jail, or were fleeing from domestic abuse. While Christian culture in the early 1980s (and really Christian culture anytime throughout the centuries) hasn't always been welcoming to those with messy lives, Pastor John DeSoto did his best to welcome everyone. John himself was a former hippie, a protester, a radicalist with long hair and sideburns who once hitchhiked 600 miles to attend a rock concert.

In terms of personality and background, John DeSoto and Pastor Victorio couldn't have been more different, but when it came to their visions of church, that was where Pete saw them intersecting. Pete's fondest memory of his dad's church was the sense of family they had created over those first ten years. It began with simple acts of service and took root in games of softball in the park. Independence Day picnics on Mira Mar Navel Base, with water balloon fights and wheelbarrow races. It deepened further in hospital rooms, as John and the boys came to pray with people through their pain.

"The best thing you can do as a pastor is show up," John told his boys.

And the DeSotos always did show up. For birthday parties and funerals and weddings and whenever people needed help moving, which was often. John and the boys showed up with the truck to load boxes and bed frames and clunky television sets.

Why did they do this? Because Jesus was nothing if not practical. More than He was moralizing or finger-pointing, Jesus was practical in that He met people exactly where they were and asked, "How can I help?"

It was through these acts of service, John taught Pete and Matt, that the people Jesus encountered felt loved. Once they felt loved, something inside them opened up in a brand new way.

Victorio was trying to do something similar here in Abelines, in his community of farmers and peasants, many of whom had a third grade education at most. This was the region of El Salvador hit hardest by the twelve year civil war, spanning from 1980-1992. It was the hub of the guerrilla uprising against the Salvadoran government and the wealthy plantation owners, and it was located about thirty miles outside Abelines. There was still a crashed helicopter buried in the surrounding jungle, right next to the former headquarters of *Radio Venceramos*, an illegal broadcast from the government's opposition. People were arrested or killed if found listening to Radio Venceramos during the war, but now it was a tourist site. If tourists ever came to El Salvador. Generally they did not, save a few adventurous backpackers with *Lonely Planet Guides* advising them to visit the War museum in El Mozote and learn of the 75,000 Salvadorans who were killed.

Even after all that violence, many people remained poverty-stricken and praying for their next meal, praying that someday they might have fair wages and running water in their villages.

Seventy-five thousand deaths, over a decade gone by, and still nothing to show for it besides echoes of the war everywhere Peter looked. It was in the people's eyes, their hunched shoulders, their sullen faces searching for hope. *Who wouldn't want to give up?*

Victorio, perhaps. Victorio who seemed relentless in his optimism. If Pastor Victorio made $100 worth of income in an entire month, he considered that a blessing and continued to serve his family and community with a joyful smile that felt like a promise. A promise that tiny strings of faith might actually move this decaying mountain called Los Abelines and transform it into something new.

Pete surveyed the interior of the leaking church. To be able to do that in Abelines—for Pete to actually be a part of it, living and working here in El Salvador—was one of the most inspiring prospects he could imagine.

The question, of course, was how.

Pete gazed across the rainy mountaintops and felt a mixture of elation and sadness.

Do you trust Me?

The words flashed across his brain, not in the form of an audible voice, but more like a question welling inside him.

Do you trust Me, Peter?

He looked down. "No, I don't," he said aloud.

The thought stung a bit.

"But I want to."

The rain quieted itself. Just as quickly as it had come, it began to fade until the only sound remaining was a persistent dripping from the orange rooftops.

CHAPTER 2

Earthquakes

El Salvador, 2001

The country of El Salvador is nicknamed *el Valle de la Hamacas,* the Valley of the Hammocks. An indigenous Indian tribe, the Pipil, dubbed it so after centuries of dwelling in a mountainous region subject to frequent earthquakes and volcanic eruptions. They found their lives were always swaying, always swinging, like a hammock hung from two trees. Back and forth, back and forth their entire world rocked. What the Pipil may not have known was that all of El Salvador is like this, not just their tiny region.

The whole country, roughly the size of Massachusetts, lies atop three tectonic plates that attract each other like magnets. They creep and crawl, sometimes crashing together, other times sliding on top of the other, resulting in earthquakes of varying magnitudes.

But while hammocks are firmly anchored and designed to withstand such rocking, a country most certainly is not.

In January and February of 2001, El Salvador experienced two of the most devastating earthquakes ever recorded there. The first came on January 13th and registered a magnitude of 7.7 on the Richter scale. It was followed by an estimated 2,000 aftershocks. For the entire month of January, the country of El Salvador shook. It shook and it shook and the feeling of insecurity grew. With each tremor, the hope for normalcy and stability grew more elusive, as though a bolt in the world had been permanently loosened.

The mountains trembled and chunks of rock broke apart and fell. Down, down, down the earth fell, gaining momentum as it landed, toppling ceilings, walls, and rooftops. Foundations cracked and faltered and the very homes where people crafted their lives seemed to betray them as everything came crashing and buried them as they slept.

From January to February, the land would not rest, and all the turmoil is thought to have triggered massive earthquake number two.

On February 13, 2001, exactly one month to the day from the first, another earthquake, this one measuring 6.6 on the Richter scale, hit El Salvador.

In the midst of it all, a young woman named Lori Margaret arrived with a group of relief volunteers and was greeted by Salvadorans with hollow eyes. She noted how they moved and breathed—their hearts continuing to beat—yet, their spirits were nowhere to be found.

Lori envisioned these spirits floating high into the sky, like pillars of smoke rising from the tops of the volcanoes.

As she peered into their hollow eyes, Lori knew not how to respond. A loving hand on a shoulder? A spirit-catching net that could reach high enough to pull them all down and give them back to their owners, one by one?

The goal of her relief team was more grounded and practical, of course. They were there to clean up, rebuild, bring supplies, and ensure the Salvadorans had all their basic needs met. Food. Water. Clothing. Shelter. Everything that had been ripped away from them.

The tangible stuff was easy, Lori thought. But how does one locate and carry hope?

CHAPTER 3

College Sweethearts

Vanguard University, 1994

Before the rainstorm in Abelines, before Pete and Dara sold everything they owned and moved their family of six to El Salvador, and most certainly before Pete found himself face-to-face with a masked gunman pointing a .22 caliber rifle in his direction, Peter and Dara's journey began with a simple love story.

And the love story began with a phone call.

Pete almost missed it, as the whirring of the cordless phone was in direct competition with U2's *Joshua Tree* album blasting against the painted brick walls of his college dorm room.

As the chorus ended, Bono's voice gave way to the slow strumming of guitars and Pete noted a ringing sound seeping into the melody. With a quick sweep of his hand, Pete lowered the volume on his boom box and picked up the receiver.

"Is Aaron there?" Dara asked on the other end.

"Nope," Pete answered, taking a swig of Lemonade Snapple. "Want to leave a message?"

"Please," Dara said, cradling the phone between her neck and shoulder as she kicked off her slip resistant shoes.

What was it Aaron had called her about? She tried to remember as she sat down on the edge of her bed and massaged the balls of her feet. They felt tender and tight from waiting tables for the last five hours. *Something about borrowing her notes from class, maybe? Or was it borrowing something else?*

"Just let him know Dara called."

"Got it," Pete said, scanning the room for a pen and paper. He traced the letters of Dara's name onto an orange Post-it note, and as he did, he got an instant visual of the girl from the campus cafeteria talking to his roommate, Aaron. She was wearing a long, flowery dress that day. Blonde hair tumbling down her back.

Pete had stuck his hand out to introduce himself across the dining table, over a half-eaten plate of french fries dipped in Ranch. Dara smiled as she shook his hand, noting that he seemed like quite a gentleman.

As their eyes met, Dara wondered: *Was he smart, too?*

That Pete was fun and energetic, Dara had already noticed, as it was hard not to on a private Christian campus of only a thousand students. Earlier in the semester, she had been walking to class and witnessed a guy with the same dark hair and olive skin as Pete climbing out the back window of a classroom that was still in session. She paused, clutching her textbooks to her chest and waiting to see what he would do next.

Pete ducked quickly under the window. With his back hunched and knees bent at near ninety degree angles, he waddled himself to the edge of the building and broke into a run. His legs carried him straight to the volleyball game that was already in progress on the other side of the quad.

"DeSoto!" one of the players shouted, and motioned for him to join.

A massive smile broke upon Pete's lips as his feet hit the grass and his eyes began to follow the ball. Dara looked back at Pete's professor, still lecturing in front of the classroom. The students scribbling notes. She observed the determined look on Pete's face as he dove for the ball. Even from a distance, she sensed his freedom, his focus, his joy. As though the classroom he just escaped from were a million miles away.

"Dara!" Pete said into the receiver with a tad more enthusiasm than was necessary. "This is Pete DeSoto, Aaron's roommate."

"That's right," she said, getting an instant visual of him climbing out the classroom window.

An awkward silence filled the phone line.

Did he care about more than ditching class and playing volleyball?

Dara crossed her legs, leaned back against the pillows on her bed, and figured there was no time like the present to find out.

"What are you up to?" she asked.

And Pete told her. About the Anthropology exam he was studying for, about his favorite professor who had grown up in El Salvador, and about how it was his mother's advice that first led him to become an Anthropology major upon transferring to Vanguard. He had been sitting at his parents' kitchen table for several hours. The pads of his right thumb and index finger were smudged with ink from leafing through page after page of the course catalog. His mother had come up behind him and placed a hand on his shoulder.

"Choose classes that make your heart come alive," she advised.

Pete knew right away which classes those were. They had appeared in the 'A' section under a subject he had never heard of called Anthropology. Each class summary highlighted a different topic that piqued Pete's interest. Words like history, people, philosophy, psychology, archaeology. He had always wanted to travel abroad, to learn another language, and to imitate the life of Harrison Ford in *Raiders of the Lost Ark*. Studying Anthropology seemed to be the closest he would get.

The more Pete learned, the more he felt like he was unlocking the keys to the universe. His textbooks taught him of science and culture and the very foundations of human existence.

The conversation continued and Dara told Pete about her family. How she was an only child and that her parents had fought a lot growing up. They had separated and gotten back together, then separated again. She told Pete about the crazy lunch rush at the seafood restaurant where she worked, how it all became a blur of balancing sodas on trays, swiping credit cards, delivering sides of cocktail sauce.

They talked and they talked and they talked as the sun traced its path across the Southern California sky. When it fell below the horizon line, Pete and Dara finally said their goodbyes.

"You've sure had that phone line tied up for a long while," Debbie Aiklen said, as her daughter Dara emerged from her bedroom.

Dara smiled and looked to the floor. In her head she thought, *I think I may have found the man I'm going to marry.*

A week later, Dara asked Pete to go out on a date. She even footed the bill. It only seemed fitting, since she was two years older than he was and she was the one with a job. Pete said yes, and they ate lunch at a Chinese restaurant off the Pacific Coast Highway in Newport Beach. They ate egg rolls dipped in soy sauce followed by plates of chow mein and sticky spoonfuls of sweet and sour chicken.

One month later, they became boyfriend and girlfriend, and two years after that, husband and wife. They got married at an Episcopalian church in La Jolla with palm trees out front and a view of the rolling Pacific Ocean. Pete was 21 years old at the time and Dara was 23. They kissed and danced and drank sparkling cider out of plastic cups.

When they set off for their month-long honeymoon—half in Hawaii and half in Lake Tahoe—Pete was already dreaming of graduate school. On the drive home from Tahoe to Newport Beach, he arranged a pit stop in the Bay Area to check out the Anthropology program at UC Berkeley. There were several universities on his radar and he spent the next several months working tirelessly to complete PhD applications for each and every one. Pete was prepared to uproot his life, if necessary, and move across the country for whatever program would take him.

The one twist Pete hadn't prepared for came shortly after his and Dara's first Valentine's Day together as newlyweds.

It was a Saturday in February of 1997. Pete was playing basketball with some friends and Dara was thrusting her head over the toilet for the second time that day. She didn't have a fever and yet she was nauseated.

"Keep in mind that you could and very well might get pregnant the first time you have sex," Dara's mother had warned her, time and again as a teenager. "So make sure you're married and make sure you love the guy."

Advice Debbie Aicklen only wished someone had told her when she was 19 years old. All it took was that one time and Debbie had found herself, along with Dara's father, in a situation that they had no idea how to handle.

Dara kept her mother's warning tucked inside her as she walked to the drugstore and bought a pregnancy test. The words grew in strength and power, becoming a tangible force inside the bathroom as Dara looked at the results and noted the blue plus sign slowly emerge.

She drew in a breath and held the air in her lungs, afraid of what might happen if she let it go. This was real.

And it wasn't that Dara didn't want the baby. On the contrary, being a mother was the one thing Dara had always thought she might love and also be good at. It felt overwhelming and beautiful, like a call to something important.

She broke the news to Pete that afternoon and they both just looked at each other in dumbfounded silence.

They would tell no one, they decided, until the following week when they were scheduled to go camping with Dara's parents.

In the meantime, several days went by and a letter arrived in the mail from American University. It was Pete's number one choice for PhD programs, as his professor, Ron Bueno had gone there, and his good friend Jamie Huff was currently working on his doctorate there in Anthropology. To study at A.U. would be an honor. Even in spite of the baby news, Pete still secretly hoped for an acceptance.

"Are you going to open it?" Dara asked, eyeing the envelope in his hand and noting how its contents made her stomach turn even more violently than her usual morning sickness.

Pete paused. "Let's wait until this weekend," he decided. "We can open it while we're camping with your parents in Carlsbad."

Dara forced a smile and tried to imagine herself giving birth at some stark hospital in Washington DC, millions of miles away from her friends, her family, and all she had ever known.

The clouds hung low over the sleepy beach town of Carlsbad, California. It was almost March and the morning air was chilly and damp. Dara sat on top of a beach blanket and dug her toes into the cold sand. Neither she nor Pete slept much that morning. As the evening's darkness had given way to light, Pete awoke and retrieved the envelop from his backpack, breaking the university seal that held it closed.

His eyes scanned the opening sentence, "We are pleased to offer you . . ." and then the words "full scholarship" popped out from the text.

Pete dropped the letter on top of his sleeping bag and sat up straight. The Anthropology program only admitted five PhD students. Not only was he one of them, but they were also offering him a full scholarship. It was all together better than he could have imagined and all together worse.

"You got in," Dara mumbled, picking up the letter and reading it for herself. She had known he was accepted already. She knew it in her bones and in the literal thickness of the envelope. She had been staring at it for days now. Thick and foreboding. Dara placed her other hand along her belly, marveling at the microscopic child that was growing inside her.

"It doesn't matter," Pete said. "I can't do it."

"Wait . . ." Dara said, trying to catch his eyes.

She reached out to stop him from getting up, but Pete inched himself away from her and made a beeline for his wet suit. It lay limp, like a puddle of black neoprene spread over the wooden picnic table at their campsite.

"I'm going surfing," he said, as though talking to no one.

Dara felt a panic rising inside her and knew she needed a ritual of her own to try to process this. She opened a packet of instant coffee and poured several cups worth of water into the Jet Boiler. Her father would be waking soon to go surf with Pete, and then her mother would begin making breakfast. In the meantime, the morning was all hers, so she poured a cup of steaming water over the decaf grounds and watched them dissolve into a frothy brown liquid. She grabbed her Bible and a blanket and found a space on the sand.

The tide was high this morning as she stared out at the ocean. The waves, quick and powerful. They beat against the shoreline, sending a gust of foam into the sky. Just watching them gave Dara a sense of powerlessness.

She opened up her Bible to John 13 and read Jesus' words to His disciples the night before He was crucified. "You do not realize now what I am doing, but later you will understand."

Dara laughed. It was like the understatement of the century. Jesus' parables were confusing and His actions ran contrary to both tradition and social customs. The disciples rarely ever understood what Jesus was doing, and frankly, neither did she.

Dara felt a torrent of emotions, each tugging and pulling her in a different direction. Pete said he was going to turn down this scholarship, but how could she let him? For the first time since her wedding day, Dara felt the weight of marriage. It wasn't an awful weight, nor was it too difficult to carry. But the heaviness of it—the responsibility, the giving over of herself—was scarier than she anticipated.

Fear collected in her stomach. The same familiar way it had when she was younger.

Few people knew this about Dara, but she had always been fearful and was fabulous at hiding it. Hiding fear was something she had gotten paid for. She had won awards for it and made an entire career out of it from ages four through eighteen.

It had started in preschool when one of Dara's friends won first place in a beauty pageant for little girls.

"Why doesn't Dara try out?" her friend's mother suggested. "The girls can compete together. It'll be fun!"

The year was 1976. Reality television had yet to be invented, which meant shows like *Toddlers & Tiaras* were not a part of public consciousness. There wasn't a bounty of Internet articles for Dara's mother to read about child beauty pageants and their potential harm, no social media forums—nothing but an assertive young mother from Texas who stood before Debbie Aiklen and declared, "Our daughters should do the next pageant together. We'll even lend Dara a dress."

And so they did. Except, this time Dara won.

She beat out her friend and all the other, heavily made-up children who had been primped and primed, practicing with their mothers and coaches for months on end. Dara was the underdog who knew nothing of poise or stage presence, but when she stood in front of those judges with her gap-toothed grin, they couldn't get enough. She was a natural.

When Debbie Aiklen realized her daughter's potential, she did what she figured any good mother would do: she nurtured it. She signed Dara up for one pageant after the next, allowing the other children's mothers to be her guide. When the other mothers enrolled their daughters in Russian ballet classes to improve posture, Debbie did the same. When they sought big, fancy agents for their kids to model in Hollywood, Debbie wanted Dara to follow suit.

By the age of six, Dara was working professionally. She didn't play Barbies, and she didn't watch Saturday morning cartoons. She went to photo shoots and go-sees. She learned and perfected the art of performance, the art of pleasing everyone around her. Yet, underneath it all was a growing fear. She could bury it, throw makeup on top of it, win another crown or the chance to model in a coveted print ad, but the fear always remained.

Will it ever go away? Dara wondered. The waves continued their rhythmic rushing sound and she stared at the horizon line, clutching her coffee mug and allowing the words to settle into her mind.

You do not realize now what I am doing, but later you will understand.

The knot in Dara's stomach loosened as she closed her eyes and felt the wind blow across her face. All she had ever wanted was a simple life. Not fame, not glamour, not money. Not even grand adventure, like Pete always craved. At the bottom of her heart was the desire to be a mom. To own a home with a big yard where her kids could play. Maybe a swing in the back and a porch where she could do exactly this—sit and pray and drink her morning coffee.

And here she was, getting the first part of her dream. Her spine tingled with the very thought of this baby. It was electrifying, beautiful, mysterious. But the setting for her entry to motherhood was off. Dara tried to imagine herself and Pete living in Washington D.C. She pictured the city she had seen in movies. The White House surrounded by snowy streets.

Dara didn't even own a pair of closed-toe shoes.

She felt another tingling sensation. This one she had experienced before and was beginning to recognize as the Holy Spirit.

Maybe.

Who could tell these things for certain?

She sensed it was prompting her to simply trust, like the disciples who didn't understand what Jesus was doing, but followed him nonetheless.

In the distance, Pete and Dara's father Dan emerged from the ocean in twin black wet suits, surfboards anchored at their hips. She watched Pete's face as they approached, his demeanor more relaxed than it had been earlier. He laid his surfboard on the sand and leaned down to give Dara a kiss. His lips tasted of saltwater and seaweed and the love she felt for him was so big, it barely fit inside her heart.

Her father, Dan Aiklen, watched the two of them and smiled. "I think I'll go check on your mother," he told Dara.

He turned toward the trailer where his wife Debbie was cooking breakfast and padded slowly across the sand.

Dara waited until her father was out of earshot and turned to Pete. "I think you should take the scholarship."

"You're sure about that?"

Dara nodded, pushing back against the fear.

Pete looked amused. "Your dad said the same thing. He said it's worth a try and that I shouldn't give up the opportunity."

"Did you tell him about the baby?"

"Yup."

Pete was quiet, his adrenaline building with each passing thought. Not only was he going to be a dad, but he had been handed a golden ticket to the exact future he always hoped for. Life was good. So good, he could hardly contain himself.

He placed his hand on Dara's stomach, noting its flatness, noting the absurdity that a little person was actually being formed there even as they sat on the sand. "I know this isn't exactly the way we planned, but I have a good feeling about it."

"We'll make it work somehow," she agreed.

Pete thought for a moment, and with all the wisdom of a 22-year-old, he added, "Of course we will! Kids can't change things that much."

CHAPTER 4

Meet the Lombardos

Hollister, California, 1982

Nestled in the sloping hillsides of Central California, the Pacheco Valley is an agricultural hub where avocados grow like wildflowers and migrant workers toil in the sun. It's a fertile country, kissing the borders of Gilroy, Salinas, and Monterey—small farming towns made famous as the settings of John Steinbeck novels.

In 1908, a family of Italian immigrants planted their first cherry orchards off the Pacheco Pass Highway and decades later, expanded them into a fruit stand, campground, and RV park called Casa de Fruta. Families stopped in while journeying from San Francisco to Yosemite. Some stopped briefly to buy vine-ripened tomatoes and artichokes the size of their fists. Others would camp for several days, letting their children play in the pool, go on hayrides, or visit the petting zoo.

One such family that came to Casa de Fruta was the Aiklens. In 1982, Dan and Debbie Aiklen brought their 9-year-old daughter, Dara, to spend the summer living there while Dan was working as an electrician in Monterey Bay. One afternoon, while Dara was swimming at the community pool, she noticed two, toe-headed boys splashing around with floaties around their arms. They were taking turns climbing to the top of the steps and then launching their 3 and 4-year-old bodies into the shallow end. With each jump, they would let out a giggle, and it made Dara want to swim over and protect them. To ensure their sweet laughter would continue and not lead to any quick slips, or skinned knees.

"Be careful," Dara said gently, swimming over to what looked to be the younger of these two blonde brothers. His skinny legs were bent and his body was arching toward the water.

"Watch this," he said to Dara, spinning himself in a half turn and landing backwards in the pool.

Dara smiled and lifted her hand up for a high-five. "Very nice," she said.

The boy met her hand with his tiny palm in a loud clap.

From the poolside, the boys' mother sat, watching this exchange and wondering who this sweet girl was that had taken a liking to her boys. Like a slender fish in a solid black one-piece bathing suit, the girl had tan skin and blonde hair that was turning a dull green color from the chlorine in the pool. She looked at least twice the age of the boys and appeared to be swimming by herself. She also appeared to have quite the nurturing impulse.

She looked to be what, eight or nine years old? *Certainly, she couldn't be more than that,* the woman thought. The woman lifted herself up from the reclining lounge chair and squatted down by the edge of the pool.

"Hey, sweetheart," she said. "What's your name?"

"I'm Dara."

"Hello, Dara. My name is Cindi." She extended her hand to Dara as she would to an adult. "Cindi Sue Lombardo."

"Nice to meet you," Dara said, offering a small, wet palm. "I'm Dara Ann Aiklen."

"Dara Ann," Cindi repeated. "That's a beautiful name."

Dara beamed.

"And have you two gentlemen introduced yourselves?" Cinid asked her sons.

"I'm Guiseppe Domiono Michael Lombardo III," said the older one, standing proud and tall.

"And I'm Antonio Michael Vincente Lombardo I," said the other, mimicking his brother.

Dara's eyes widened and she looked at Cindi. "Those are really long names!"

Cindi laughed. "Call him Nino, and him Guiseppe," she said.

For the rest of the summer, Dara tagged along with Cindi, Nino, and Guiseppe as though she were a natural extension of their family. Together they took trips to the petting zoo, ate meals, and sang songs about Bible stories that Cindi taught them.

Cindi was a young mom in her mid-twenties. She had chocolate colored eyes and wavy blonde hair. She graduated from Bible college only a few years earlier, and it was there she studied both Greek and Hebrew and discovered her love for reading Scripture. Once, she came across a verse in 2 Timothy about weak-minded men and women, and she asked God in prayer, "What makes people weak-minded?" The answer she felt He gave her was *Not knowing my Word.*

Cindi then vowed to study God's Word with fervor, and passed all she learned on to her boys, who even at the ages of 3 and 4, had over 30 different Bible verses memorized. Cindi and her husband Butch were from Kansas and had also come to Casa de Fruta because Butch had taken a temporary job in Monterey Bay.

What Dara loved about Cindi was that she was kind and did fun things most other mothers wouldn't ever try. On several afternoons, Cindi lugged a picnic table underneath a massive oak tree and used it to climb to the lowest, sturdiest branch she could find. From there, she hoisted blankets over the branches and lifted the children up, one by one, until Dara, Guiseppe, and Nino were all leaning against her, staring out at Casa de Fruta like kings and queens of the world. The hay colored hills of the Pacheco Mountains surrounded them in the distance, and Cindi read Bible stories and sang her own rendition of "Mary Had a Little Lamb":

> Mary had a little lamb
> Whose heart was pure as gold.
> Ever since the dawn of time,
> His story has been told.
> He lived his life so full of love
> That all the world could see.
> And then this lamb laid down his life
> And died for you and me.
> Baa, baa, little lamb, born in Bethlehem.
> Baa, baa, little lamb, he died and rose again.

By the time Cindi finished singing, both boys were asleep, leaning against their mother and taking small, peaceful breaths. Dara looked at them from her tree branch, hummed the tune Cindi had just finished, and thought how this was exactly the type of mother she wanted to be when she grew up.

As the summer came to a close, the Aiklens went back to their Southern California home, but they vowed to keep in touch with the Lombardos as best they could. Two years later, Cindi called Dara and gave her the news that her husband Butch had been offered a job in Huntington Beach and he was going to take it, which meant they would be moving only one city over from where Dara and her parents lived.

For the next four years, the Aiklens and Lombardos hung out every week.

Dara and Cindi baked bread together while Nino and Giuseppe played in the yard. Dara watched Cindi closely as she added sugar and warm water to the yeast, waiting for it to proof.

"How do you know when it's ready?" Dara asked.

Cindi explained each step, from the kneading of the bread, to the many hours of patience it took to wait for it to rise. Whenever Dara didn't understand something, she tapped Cindi's elbow and asked her to do it again. Asked her why. Asked her how. Dara was always asking questions, and as Cindi had no daughters of her own, she was more than happy to answer them.

As Nino and Guiseppe grew to the ages of seven and nine, Cindi became adamant that they learn to be gentlemen. When the foursome set out to go anywhere, be it the park, the beach, the mall, or the grocery store, the boys charged ahead, running to the car and climbing into the backseat.

"Excuse me!" Cindi shouted after them, urging Dara to stay put at her side.

Dara watched as the look of recognition came upon Nino and Guiseppe's guilty faces.

"What did you forget?" Cindi asked, hands on hips, eyes meaning business.

The door to the backseat swung open and the two brothers raced each other to the passenger side where the first one to get there opened the door as the other motioned for Dara to step inside.

Dara smiled, took her seat inside the car, and waited as the boys closed the door behind her.

"That's more like it," Cindi said.

Dara loved the stability of the Lombardo family, the peace and love and discipline they provided. It was a stark contrast to her own home, which was filled more often than not with chaos and fighting.

Dan and Debbie loved their daughter more than anything, and did the best they could to get along with each other for her sake. They wanted their daughter to feel safe, they wanted to give her a stable home, and they tried over and over again to make their marriage work. But each attempt ended in angry outbursts. It ended in accusations and threats and the decision to "take a break" for the umpteenth time.

When Dara turned fifteen, the Lombardo family left Huntington Beach and moved back to Kansas. Dara cried in her room for hours.

"No matter where we go, we will always be in each other's lives," Cindi promised.

And she meant it.

Throughout high school, Dara flew to Kansas to spend weeks of her summer break with them. When she and Pete got married, Nino and Guiseppe—grown men who now towered over Dara with their six-foot frames—filled in as altar boys and ushers.

And in December of 1997, as Dara laid in bed at the birthing center in Bethesda, Maryland, about to give birth to her first son, the thought that kept her calm was an image of herself, holding her newborn in her arms at night and singing "Mary Had a Little Lamb" while his eyes got droopy and he drifted off to sleep.

CHAPTER 5

The Birth of a Salesman

Washington, D.C., 1998

"First things, first: Lay the receiving blanket down like a diamond," Scott Anderson said as he smoothed the pale blue cloth across Dara and Pete's dining room table.

Dara watched closely, feeling the weight of PJ, her eight pound newborn, grow heavier by the minute as she cradled him across her shoulder.

Scott folded the top corner of the blanket downward and then turned to Dara.

"Now I'm ready for this little guy." He smiled and continued narrating the swaddling process, grabbing PJ from Dara's arms and placing him in the middle of the diamond shaped blanket.

"Babies love being swaddled for so many reasons," Scott explained.

And Scott would know. Although he had no children of his own yet, he had grown up on a farm in rural Montana, the oldest of six siblings. Just watching him with PJ put Dara at ease. Here was someone who actually *knew* what to do with her baby. Who held him with confidence, having arrived on her doorstep with an arsenal of techniques, far superior to the methods she and Pete had been attempting. Their methods involved little more than holding PJ close, pacing around the room, and pleading with God that he would please, oh please, oh please stop crying.

Scott tucked the last little corner of the receiving blanket into the bundle he had created around baby PJ just as the front door to the apartment was forced open. Pete walked inside followed by a drift of icy air. He pulled the gloves off his hands and the knit cap off his head, causing his hair to stick out in various directions. His shoulders were slumped and he moved like a man walking against a head wind, every step slow and forceful. He mumbled a hello to Scott and Dara and felt the softness of the couch rising up toward him as he sat on it. It felt insanely good to sit.

"Dude, you look like a refugee," Scott said.

Pete smiled and ran his hand through his hair. His day had begun by attending grad seminars at American University and then teaching an SAT Prep class, one of his many side jobs. Tomorrow, he would spend his morning with the baby, then head to the library to write a paper, and finally to the restaurant where he waited tables in the evening. Each day stacked on top of the one before it, the weeks morphing together to become a mass of indistinguishable fatigue.

The moment Pete and Dara had driven away from the birthing center with PJ fastened safely into the back of their red Nissan Pathfinder, Pete had noticed something inside him shift. His world of surfing and anthropology and academic accolades distilled into a single thought:

This precious little life.

Scott watched Pete closely from the other side of the living room. This was a different version of his friend than he had ever seen before. In college, Scott had been Pete's resident adviser in the dorms. They had spent hours listening to Pearl Jam and brainstorming ways they would use their Anthropology majors to help eradicate poverty.

At the tail end of Scott's senior year at Vanguard, he decided to propose to his girlfriend Shawna. He set up a lunch date with Shawna's father in hopes of procuring her father's blessing, but instead of smiling and welcoming Scott into the family, the man was silent.

Scott watched nervously, as Shawna's father pulled a pen from his pocket and began writing something on the top of a paper napkin. It looked like a bunch of numbers.

"Before I answer your question," Shawna's father said, "I'd like you to answer mine." He shoved the napkin across the table at Scott and said, "This is the amount of money you're going to need to take care of my baby. How exactly do you propose you will come up with it?"

Scott was silent. He shifted in his seat and stared down at the Formica table top.

"I've been working two jobs all throughout college," Scott began. "I'll be graduating with two degrees next month, I grew up on a farm in Montana where I worked hard all my life, and I also don't believe in debt."

Shawna's father smiled.

"Whatever else it takes to be with Shawna, I'll do it," Scott added.

"That's a good answer," her father said. "But I think I may have an even better one. What do you say you come work for me?"

Two years later, here Scott was, working for a commercial lighting company as the head of National Sales. Scott had just secured lighting contracts with a whole slew of hair salons in Florida, as well as all Sunglass Hut retail chains. With every new client he signed on, he became more convinced that this was the job he was made to do.

Scott looked at Pete hunched over on the couch and what he saw was a man who needed a napkin passed across the table to him.

"What if I offered you a job?" Scott asked.

Pete lifted his head. "Doing what?"

"Working for Regency. Selling commercial lighting in California. You'd be on my team and I need a new salesman."

"Sales?" Pete laughed. "I'm an academic. I just finished deconstructing the arguments of Karl Marx. His whole theory of commodification and the way it erodes the very soul of capitalist nations."

"Look, I was an Anthropology major too, and if I can transition from egg head to salesman, then so can you. In fact, about sixty percent of college graduates end up in careers that do not utilize their majors. It's true. Look it up."

Pete put his head in his hands and groaned.

"Statistics. You'll find in sales they work like magic. They make people feel comfortable about their purchase, make them feel less alone. Did I mention the commissions are really solid and that you'll have medical benefits for you, Dara and the baby?"

The word *benefits* caught Pete's ear.

The thought of earning big commissions was not enticing, although Pete noted that perhaps it should be now that he had a son to look out for. Pete never cared much about earning lots of money. During his senior year in high school, he and his classmates were asked to grab colored markers and write predictions as to where they saw themselves in ten years on a massive piece of butcher paper that had been rolled along the floor of the classroom.

"I'll be the next Prince!" one student wrote, followed by a musical note and a cartoon image of himself dancing.

"I'll have designed the next wave of personal computers and made loads of money off my patent!"

"I'll be a teacher!"

"I'll start my own business and be rich!"

Pete thought for a moment about what he really wanted for his life. He envisioned his mother sitting in her office at the San Diego Rescue Mission, counseling women who were victims of domestic abuse. He saw his father praying at the bedside of one of his church members whose son had cancer.

Cancer. Pete hated the word. It reminded him of his two grand-mothers, both of whom were hardworking women and both were diagnosed with terminal cancer. Yet, their experiences with the disease couldn't have been more different.

One grandma was married to a lawyer who had gone to UCLA and had access to all the best doctors and latest technology. She was given state-of-the-art treatment and had died in peace. His other grandma, on his dad's side, was a single mother of Mexican ancestry who had neither health insurance nor a savings account. Forced to take what she could get, her battle with cancer was wrought with negligent doctors and social medicine. Her immune system weakened with each passing day, and she died in immense pain.

The stark contrast of their narratives angered Pete. It wasn't fair. Someone had to fight for people like her.

Pete picked up one of the blue Crayola markers rolling around the edges of the butcher paper, selected a blank space amidst all the other penned out hopes and dreams, and he wrote this:

"In ten years from now, I probably won't be rich, but I will be working to end the suffering in this world." He signed it *Peter DeSoto* and he meant every single word.

"Just think about it, alright?" Scott asked. "I know you love this program you're in, and I know it's an amazing opportunity, but I'm worried about you. I've never seen you looking like this, and if I were in your shoes and had a brand new baby to take care of, I'd probably look the same way. Hell, anyone would."

Scott paused for a moment. "But this job will give you a ton of freedom and alleviate some of the pressure at least."

Pete was quiet. PJ opened his tiny mouth to let out an exclamation. His eyes swiveled around the room and he began to whimper in short, frantic spurts.

"The crying baby that doesn't sleep at night, I can't do much about," Scott added.

Pete smiled and looked over at Dara, whose face was pleading.

"We should definitely think about this," she said, patting PJ's back. "Shouldn't we honey? Maybe talk it over, pray about it?"

PJ's whimpering to turned to full out shrieks and Dara motioned that she was going to change his diaper. Pete watched the curve of her back as she exited the room. Her long hair had been pulled back into a ponytail, and he noted that she looked more beautiful than ever.

"You'd be an awesome salesman," Scott said. "I mean that sincerely. You're great with people and you have a natural sense of confidence."

Pete smiled. He felt heavy inside. "Thanks, Scott."

Scott extended his hand and Pete met it with the same parting handshake they had done throughout college.

"I'll let you know," Pete said.

Behind the bedroom door, Dara was quietly praying as she finished fastening a new diaper onto PJ's little body. *Please let him take it. Please let him take it. Please let him take it.* Was it wrong of her to want this so badly?

She sighed, looking down at her son's brown eyes. They were bright and glinting and curious. She lifted up his body and nuzzled her nose into his soft stomach. PJ smiled and let out a squeal.

"Can you go tell Daddy to take this job for us?"

Dara tickled him again and he smiled.

"Can you?" she teased. "Can you?"

PJ laughed and grinned, as though totally on board with this plan.

Dara imagined how much safer she would feel—back in California, living like grown-ups instead of college students struggling to pay bills. This job sounded so comfortable and steady, like a promise for the future that she could actually lean into. It seemed to come with guarantees, unlike the situation they were in right now where Pete's primary source of income was waiting tables.

On certain nights, the restaurant would be really slow, or the people sitting in his section wouldn't feel like tipping as generously. There was no controlling or predicting it. Each dinner shift was a toss-up, and all they could do was pray that at the end of every week, they would have enough to buy diapers.

Their student housing was paid for by Pete's scholarship, and for that she was incredibly thankful. But how great would it be to live in a house one day. With a yard, and maybe a little garden.

Dara's thoughts were interrupted by a slight knocking on the bedroom door. Pete opened it and poked his head in.

"So that was unexpected," he said, walking over to PJ's crib and picking him up. "What do you think I should do?"

Everything inside Dara wanted to scream the words, TAKE IT!!! But instead she steadied herself and said, "I think we should pray about it."

"Well, yeah," Pete agreed. "Of course I'll pray about it, but you want me to take it, don't you?"

"I want you to do what's going to make you happy," Dara said.

"Great. This PhD program makes me happy, so I guess I'll tell Scott no and we'll just stay here."

"OK," Dara mumbled, turning to look out the window.

"See! You're not OK, you want me to take it and I can hear it in your voice."

"What do you want me to say?" Dara asked. "I can't tell you to take it because I'm not the one who's going to have to show up for work every day!"

"Well, duh! But we're a couple and we have to make these decisions together because this isn't just about me anymore. So tell me honestly, Dara, what do you want?"

Dara sighed. "If going back to California is really an option, and if *you* feel positive you're at peace with giving up this program—giving up this dream of yours, which really is kind of a big deal—then I would be more than happy to go."

Pete nodded.

"It's not just about California," Dara said softly. "It's about stability. I would love having that stability for us, and I'm just not sure if it's selfish for me to want that."

"It's not selfish," Pete said.

Tears began to form in Dara's eyes. "I'm scared sometimes," she said. "I'm scared about what four more years of this is going to look like."

"I know," Pete said. "Me too."

He walked over to Dara and with PJ in one arm, Pete took his other free arm and wrapped it around the small of her back. He drew her closer him, and with the baby sandwiched in between, Dara placed her head on Pete's chest and they hugged each other in a tight embrace. The three of them against the world.

CHAPTER 6

La Matanza (The Massacre)

El Mozote, 1992

War is never an easy topic of discussion. It doesn't matter where it happened, why it happened, who was involved, or how noble the initial motives were behind it. Somewhere along the line, winning takes precedence over dignity and when that happens, war gets especially ugly.

In the fall of 1992, four members of the Argentine Forensic Anthropology Unit drove a convoy of vehicles into an abandoned Salvadoran village called El Mozote. There, they began to poke and prod the overgrown dirt, digging carefully into the remaining foundation of an old church that had once been called Santa Catarina. Underneath the crumbled adobe and burnt wooden frames, the group of anthropologists uncovered a total of twenty-five skulls hidden deep within the earth, twenty-three of which belonged to children.

This dig was important because it confirmed the story of an elderly woman named Rufina Amaya, one of the few survivors of a massacre that wiped out an entire village of nearly 900 people at the start of El Salvador's civil war. The massacre occurred in December of 1981 when the residents of El Mozote were taken under siege and divided into groups based on their sex and age. The men were killed first. Then the women, and finally the children.

The violence was senseless, it was diabolical, and part of it was funded by the United States military.

Why would they help to fund something like that?

In fairness, they didn't know that *this* was how their money would be spent. And even if they did, their initial motivation was not to kill innocent people. It was to stop communism. This was the early 1980s and the US was utterly terrified of the spread of communism. Ronald

Reagan had just been elected president and communist takeovers were happening all over the globe. They captured South Vietnam in 1975. A year later, the Soviets and Cubans joined forces to install a communist government in Angola. In 1979, the Red Army invaded Afghanistan. Also in 1979, a socialist group called the Sandinistas took control of Nicaragua.

When civil war broke out in neighboring El Salvador one year later, the Sandinistas jumped right in to provide aid. And that's when everything came to a head. The US saw the possibility of El Salvador becoming communist and it was too much to bear. In a moment of desperation, President Reagan said this in an impassioned speech: "San Salvador is closer to Houston, Texas than Houston is to Washington, DC. Central America is America. It's at our doorstep, and it's become the stage for a bold attempt by the Soviet Union, Cuba, and Nicaragua, to install Communism by force throughout the hemisphere."

The United States government broke out their checkbooks and began investing millions to support the Salvadoran government, filled with conviction that what they were doing was right. Any side backed by communists was clearly evil, they presumed; therefore, they were on the right side of history.

But in thinking this way, they forgot to ask one important question: *What does the word* communist *mean in El Salvador? Who does it describe?* Does it only describe those who hate democracy, or does it describe other disenfranchised members of society who are fighting for nothing more than basic human rights?

Take the average Salvadoran worker on a coffee plantation, for example. Let's say he worked twelve hour days picking coffee cherries and barely made enough money to feed his family. Let's say his home had neither electricity nor running water. Let's say he had little access to education or upward mobility, but he knew somewhere in his heart this wasn't fair. He knew he couldn't continue living like this, and didn't want his children to have to live like this either, so he banded together with other plantation workers and they staged a plan to fight for fairer pay.

Those plantation workers? They were labeled communists.

No, war is not easy to talk about. It never is. Especially, as motives become skewed and important questions remain unasked.

CHAPTER 7

The Car Accident

Valencia, California, 2003

Scott's instincts about Pete had been right—he was a good salesman. One of the first major clients Pete helped sign for Regency Lighting was the banking giant, Washington Mutual. After that, the floodgates opened. Pete signed The Disney Store and Cinemark movie theaters. He developed a team to work under him and began traveling around the US. He went to New York, Las Vegas, San Francisco, Chicago, Atlanta, Dallas, Palm Springs. There were deals made on the golf course and over rounds of beer at the House of Blues. His conversations were a flurry of chatter about the next great vacation someone was taking, the stock market, the accounts they were about to land, whose wife was getting a nose job, the fastest route to flying first class by compiling credit card points and frequent flier miles.

Pete became well-versed in the latest lighting technology and felt a noticeable pressure to upgrade his home and shop around for timeshares. It was what everyone was doing. The atmosphere was competitive and exhilarating. Pete had to admit, he loved winning. He loved networking and team building. He loved watching the numbers rise with every account they signed.

Dara was thriving, too. She gave birth to their second son, Isaac, in December of 1999. Then came their first daughter, Hannah, in November of 2002, just as PJ was about to turn five.

PJ had grown into a contemplative child with dark brown eyes and chipmunk, rosy cheeks. His brother Isaac was his opposite in many ways. While PJ was lost in thought, three-year-old Isaac was searching for adventure. Dara and Pete nicknamed Isaac *the Little Lion*, as he liked to grow his hair long—a golden mane streaked by the sun. Yet, for all their personality differences, the two brothers were inseparable. PJ and Issac shared a bunk bed, built forts out of sheets, and crafted a Lego universe in their garage.

When Pete wasn't traveling, he taught the boys to ride bikes and to run a profitable lemonade stand in their Valencia suburb. He and Dara had bought a cottage home in 2002 that was nothing short of magical. The yard was lined with rose bushes and fragrant jasmine trees in the backyard. Dara loved the smooth, white petals that bloomed every spring and attracted a flurry of hummingbirds. She watched one morning as they dipped their long, slender beaks into the center of the flower and noted how freeing it felt to not be so afraid. Dara was thirty years old now and her life was bordering on perfection. She had a beautiful baby daughter, two boys that brought her joy, a husband she dearly loved, and a neighborhood that was safe and bursting at the seams with great amenities. What was there to fear at this point?

Bonner Springs, Kansas, 2004

When the Kansas state troopers pulled up the dusty driveway, Cindi Lombardo was in her kitchen sautéing minced garlic and onion in a pool of grassy olive oil. The smell of garlic wafted through the room as she stirred it with a wooden spoon, waiting patiently for the moment to start adding the red wine and scraping the bits of onion that had stuck to the bottom of the pan. Next came the tomatoes, the salt and pepper, and lastly, the fresh chopped basil. But not until the very end.

Today was Guiseppe's 26th birthday, and both her boys—men now, really—would be arriving soon. Cindi's husband Butch had called less than an hour ago to say they had finished working and were on their way home. She hummed to herself as she noticed the car approaching from her kitchen window. It left a trail of dust in its wake and stopped right in front of her house. Two men exited the vehicle wearing button-down shirts, black ties, gray trousers, and their signature black-rimmed hats with the Kansas highway patrol logo emblazoned on the front in gold. Their faces were somber as they approached her doorstep.

Cindi lowered the heat on the stove and walked to her door before they even had time to knock.

"Are you the mother of Guiseppe Domiono Michael Lombardo III?" the first man asked, standing on her porch?

"Yes," she answered.

"Are you the mother of Antonio Michael Vincente Lombardo I?" Cindi nodded.

"And are you the wife of Joseph (Butch) Dominick Lombardo, Jr?"

With each name she was asked, her heart pounded louder in her chest, like a drumbeat threatening to go haywire. The men's faces began to blur and she managed to ask the one question her lips were begging her not to form. The question she already knew the answer to because she felt it the moment they began saying her husband's name.

"Stop," Cindi said, searching the eyes of both men for an answer. "Please just tell me that one of them is still alive."

The state troopers averted their eyes and Cindi watched as the one talking paused to take in a deep breath of air. She watched his chest rise and fall and felt her own body fade into the distance as he said these words: "I'm sorry, ma'am. There were no survivors."

Cindi's legs felt light and the familiar front yard of her home transformed into a wobbly haze. She fell to her knees as the words and their meaning sunk deeper inside her chest. The only man she had ever dated, the only man she had ever loved, her high school sweetheart from the age of 16, her baby boys, her baby boys, her baby boys . . . *All of them were gone.*

———————————

Valencia, California, 2004

Pete opened the door to his office at Regency Lighting and slid into the black swivel chair facing his wooden desk. His eyes traveled to the framed photograph that sat atop it. It was of him and Victorio, a pastor Pete met one year earlier when his former Anthropology professor, Ron Bueno, had invited him to go to El Salvador for a week.

Just looking at the photograph brought back the smell of the pupusas they had eaten for lunch that day, the image of Victorio's wife and daughters huddled together in cotton dresses, sweat dripping down their foreheads as they each patted balls of cornmeal in their hands, molding and shaping them into perfect circles and then placing them on an oiled grill. The women churned out dozens of tortillas, stuffing them with cheese and black beans, searing their edges together to form an enclosed disk around the filling, then placing them back on the grill so the cheese could melt and mix with the beans.

That first meal of pupusas in Abelines had forged a bond between Pete and the Salvadorans that he still couldn't shake. As they ate, Pete watched the lone patch of sunlight slanted across the doorway of Victorio's dark, cement home. It was the middle of the day, but his house had no windows or electricity, so they ate by the door, letting in as much sunshine and air as possible.

His wife smiled a large toothy grin as she presented each person with a bottle of Coke and a plastic straw. A luxury they reserved mainly for guests. Pete sensed this, both in her eyes and the way she placed each Coke on the table with a flourish of deliberate pride.

They gathered round the table—Pete, Ron, Pastor Victorio, several others from Ron's nonprofit, ENLACE (pronounced *en-lah-say*)—and bowed their heads. Victorio gave a prayer of thanks in Spanish. Pete caught himself bristling with every word he didn't understand. A hint of shame crept in as he thought of his last name: DeSoto. Pete was of Mexican heritage and this language was a part of him; yet, he was clueless about what was being expressed.

Mid-prayer, Pete opened his eyes and watched Victorio's facial expressions as he spoke. Victorio had a deep, ruddy tan line across the top of his forehead from the hat he always wore while working in the sun. His eyes were closed, his face was filled with contentment and his words were soft, as though he were speaking to a good friend.

"*Gracias*, amen!" Victorio proclaimed, clasping his calloused hands and lifting them upward.

Victorio caught Pete's eye as he finished the prayer, and there was a glint in them, as if to say, *I see you were watching me.*

Pete smiled back and looked away as if to say, *Yes I was.*

Christian culture had many rules, both spoken and unspoken. The rule that everyone must keep their eyes firmly shut while praying fell into both categories. It was verbally reinforced throughout all of childhood and mentally reinforced from then forward as that twitch of guilt arose whenever Pete was tempted to open his eyes during prayer. It felt like cheating. Like spying on a private moment between other people and God.

As a kid, Pete cheated a lot during prayers, especially to watch his father pray. There was something electrifying about it, like peering into the forbidden. Pete watched his dad's brow furrow, or watched as he searched for the right words. Sometimes Pete hoped he might see an angel hovering around the circle of people his dad was praying with, or some visible manifestation of the Holy Spirit they were crying out to. When that failed, Pete snapped his eyes shut again in hopes of listening and feeling the spirit moving, getting in the groove with everyone else. But even as he tried to concentrate, he could rarely shake the feeling that with his eyes closed, he might be missing something.

Ron hunched over the table, pulling apart his pupusa with his fingers. He sat next to Victorio and was over a foot taller than him. Pete tried to imagine Ron growing up in El Salvador as a missionary kid, a lanky young gringo playing soccer in the streets with his Salvadoran friends. Pete's mind then shifted to a vision of his own boys, Isaac and PJ, learning Spanish, going to school here, coming along with him to Abelines and other remote villages where he would give them piggyback rides up the hills and teach them to carry bricks for the building projects. Maybe even wield a machete like the local village kids.

These memories flooded Pete's office at Regency Lighting, even as he knew they didn't belong there. They belonged within the confines of the picture frame, a convenient, 4x6 inch space with boundaries that could keep them in check. But instead, these thoughts had grown a life of their own over the past year since his trip. They followed him around like stubborn little children yanking on the bottom of his t-shirt until he was willing to stop and listen and finally acknowledge whatever it was they so desperately wanted to tell him.

Move to El Salvador, they said. *You know you want to.*

And he did. More and more every day.

The moment Pete encountered God in the Abelines rainstorm, everything he had been burying for that past four years cracked wide open: his passion for anthropology, for culture, and for people whose hearts were aching for something. He had wanted to meet people in that place— right in the middle of the aching and give them something to hope for. Maybe it was faith? Maybe it was clothing or food or something basic, like listening? Listening and showing them they mattered. Their needs mattered and they weren't invisible, even though their lack of resources made them feel that way.

Jesus had done the same thing. And while Pete may not have trusted God as fully (God could be angry and mysterious at times), Pete did trust Jesus. Jesus, he could visualize. Pete imagined the sights and sounds of Jesus walking through the dusty streets, encountering a paralyzed man and telling him to get up and walk. Jesus, eating meals with social outcasts and urging the disciples to take more risks. To be bold. To have faith that uprooted mountains and changed the chemical composition of water.

These snapshots of Jesus grounded Pete and gave him strength to stand tall when a God he didn't know very well tapped him on the shoulder in Abelines and said, "I have an invitation for you. If you'd like to take it."

The invitation was to reexamine his life and the role that faith was currently playing in it—now that Pete was nearing thirty and had reached every major milestone American culture laid out for him. He had the wife, he had the kids, he had the house and two cars and the burgeoning career with several options for advancement. He had a retirement package, he lived near a good school district, and God had peered in and said, "So, where do I fit into all this?"

A fair question. Pete had been wrestling with it since returning from El Salvador, especially as he watched his boys grow and considered what type of faith he wanted to model for them. What type of faith was even necessary in this life of safety and comfort he had created?

Not that there was anything wrong with safety and comfort. They were blessings. But Pete's parents always taught him that great faith requires risk. It requires stepping out on a narrow ledge, which looks different for every single person. For some, it may look like saying sorry, restoring an old relationship that has felt hopeless for a long time. For others, it could look like adopting a child with a disability, or quitting a job, or doing anything at all that is uncomfortable and scary and feels downright impossible if not for God offering to walk with them the entire time.

For Pete, the narrow ledge was moving to El Salvador.

That day in Abelines, it almost felt like God was urging him to go for it. But now Dara was pregnant. Again. With baby number four.

She had just cleared the first trimester, and unlike with their first three children, she and Pete had made the decision not to find out the sex of the baby.

The phone on Pete's desk began to ring and he picked it up, thankful for the distraction.

"Dara's on line one," his assistant told him. "She says it's an emergency."

The word emergency made his chest clench.

The baby.

Something is wrong with the baby.

Pete stabbed at the button for line one, and clutched the phone against his ear.

"Honey?" he asked.

At the sound of his voice, Dara began to sob. Short, guttural cries with labored breaths in between. She kept opening her mouth, trying to force the words out but they wouldn't come. Just tears. Only tears.

"Dara, you're scaring me. Did something happen to the baby?"

"No," she uttered between breaths.

The thought of the baby cleared Dara's head for a minute. Helped her focus.

"Not the baby . . .. Cindi."

"What about Cindi?"

The sobs came even harder this time as Dara imagined herself saying the words.

"There's been a car accident," she whispered.

The Lombardo men had been driving on the turnpike when their tire blew out only minutes after hanging up the phone with Cindi. They had attempted to pull over and fix it when their minivan lost control and collided with a guardrail and sign, causing the entire vehicle to spin out like a football, roll over several times, and finally crash into a bridge pillar.

Upon hearing about their deaths, Dara booked the soonest flight she could and spent several weeks with Cindi at her home in Bonner Springs, Kansas. Much of the time, Cindi sat on the couch and stared numbly into the distance. Her brain couldn't register the loss in its totality, so it went into a trance-like state. Dara tried her best to fill in the gaps.

She brushed Cindi's teeth and reminded her to spit into the little cup she held out. Dara then wiped her mouth and led her to the bathroom. There, she got down on her knees and washed Cindi's feet in the bathtub, using soap that smelled like lilies and ensuring the water was just the right temperature.

"Nino taught me so much about kindness" Dara said, as she dried Cindi's feet with a towel.

At the mention of her son's name, Cindi's eyes regained their light for just a minute. "What did he teach you?" she asked. "What do you remember?"

"Remember the time I dropped his birthday cake on the floor?" Dara asked. Smiling, she blinked back tears, grabbed a bottle of lotion, and began to rub it into the balls of Cindi's feet.

"I think Nino was about six or seven years old. Whatever year it was that my mom and I brought him that chocolate yogurt cake."

"From Heidi's Yogurt," Cindi mumbled.

"Yes," Dara said. "We'd brought the cake and put candles in it and we were all singing *Happy Birthday* to him when the whole thing slipped out from under my hands and crashed on the floor."

Cindi's mouth relaxed into a slight smile.

"I was mortified," Dara continued. "I thought I had ruined the whole day and I was waiting for him to burst into tears, like any other six-year-old probably would have. But then he just came up to me with the biggest grin and said, 'It's OK, Dara. It all goes down the same way.' And I couldn't believe it. He and Guiseppe just started scooping the cake off the floor, like it was no big deal, and looking back on it now, you know what it was?"

Dara paused, working out the exact words she wanted to say in her head. "It was gratitude. They were both so grateful for absolutely everything."

Cindi looked down at Dara for a moment and what she saw was a 9-year-old little girl, her body like a slender fish in a solid black one-piece bathing suit. Cindi saw the curious look in her eyes, the beads of water dripping down her long, greenish blonde hair. She saw Dara sitting in the oak tree at Casa de Fruta, singing songs and asking questions. Always asking questions. She saw Dara in her Huntington Beach kitchen, covered in flour and kneading bread dough with her adolescent hands. Later, she envisioned Dara on her bed in college, calling Cindi in Kansas to gush about the guy she had just met named Peter.

The tears spilled down Cindi's cheeks and for the first time since the car accident, those tears weren't for Butch. Or for Nino, or for Guiseppe. They were in response to this little girl kneeling at her feet. A daughter in Cindi's heart, whom after all these years, was now parenting *her*. The pride Cindi felt was overwhelming and she began to sob. She sobbed over this bizarre intermingling of joy shoved up against heartbreak.

The funeral for the Lombardo men took place a few days later on a sunny morning in Kansas City. Several hundred people gathered at the cemetery and eulogies were read for all three of the men. Because their bodies had been unrecognizable after the accident, there were no open caskets. Once the prayers had been said, a woman came up and sang a worship song by Matt Redman called "Blessed Be Your Name."

Dara opened her mouth and the words she knew by heart came tumbling out, joining together with a chorus of other mourners singing to God:

Blessed be Your name
On the road marked with suffering
Though there's pain in the offering
Blessed be Your name.

The tempo increased for the final refrain and Dara could barely choke out the lyrics:

You give and take away
But my heart will choose to say
Lord blessed be Your name."

Dara had sung this song countless times in church, but the lyrics had never pierced her like this. They had never felt like a bitter offering. *You give and take away, You give and take away, You give and take away . . .* Even when it doesn't make sense.

Dara stopped singing and opened her eyes. She saw a church filled with 5,000 people who had traveled all over the world to celebrate the lives of these men. Five thousand people had come to Kansas City with only a few days' notice because the Lombardo men had touched them in some way. They had used their time well on this earth.

How am I using my time? Dara wondered.

She recognized with intense clarity that her life could end just as swiftly. There was no choosing or bargaining. No controlling the outcome. It was God's call and He could call her at any moment.

Dara closed her eyes and prayed. "Please use me," she said. "Please use me and guide my life. Wherever you want me to go, whatever you want me to do, just let my life matter somehow."

A week after the funeral, Dara flew back to Valencia. She opened the front door of her cottage home and rolled her suitcase along the hardwood floors, grateful to be back. She had fallen in love with this house the moment she and Pete laid eyes on it.

Dara left her suitcase propped against the bed and wandered out to the back patio. This was a rare moment to herself when the kids were still with her parents and Peter was at work. She took full advantage of it and plopped down in the chair where she and Pete often enjoyed a cup of tea while the sun was setting. She felt tired, jet lagged, and emotionally spent after the last few weeks in Kansas.

She sighed and allowed her body to fully relax into the chair. The baby kicked inside her stomach, and it reminded Dara of how bittersweet the cycle of life could be. Here was this child about to enter the world, yet Nino, Butch, and Guiseppe wouldn't be there to witness it.

Her eyes surveyed the yard around her and she felt a tightness in her chest that bordered on nostalgia. As though everything was temporal, and even the very yard she sat in would soon be nothing more than a distant memory.

The streets were bathed in golden rays as Pete and Dara headed out for an evening prayer walk through their neighborhood. They selected one of several *paseos*, a network of interweaving pathways that crisscrossed through the community, like arteries in a heart. They strolled past Spanish-style homes, each having their own conversation with God inside their heads. Dara felt Him asking her to follow. She had sensed it several times since the Lombardo funeral, although she could never quite figure where.

As Pete walked, he analyzed the relationship between faith and risk, risk and faith. He thought of how Jesus had oriented his entire life around easing the world's suffering. Other than donating money, Pete noted that he wasn't doing much else to ease the world's suffering.

Suddenly the words: *You can trust me.*

A statement this time. A statement that felt so much different than the question he felt God posing to him in Abelines. Pete noted how solid these words were, like a surface that would support him if he leaned into them.

The sun dropped even further behind the houses dotting the horizon. Pete and Dara passed the stairway leading up to the Olympic-sized pool that sat atop the bluff in their neighborhood. The one with the panoramic view where Dara loved taking the boys to swim on hot afternoons. They turned a corner and both Pete and Dara stopped walking at the same time. They stood still and just looked at one another.

"What is God saying to you?" Pete asked.

"He's reminding me of that verse about storing up treasures in heaven."

Pete's eyes grew larger and he opened his mouth as if to say something, but then closed it again.

"What?" Dara asked.

"It's just . . . that's what I'm hearing, too," Pete said.

Dara was quiet for a minute. "I almost feel as if he's asking us to sell everything and go somewhere."

"Luke 18," Pete said. "'Sell everything you have, give it to the poor, and you will have treasure in heaven. Then follow me.'"

"It's not a verse people usually take literally."

Pete laughed. "I know."

The sky became orangish-gray and a chilly breeze brushed across Dara's arms.

"But what if we did?" Pete asked. "What if we took it literally?"

"OK, so we'd sell everything . . . and go where?"

"You know my heart has always been in El Salvador," Pete said.

Dara nodded. "How long would we stay?"

"Not forever," Pete said.

Dara's face softened. "How about three years? I think I could handle three years."

"Three to five?"

Dara rolled her eyes. "You're such a negotiator."

Pete laughed.

"Fine. Three to five."

Dara smiled and wrapped her arms around Pete. "Why don't we just see how things go before we get too ahead of ourselves? You can talk to Ron and ask if ENLACE even needs you, we can start the ball rolling with raising support funds to be missionaries, and if everything falls into place, we'll know it's God's plan for us."

Pete nodded and gave her a kiss. "Sounds perfect."

It took less than twenty-four hours for Pete to pick up the phone and make an international call to Ron Bueno in El Salvador.

"Is ENLACE hiring?" Pete asked.

"Who wants to know?" Ron asked.

They bantered back and forth like old friends and Pete told Ron about the Lombardos' funeral, about his prayer walk with Dara, and their desire to move to San Salvador and work with ENLACE.

Ron was quiet for a moment. When he had first met Pete, Ron was a 24-year-old adjunct instructor who knew very little about teaching college. Ron would pace around the classroom with a small stub of chalk in his palm, pausing periodically to write something important on the board, and then turn that main point into a question for his students to discuss in small groups.

"Poverty and inequality have many roots," Ron said to his Applied Anthropology class of six students, "but if you could boil it down to one—one main factor that lies at the center of all inequality, all systemic poverty—what do you think it would be?"

Ron took a seat at the head of the conference table and watched his young students, pens cocked at an angle, eyes looking to the ceiling as they pondered.

"Greed?" one student posited.

"Government corruption?" suggested Pete.

"Dehumanization," Jamie Huff said. The flat tone of Jamie's voice indicated that he meant it as a statement, not a question.

Ron looked at Jamie. "Can you explain further?"

"Sure," Jamie said. "Say, you've got a country like El Salvador that just came out of a twelve year civil war. From what you've told us, the whole reason they started fighting was because the wealthy plantation owners didn't want to pay their workers a fair wage, right? So the workers got sick of being exploited and decided to demand they be paid enough to actually put food on the table. A pretty reasonable request. But instead of conceding, the plantation owners decided to fight back and kill them. Partially because they are greedy, sure. And fearful and selfish. But more than anything, I think they just couldn't recognize that their workers were actual people. They saw them as lower class citizens, as *mestizos*, as Indians with an inferior culture, no education, not even worthy to eat at the same table as them. They couldn't see their humanity, and the more they fought against each other, the more they lost sight of it."

Ron nodded. "Nicely put."

He walked to the chalkboard and wrote the words *BROKEN RELATONSHIPS*.

"This is another name for it," Ron said. "You can call it *dehumanization*, or you can call it *broken relationships*, but the more I do this work, the more I'm beginning to recognize that broken relationships are the root of it all. If we could fix that somehow, if we could find a way to mend these broken relationships, or this *dehumanization* as Jamie calls it, I think we would be on to something."

"But how?" Pete asked.

"I don't know," Ron answered. "That's the part I'm still trying to figure out."

Ron cradled the phone on his shoulder and peered out the window of his office in San Salvador.

"Remember that conversation we had in class all those years ago—the one about broken relationships being at the root of inequality?"

"Yeah," Pete said. "I still think about that quite a bit, actually."

"Remember Pastor Juan? He and his wife live in San Martín, in the heart of one of the worst gang-infested neighborhoods in all of El Salvador and they are trying to clean up their community. Juan wants to build a medical clinic and a well to bring running water. The guy's a visionary and a great storyteller, really good at motivating and mobilizing people. He's even good at reaching out to the gangs. He invites them to come eat at his church potlucks, and they actually do."

"Really?" Pete asked.

"Yes. Juan's built a rapport with MS-13 in his neighborhood and they seem to respect him. Anyway, if we're going to help him carry out even a fraction of what he hopes to accomplish, we'll need money. And that's where I think you can come in. How would you feel about being in charge of fundraising for ENLACE? You've got the business and marketing background from working in lighting for all these years."

"I'll do it," Pete said before Ron could even finish the sentence.

Pete began researching the cost of flights, food, and rent in San Salvador. He made spread sheets, pored over credit card statements, budgeted for things like diapers and baby wipes and medicine. Next, he studied the real estate market, predicted what he could get for the house, and came up with a formula to determine how much money they would need to live off of as a family of four for an entire year.

Pete scheduled a breakfast meeting with his friend who was a real estate agent. They hatched a plan over coffee and omelets, and by the end of that very same day, the agent had Pete and Dara signing a bill of sale on their beloved cottage home off Garland Court. It took less than twenty-four hours for their house to both go on and off the market.

The DeSotos loaded up U-Hauls, sold their most expensive and cumbersome furniture, and settled into a two bedroom apartment on the other side of town. Three days after the move, Dara went into labor and their daughter, Kaya, was born.

"I'll give you one year to find my replacement and to help train him," Pete told Michael Goldstone, his friend and boss at Regency Lighting.

From that point forward, there was no going back. With little time to breathe or think, Pete and Dara continued to place one foot in front of the other, scrambling to catch up with the pace of their lives in hopeful, yet anxious obedience.

PART TWO

RISK

Risk has many faces. At its best, it can be an exhilarating friend, a fortune teller predicting visions of glory. It can be a humbling teacher, or a doorway into unseen possibility.

At its worst, risk can be a train wreck. It can rip you in two and leave you with nothing.

The toughest part is never knowing which version you will get.
But choosing to do it anyway.

CHAPTER 8

Culture Shock

Los Angeles, April 2005

The Tom Bradley International terminal at LAX airport was abuzz with squirming children, humming conveyor belts, and the flutter of passports being exchanged from one hand to the next. High heels clicked along the ceramic floor and suitcases rolled beneath fluorescent lighting.

Just outside the check in line for TACA Airlines stood Debbie Aiklen with arms crossed and a pained look on her face. The words *they're taking my babies to El Salvador* kept running through her head on repeat. It was all she could see or think. It wasn't just her only daughter—that was bad enough. But her *grandchildren.* Debbie watched as seven-month-old Kaya wiggled in Dara's arms. She was still nursing for heaven's sake.

And this country they were going to. Debbie had been there.

She and Dan had visited it before the civil war. Back in 1970-something. They had left baby Dara with her great aunt so they could take a surfing trip to El Salvador. An undiscovered patch of ocean Dan wanted to conquer. Was it ever beautiful! In parts, the sand was thick like clay and the pristine water was every bit as warm as it had been in Florida where Debbie grew up. The people she met in El Salvador were beautiful, too. They were poor as all get out, but kind. So kind.

Safety in this country was an entirely different story. You could easily get sick and diseases were running rampant, as the very same river they used to drink out of was the place they chose to wash everything else.

An image of PJ and Isaac playing in the river filled Debbie's thoughts. She envisioned her grandchildren drinking the polluted water, their bellies beginning to expand as though they might pop. *This whole thing was crazy. Why couldn't she stop it?*

Debbie had tried. She'd made a fuss. She'd researched crime statistics—probably one of the worst ideas she could have come up with because now there were tattooed gang members haunting her thoughts alongside everything else—but her hope had been that maybe, just maybe, she could talk some sense into Dara and Pete and the whole rest of this crew standing in the check in line at LAX.

There was Jamie Huff, Pete's best friend from college and "certified" El Salvador expert. Jamie was coming along to help them get settled because he had lived in El Salvador while doing research for his PhD dissertation. A smart man, Jamie was, and always so sweet to Debbie. But right now he wasn't on her list of favorite people.

Neither were John and Lucia at this very moment—Pete's parents, who were also in support of this grand El Salvador scheme. Debbie knew this type of thing was somewhat normal for them, having dedicated their entire lives to Jesus and ministry. Debbie respected that, most definitely. She loved Jesus herself and tried to follow Him as best she could. Admittedly, she had screwed up about a million and one different times, but all that aside, was Jesus *really* dragging her daughter and grandchildren to a death trap?

Debbie's heartbeat quickened at the thought of it. Yet there in front of her was Lucia holding Hannah's hand as they waited in line. Lucia quieting PJ and Isaac, both boys teeming with energy and nerves, absorbing the chaos around them as children often do.

Meanwhile John, poor thing, was doing his best to manage the luggage. On the floor next to them, behind them, and in front of them, were three rolling carts that contained 27 bags filled with the DeSoto family's most prized and essential possessions. Everything they might need to live for the next three to five years in El Salvador.

They had packed surfboards and surf wax, a can of play dough in every color of the rainbow, and a collection of *Barney and Friends* sing-along DVDs. They packed essential oils because Dara had read that geranium oil is a natural mosquito repellent. Dara also brought Costco-sized cases of granola bars and Kraft macaroni and cheese, plus her favorite robe and coffee mug, the two items she used every morning without fail. Pete had brought a Spanish dictionary, a guide to fundraising, his beloved iPod crammed with all his favorite albums, and the complete set of William Barclay's New Testament commentaries on the gospels of Matthew, Mark, Luke, and John. He had packed several anthropology textbooks he couldn't bear to part with after grad school, and the director's cut edition of *Raiders of the Lost Ark.*

Their 27 bags also held wet suits, Legos, playing cards, and vitamins. They packed their favorite worship albums, baseball caps, *Power Ranger* DVDs, diapers, and swaddling blankets. In truth, the DeSotos packed everything they owned because all that was left after selling their home and cars and expensive baby toys was just enough to fit into 27 bags—approximately 4.5 per person.

The crew waved a final goodbye to Dan and Debbie who stood at the bottom of the escalator, wiping their eyes and watching them disappear, one by one, into the airport security line. On they continued through the airport, Jamie, John, Lucia, and the DeSoto family. They shuffled through metal detectors and down the narrow airplane aisle. When it was nearly midnight, seven-year-old P.J. was buckled into his window seat, eyes closed and head propped against a nylon pillow given to him by a flight attendant. His five-year-old brother Isaac sat next to him, leaning against Pete's upper arm and breathing softly.

Dara sat across the aisle with their two-year-old daughter, Hannah, and their seven-month-old, Kaya, who wiggled in her arms, awake and smiling and hoping to be entertained.

The lights in the cabin grew dim and the captain told everyone to prepare for take off, first in Spanish and then in English. The plane traveled through the night until a golden band began to form, casting orange and pink ribbons above the horizon.

Dara's legs felt stiff, like iron stilts that didn't want to move. If she could have stayed on that plane forever, she might have. It would have been superior even to going back to the US, as the home they once knew was now in the possession of a new family and filled with furniture she wouldn't recognize. Pete's job at Regency Lighting was no longer available either, as he had given it to someone else. Whether they moved forward or backward, nothing would ever be the same.

They landed in San Salvador at 5:30 a.m. The group headed straight from the airport to an apartment complex where the DeSotos would be living for the next six weeks. It was called Torres del Bosque. A tall building with a swimming pool and tropical garden at its base.

The sky in San Salvador felt bluer, the air more thick. Lush greenery sprouted out of every corner, vibrant and inviting. There was something healing about the presence of so much nature everywhere. Amidst the crumbling homes pieced together with random materials and the street corners marked with gang insignia, nature continued to juxtapose itself as a thing of beauty, a moment of reassurance amongst these other foreboding elements.

The first peculiarity Dara couldn't help but notice was that men, women, and even children seemed to be riding in the beds of pickup trucks, most of them standing up as they rode, gripping a bar that had been installed along the top of the pickup's rear window.

It was a shocking sight. Dara cringed as she imagined them in a car accident—being flung from the back of the pickup without seat belts or any sort of barrier to keep them safe.

The trucks barreled past the ENLACE bus and Dara watched the standing passengers in the back, their dark hair and tee shirts whipping behind them with the force of the wind. As the paved highway angled, so too did their bodies. Yet, the passengers stood firmly and increased their iron grip on the bar while they whirred past patches of green jungle. Like the graffiti, this too felt dangerous. Lawless. It made Dara question how much rules and laws actually mattered here in El Salvador. That question, along with the drive, the flight, and all other excitement, made her stomach uneasy.

"Look at the dog!" Isaac said, pointing to a golden mutt on the side of the road. It had matted fur and a tail that hung low. Its ribs and haunches were protruding from taut skin and it seemed to be having trouble walking.

"Yeah, look!" PJ quipped. "What's wrong with it?"

"It looks like he doesn't have an owner to take care of him and feed him," Dara said.

"You'll see lots of stray dogs. Pretty much everywhere," Jamie said.

Pete smiled. "Last time I was here, my running joke was that not all dogs go to heaven. Some dogs go to El Salvador."

Jamie laughed, and Dara shook her head with amusement. She placed her hand on top of Pete's and felt grateful she could always count on her husband to lighten the mood.

The van made a sharp turn off the highway and into the driveway of Torres del Bosque, where Ron Bueno and his wife Michelle were standing with big signs that said "WELCOME," "BIENVENIDOS" in bright marker. They started waving and jumping up and down. Even Ron attempted a mini-jump with his 6-foot, lumbering frame. His wide smile was adorned by a thick, blonde beard and Michelle stood half a foot below him, radiating a warmth that was welcoming, yet understated.

Their son Jack was the same age as PJ and came running toward the van to ask if they could play soccer together.

"In a minute," Dara said. "We need to unload all the bags first. Can you guys help us with that, please?"

PJ and Jack nodded as Dara handed them small bags to carry.

The next hour was spent choosing beds, shuffling around, mopping sweat off of foreheads, learning the layout of the apartment, and drinking pot after pot of coffee. Dara strapped Kaya to her chest and clutched a warm mug filled with fragrant, Salvadoran *café*. She and Michelle wandered over to the poolside while PJ and Jack kicked a soccer ball in the grassy courtyard. Pete approached them with a ring full of house keys, and as Ron started to explain which key served what function, they heard a sudden splash coming from the pool behind them.

"Hannah!" Dara said, noting that her two-year-old daughter had taken it upon herself to jump in the water. Hannah splashed around and emitted a small giggle.

"At least she's known how to swim for the past year and a half," Dara said, looking at Pete and then warning her daughter not to go past the shallow end.

"Can I swim too?" Isaac asked, and Dara nodded in approval. Then he could keep an eye on his sister.

Less than an hour later, after the kids had been splashing around and Pete had joined Jamie and Ron in the backyard, Dara was laying at the poolside and feeling loopy from the lack of sleep on the airplane ride. Out of the corner of her eyes, she noticed something floating in the water. It was soft and brown and bobbing next to Hannah. She squinted, and leaned closer, Kaya still strapped to her chest.

Dara face grew warm and her eyes widened. Her daughter had pooped in the pool.

At the community pool in Valencia, this would have been major cause for alarm. Dara had seen it happen with other families. The entire pool was shut down. They were escorted out in shame alongside the rest of the whiny, dripping children, all staring at the culprits with eyes that were pointed and accusatory. *What could she do?* Dara wondered. *Did this pool even have chlorine in it?*

In a moment of panic, she lowered herself and Kaya to the water's edge and began scooping the poop out by the chunk load. She pictured the other residents using this pool, not knowing that her daughter had contaminated it. Should she warn them? Who would she tell? *And how would she say it in Spanish?*

Dara dumped the remaining bits of evidence in the trash and walked back to the poolside to gather Isaac and Hannah.

"Isaac, swim time is over," she said. "Please get your sister and come dry off."

Dara headed for the bathroom and scrubbed her hands with soap three different times. *Why is this water not getting warm?* She wondered.

A fair question, and one she would soon find the answer to, as the majority of Salvadorans do not have hot water in their homes. Not for showers, not for dish washing. Not for anything.

Dara held the laminated menu for the *pupusería* between her fingers and stared at the sea of words she did not recognize. Although her children were back at the apartment with Michelle, Dara imagined them sitting across the table and staring up at her expectantly, waiting for her to order something—to feed them, but she would have no idea how.

She could feel her throat closing. "It's all in Spanish," she whispered to Pete.

He noted the worried look in her blue eyes. The reality of Dara never having traveled internationally dug into his conscience yet again. He would need to guide her through every step. Explain things. Teach her.

"It is," he said. "And honestly, I don't understand half of it, but we'll use the few words we do know and go from there. We'll learn together."

Pete grabbed her hand in his and Dara softened. She did love this man. That much she knew for sure. And she trusted him more than she trusted herself.

"What's good here, Ron?" Pete asked.

"Everything," Ron answered, a huge smile spreading across his face. He had grown up in El Salvador as the son of American missionaries. This had been the food of his childhood.

The waiter approached the table and Ron ordered for everyone. Pupusas stuffed with shredded chicken, some with beef, and still others with red beans and gooey cheese popping out the sides. He ordered *curtido*, shredded cabbage marinated in vinegar to help with digestion, and then a round of papaya juices blended with crushed ice. The drinks were sweet and refreshing alongside the warm, savory pupusas.

"As we drove up to the restaurant, you probably noticed the guard outside with the single barrel shotgun?" Ron asked.

Dara and Pete both nodded.

"Almost every business or parking lot has at least one," Ron explained. "I know it's probably alarming at first, but you'll get used to it. They're meant to keep you safe in case there's any trouble."

Dara felt her heart quicken.

"I don't mean to scare you," Ron insisted, "but I also don't want to sugarcoat this. The two major gangs that control the streets are called *maras*. *Mara Salvatrucha*, otherwise known as MS-13, and Barrio 18. Each gang controls certain neighborhoods and streets, meaning that they charge 'rent' to all business owners within their territory."

"Rent?" Dara questioned.

"Yes. They call it rent, but it's really more like extortion because the business owners have to pay them what they ask, or risk getting killed—either by them or their rival gang. The one benefit of paying rent is that it is supposed to provide protection for the business owners. So the rival gang can't hurt them."

"Why would the rival gang hurt them?" Dara asked.

Ron sighed. "Because their business happens to be located on a street that's controlled by their rival. It's about territory and power."

Dara looked at him quizzically. "So all people who sell things have to do this? Like that woman we saw earlier selling coconuts on the side of the road—she has to pay the gangs a portion of her profits?"

"Probably," Ron said. "It's hard to know for sure, but I would guess based on the neighborhood that she does."

Dara imagined the woman: long cotton skirt, dark hair tucked back into a ponytail at the nape of her neck, gun pointed at her head as she stood behind a table of brown coconuts. Goosebumps traveled the length of Dara's spine. How did people live like this? How would *she* live like this?

Ron and Pete exchanged glances as Dara slumped lower in her chair.

"If you take the necessary safety precautions, you should be just fine," Ron assured her. "And that is mainly what I want to get across right now. Not focusing on all the particulars of the gangs and how they work and why they do what they do, let's focus on what's most important: *keeping you safe.*"

Dara's mind began to drift as Ron rattled off the safety precautions. She felt her world shrinking with every sentence that he spoke. She couldn't go out after dark. She couldn't leave the apartment, period, unless Pete or someone else was with her and the kids. Someone who spoke Spanish. Someone who knew the neighborhood.

Pete had warned her of this back in California. He'd told her it would be different in El Salvador, that she would have less freedom. And Dara had heard him, but not really understood.

"It won't always be this way," Ron said. "Once you become familiar with what streets and stores are safe to visit, and once you learn how to communicate, you'll have more freedom. But for now, we've got to err on the side of safety. And the safest place for you and the kids is at the apartment."

———————————

The first major purchase Pete and Dara made in El Salvador was a 12-seater *microbús* with a stick shift engine. It seemed just large enough to transport their entire family of six, plus a handful of ENLACE staff members and volunteers. Pete drove the *microbús* each morning to his Spanish classes at the Universidad Centroamericana, otherwise known as UCA, a Jesuit university in San Salvador. While there, he studied grammar, memorized vocabulary, and practiced stringing together broken sentences with his classmates.

As someone who loved being a student and felt at home in the classroom, this was the easiest part of Pete's day. The rest was a different story. It was an exercise in extreme patience, as the everyday minutiae of life became increasingly complicated.

Bills needed to be paid—in person—which meant driving to a specific location, finding said location, figuring out exactly who to talk to once he was there, waiting in line, and then walking back to the *microbús* and finding that a tire was flat. In El Salvador, tires were always going flat from the jagged pathways they were forced to traverse on a regular basis.

As someone who took pride in functioning efficiently, this utter lack of it was wearing Pete down. He made daily checklists of immigration papers that needed to be filed and specific items that needed to be bought, like mosquito netting for the kids so they wouldn't get bitten to death each night while they slept. Try as he may to get it all done, he inevitably seemed to fail. Like a character in a video game who couldn't manage to outsmart the obstacles being thrown at him.

He sat down in the ENLACE offices and let out a long sigh. His coworker, David McGee, a fellow American expat, pulled up a chair next to Pete and asked how he was doing. David smiled as Pete spoke, knowing all too well what he was feeling.

He and his wife Jenny were a young couple who had been living in El Salvador for the past three years. They had come for their honeymoon in 2002 because their friend, Ron Bueno's brother, had offered to pay for their plane tickets if they would be willing to spend part of their honeymoon volunteering with ENLACE.

The original plan was to stay for three months, but since neither David nor Jenny had jobs or apartments or much of anything to go back to in the US, they decided to stay longer. They began to bond with the people they were meeting in El Salvador and they loved the ways ENLACE was working with them to improve their communities.

As a photography major in college, David had brought all his equipment and started using it to document everything he saw. He photographed the landscape, the villages, the food they ate, the smiles on their faces. David recognized that he could use his camera to tell stories, and his wife Jenny could help arrange these photos in a brochure or on a website, as she was a graphic designer.

Together, they became the communications team for ENLACE, reporting on the work being done in the communities and sending those stories out to the donors. One month piled on top of the next, until David and Jenny had been living in San Salvador for three years and had little interest in leaving. This place had become home.

David waited until Pete was finished venting about his immigration paperwork, which was still going to take three more days to process.

Finally he said, "That immigration paper you were able to file today? That's a success."

Pete just looked at him.

"I know it doesn't sound like much, and I know you're probably more of a Type A personality."

Pete laughed.

"But here in El Salvador, just getting one thing done each day—not ten things, not five things, just one thing—is considered a victory. Don't expect much more than that because you'll make yourself crazy if you do."

Pete nodded and smiled. It was a humbling prospect.

"One thing," David repeated.

Pete parked the *microbús* in the driveway after Spanish class and noticed the winds were picking up. The front door slammed shut behind him as PJ and Issac ran across the tile floor.

"Daddy!" Isaac shouted. "There's gonna be a storm!"

"A big one!" PJ added. "Mom says it's going to rain more than we've ever seen."

Pete looked out the window as a gust of wind dismembered a tree branch and sent it skidding down the streets of their new neighborhood in Plazuela Rosales. Their six-week stint at Torres del Bosque was up, and now the DeSotos were living in Ron and Michelle Bueno's house—a spacious, two story home with a grassy yard and hammock hanging in the back. They had it all to themselves, as Ron had taken a consulting job in California for the next six months, partially because it would give him opportunity to do more fundraising for ENLACE while he was there.

Plazuela Rosales was a gated community with armed guards and an actual playground inside where the kids could swing and go on the slides. Dara still wasn't comfortable venturing outside the *plazuela's* walls, but the fact that she could walk freely outdoors, smell the flowers growing around the playground, inhale gulps of fresh air, humid or not, gave her moments of extreme gratitude.

A torrent of rain fell from the sky, landing against the rooftop like nails on a metal shed. Little Kaya sat on a blanket in the middle of the living room, quietly selecting one toy after the next, picking each up, examining it closely, and then putting it in her mouth.

"This is awesome!" Isaac shouted.

Dara picked up Kaya from her blanket and motioned for Hannah, who was coloring, to come join Pete and the boys at the window.

They watched as Hurricane Adrian tore through the landscape with 80 mile per hour winds. The storm first landed in the beach town of La Libertad, about twenty-four miles south of San Salvador. The torrential rains toppled trees and washed away roads. An estimated 14,000 people in the low-lying areas were forced to evacuate, and the DeSotos lost power in their home for several days.

The Salvadoran government would spend the next four months trying to repair and re-build an estimated 12 million dollars' worth of damages Hurricane Adrian inflicted on their country.

But their relief efforts would be thwarted on October 1, 2005 when the Santa Ana volcano erupted into a violent explosion, sending a column of gas and ash six miles into the sky. A flood of boiling mud and water damaged 34 acres of agricultural crops in a nearby village. Santa Ana residents reported seeing boulders the size of automobiles rolling down the mountainside.

Just when the ash from the volcanic eruption was starting to dissipate, and the air was feeling clearer, another tropical storm rolled down from the Gulf of Mexico. This time, it was the tail end of Hurricane Stan, which struck El Salvador with a vengeance. It caused flash floods and mudslides, left 71 people dead, and eradicated three quarters of the country's food supply. Grains, vegetables, and coffee crops all suffered major losses.

When the weather finally cleared and the ENLACE offices went back to work, their first order of business was to find a way to prevent further erosion in at-risk communities. In the town of San Miguel, some residents were trapped because the roads they usually took—to get to the bus, to go into town and buy food or supplies—had been completely washed away. An entire cliff side disappeared, as though it had never been there.

Ron Bueno was pacing around ENLACE's conference room with a large cup of coffee in hand and a PowerPoint presentation on the projector screen behind him. The air conditioning was on full blast to combat the relentless humidity outside, and the staff was gathered around the table, elbow to elbow, enjoying a typical Salvadoran breakfast of scrambled eggs, fried plantains, and red beans. Sonia, the office housekeeper and cook, could whip up any breakfast for the bargain sum of three dollars. It was a luxury Pete took advantage of whenever possible, as these air conditioned breakfast meetings were fast becoming a major highlight of his week. He loved the camaraderie of the staff and the endless strategy sessions with Ron at the helm.

"Tires," Ron said. "Used tires."

He took a swig of coffee and walked to the other side of the room.

"We'll buy a truckload of them, fill the insides with cement, dirt, whatever we can find, and line them up along the hillsides with major roads."

Ron clicked the PowerPoint and an image popped onto the screen of a rural hillside supported by dusty tires, layered and stacked on top of each other like bricks.

"Erosion prevention at its finest," he said. "It's cheap, it's effective, it's environmentally sound, and best of all, it's a hands-on activity that the people in the communities can take part in."

Ron was beaming. Pete swallowed a bite of eggs dipped in *crema* and marveled at Ron's enduring optimism. From where Pete sat, the entire country was in shambles. Just that morning, he had seen a photo of a six-year-old Salvadoran girl who had been smashed by a massive boulder that fell through the roof of her home. Her body wasn't visible, thank God, but next to the boulder was a teddy bear and one little shoe. The sight of it had strangled his heart, especially when he thought about his own two daughters.

Yet, here was Ron—always moving forward, always reassessing and brainstorming a new plan to improve things for the next time around.

Pete had learned from Ron and taken a similar approach to learning Spanish. After the meeting ended, he decided to practice by having a conversation with Absalon Rivas, ENLACE's resident computer technician. Pete used the vocabulary and sentence structures he had learned so far to tell Absalon about his weekend and about getting so lost in one section of San Salvador that he couldn't find his way home. Mid-sentence, Pete realized that he didn't know the word for "embarrassed" in Spanish, so he did what he always did in these situations. He improvised.

When it was a noun he didn't have the word for, he would use the English word and put an 'el' in front of it, plus an 'o' at the end. Like, that day when he and Dara first moved there and he couldn't find the freeway. "*Dónde está el freeway-o?*" he had asked the man behind the counter at a gas station.

Dara had nudged him afterward and said, "Is that really the word for freeway?"

"Who knows?" Pete said, smiling and shrugging his shoulders. "He gave me directions to something, so I think he understood me."

Pete racked his brain for some way to tell Absalon he was embarrassed.

"*Estoy muy embarassado,*" he said.

Absalon's eyes widened behind his silver-rimmed glasses. A smile spread across his lips and he nodded his head.

"*Desconcertado,*" Absalon said quietly.

"*Cómo?*" Pete asked.

Absalon laughed. "*En español, embarazado* means . . ." he stopped speaking and held his hands out in an arc around his midsection.

"Pregnant?" Pete asked. It was always a game of charades, this learning to communicate.

"*Sí!*" Absalon said.

Pete nearly bent over laughing. "Did I really just tell you I was pregnant?" he asked in English.

"*Sí,*" Absalon said, laughing along with him.

"So how do I say *embarrassed?*"

"*Desconcertado.*"

A realization struck Pete and he looked at Absalon. "You know more English than you let on."

"No, no, no," Absalon contested. "*Mi inglés es muy malo.*"

"Mmmm hmmm," Pete said, knowing fully that he would go to Absalon the next time he needed to know how to say an English word in Spanish.

Faded, golden light shone from the lamp in the corner of the bedroom and it pierced Pete's eyes like a sudden jolt of electricity. He squinted them shut again as a reflex and rolled onto his other side. He didn't know why the lamp was on at this time of night and he didn't care.

Two tiny mosquitoes danced across Pete's nose and buzzed lightly in his ear. His left hand waved at them violently, and he emitted a slight groan, pulling the covers over his head for protection and nestling deeper into his pillow.

THWACK! THWACK!

Pete's brow furrowed and he dared to open his eyes again, this time forcing them to remain that way in spite of the painful rays of light that dared to reveal themselves once he pulled the covers from his face. He did so slowly, unsure of what he might find.

Another mosquito buzzed by his head, drawing awareness to the itching sensation he felt on his neck. He placed his hand along the skin underneath his jaw and felt three swelling bumps. They itched like crazy.

In front of him was a disheveled Dara, standing on a chair she had drug in from the dining room and waving a paperback book in her right hand. THWACK! went the sound of the book as Dara drove it against the ceiling with all her might.

"Dara, what are you doing?" Pete asked, not bothering to mask his irritation.

"I'm killing mosquitoes, that's what I'm doing," she said.

THWACK! THWACK! THWACK!

Dara was in her pajamas and her long blonde hair fell heavy down her back, swinging from side to side as she used the weight of her entire body to swing the book with her right arm. The ceiling above her was covered in black dots, a colony of what must have been hundreds of tiny mosquitoes, some lying still, but many flying from one spot to the next, clashing into each other in confusion as they tried to evade the paperback book threatening their lives. The few she had managed to kill left messy red streaks across the white plaster ceiling.

THWACK!

"You really need to be doing this now?" Pete asked.

"Yes!" Dara exclaimed. "I am defending our children whom these mosquitoes have been feasting upon all night long."

THWACK! THWACK! More blood sprayed across the ceiling as Dara's aim and determination grew more pronounced.

After the floods and the tropical storms had come the mosquitoes in gray buzzing clouds too numerous to count. They had been pestering the entire family for the past several weeks, hiding expertly in the crevices of curtains and bedspreads. A quick wrestling or patting of either would release a swarm of hundreds flying out in all directions, only to then find yet another hidden corner to nest and reproduce inside their home. By day the mosquitoes remained dormant, but at night they went to work, leaving few patches of human flesh unbitten.

Nine-month-old Kaya was unaccustomed to sleeping with mosquito netting, and often pulled it down in her sleep. With little recourse to defend herself, she had woken up with a fever and a tender, swollen body. Kaya spent the past few mornings sobbing in pain and Dara held her close, giving her Benadryl to try to ease it.

"I'm sick of it, and they are not going to win anymore," Dara said, squinting in concentration as she aimed the book at a small patch of mosquitoes clustered together on the ceiling. THWACK!

Pete sighed. There was no stopping her. He shoved aside the covers and pulled himself up from the bed.

"Give me a book," he said.

Dara smiled. She handed him the first book within reach and Pete jumped in the air, smashing several mosquitoes with brute force, blood smearing alongside their mangled little bodies.

"Nice," Dara nodded in approval.

With that, Pete and Dara began to take turns, jumping, thwacking, and converting their bedroom ceiling into the likes of a Jackson Pollock painting.

"This is kind of fun," Pete said, smacking yet another.

Dara laughed in agreement. Then Pete began to laugh, and before long they were both close to hysterics, laughing, thwacking, and reveling in the sheer lunacy of it. With every mosquito they obliterated, their excitement grew, and by the end of the massacre, they both laid in bed next to each other. Tired, giddy, and grinning with satisfaction.

CHAPTER 9

Innocent Voices

El Salvador, 1980-1992

The United Nations estimates that 80 percent of the Salvadoran military soldiers who fought during the civil war were merely boys— boys under the age of 18.

Eighty percent.

The 2004 film *Voces Inocentes* brings this statistic to life through the story of an 11-year-old boy named Chava. The film is loosely based on the experience of the producer and screenwriter, Oscar Orlando Torres, who grew up in El Salvador during the civil war. From the start, the story pulls viewers into the constant juxtaposition of his life. On the one hand, Chava and his friends are being typical kids— goofing around, running through the streets of their neighborhood, getting lectured by their parents. On the other, they are fearing their twelfth birthdays because at the age of 12, they are old enough to be drafted to fight for the Salvadoran government.

The drafting process is brought to light in one particular scene where a convoy of army jeeps arrives at Chava's elementary school right in the middle of recess. Several men jump out in camouflage fatigues and smooth green helmets. The shrill sound of a whistle shrieks through the playground as the army men and the school principal march into the middle of the schoolyard. All the jump rope and games come to an abrupt halt as the kids fall silent and clear to the sides. Fear enters their eyes as they stare up at the principal who begins to read the names of the boys who are being drafted.

One by one, the boys line up in the middle of the playground. One cries. Another looks confused. Yet another wets his pants, urine dripping down his leg and spilling over the tops of his shoes.

"It's not fair!" a female teacher yells, lunging toward her student as he walks forward. "He's only ten!"

The army men ignore her outburst and continue reading their list of names. When they finish, the captain addresses the boys with a long shot gun cocked over his shoulder.

"You should feel proud," he says. "You're going to be soldiers like us. You're going to defend your country."

The men with the rifles and black combat boots lead the boys away from the schoolyard and into trucks that will drive them far away from the lives they have always known. The boys take nothing with them and they say goodbye to no one. Not even their parents who are likely working their jobs as usual. Assuming that their sons will be home for dinner.

In addition to the 80 percent of underage fighters in the Salvadoran military, their opposition—a group of peasants and guerrillas known as the FMLN (*Farabundo Martí Liberation National Front*)—was estimated to have about 20 percent of its fighters under the age of 18. The one difference is that most FMLN soldiers (some of whom were female) joined willingly and for various reasons. Some wanted revenge, some wanted to stop feeling helpless, and most all thought they would be fighting for a better life.

Willingly or unwillingly, the grand sum of this equation is a whole lot of young people who were yanked out of school for years at a time, estranged from their families, and indoctrinated by a culture of ruthless violence.

What became of them all?

Think of their experiences like a vast mosaic with intricate patterns. Each piece different than the one next to it. Some pieces containing elements that overlap.

Many died in combat. Some were maimed, injured, and suffered loss of hearing or eyesight. Around 40 percent of the child soldiers interviewed for one case study discovered their parents had been killed while they were fighting. Their re-adjustment to life after war was especially difficult. Others joined their families in refugee camps in Honduras, while others were sent to Mexico and smuggled over the border by paid "coyotes" so they could then live with relatives in the United States.

This last group is the one I would like to focus on for just a minute. Imagine, if you will, a growing community of Salvadoran refugees sprinkled throughout Los Angeles in the 1980s.

Not the glitzy, Hollywood version of Los Angeles, but the gang-infested, racially divided neighborhoods near MacArthur Park and Pico Union where the Mexican Mafia ruled the streets. There were also the notorious Bloods and Crips, the Laotian gangs, Cambodian gangs, Vietnamese gangs, and the oft-overlooked white gangs comprised of Skinheads, Ku Klux Klan members, and other hate-wielding supremacists.

The streets of East Los Angeles were like a war zone all their own, and in the midst of it landed the young Salvadorans who knew little more than to do what they had already been taught in situations such as this—to meet violence with more violence. A reflex muscle finely tuned. In the war, they had learned how to make weapons, build defenses, and band together in an effort to save each other's lives.

Some joined Barrio 18, an already-established gang that is rumored to have started in Los Angeles as early as the 1940s. For other Salvadorans, banding together resembled little more than a disgruntled group of teenagers standing on street corners, smoking weed, and listening to heavy metal. According to the oral history of the *Mara Salvatrucha*, these were their humble beginnings. They started fights at school, stole cassette players out of random cars, and engaged in low-level drug trafficking.

As these teenagers began committing crimes, they were also sentenced to jail. And it was in jail that their desire for power and respect was finally realized. In jail, the Salvadorans found mentors. Experienced gang bangers well-versed in the art of organized crime. These mentors taught them how to compete against other gangs with the hopes of both gaining control and learning to profit from it. As journalist Geoffrey Ramsey states, "Controlling the streets made no sense if you could not get financial benefit from it."

As they were released from prison, they took these new skills to the streets and taught them to their peers. In time, MS-13 had gained enough respect to approach the Mexican Mafia and form an alliance. Together, the two gangs expanded in members, territory, and enterprise. They spread throughout the US, crossed the border into Mexico, and added to their laundry list of criminal activity which then included extortion, kidnapping, and trafficking of firearms and drugs.

In February of 1992, the civil war finally ended when the Salvadoran government signed an official peace treaty with the FMLN. Two months later, the verdict for the Rodney King trial was announced and the streets of Los Angeles erupted into violent riots.

Why? Because the African American community was outraged. Video footage had been released of white police officers senselessly beating a black man named Rodney King. Throughout the trial, they had been hoping and praying for justice—that the offending police offers would get sentenced to jail. This didn't happen.

The community fought back by starting fires, looting stores, pulling people out of cars that were stopped at intersections, and beating them in the streets. The worst case was of a man named Reginald Denny who was yanked from his vehicle, nearly beaten to death, and who suffered acute brain damage after his head was bashed in with a cinder block. The doctors found a total of 91 fractures in his skull.

News coverage of the LA Riots sparked more riots in major cities throughout the US. As the situation grew in volatility, President Bill Clinton decided it was time to act. He assigned a task force who realized that much of the violence was a result of gang activity. The best way to stop it, they reasoned, was to "get tough on crime." First, Clinton enacted the "Three Strikes You're Out" law, which meant even misdemeanors and nonviolent offenses could result in a lifetime jail sentence if it was a third criminal offense.

Second, the Clinton administration found that many of the criminals clogging up American jails were actually foreigners, and perhaps it was high time to send them back to their own countries. In 1996, Clinton signed a policy deporting all foreign criminals. From 2000-2004, an estimated 20,000 prisoners were sent back to El Salvador, Honduras, and Guatemala.

In 2001, two major earthquakes hit El Salvador, which further weakened an already suffering economy that had never quite recovered from the twelve year civil war. As the MS-13 and Barrio 18 members returned to their home country, they hardly recognized it. Many of their family members and friends had died in the war or relocated. The job prospects were sparse, and even if there had been jobs available, most of the deportees were uneducated and under-qualified.

Under-qualified for everything, except the lifestyle they already knew.

CHAPTER 10

Spanish Lessons

El Salvador, 2005-2006

The Centro de Intercambio y Solidaridad, otherwise known as CIS, is a grassroots organization that teaches Spanish classes and promotes social justice in San Salvador. They began in 1993 after the peace treaties were signed that ended the civil war, and their main objective was to promote positive change and spread awareness of the Salvadoran government's human rights violations against their own citizens. They converted an old brick home into a language school and painted colorful murals all over the outside. It was located down the street from the University of El Salvador, in a part of town known for being leftist and revolutionary. A part of town Dara had never ventured to.

She sat in the driver's seat of the *microbús* with her hand hovering over the keys which dangled from the ignition. All she had to do was turn them and the vehicle would spring to life. She imagined herself putting the *microbús* in reverse, backing out of the driveway, waving to the guards at the gate to their housing community, and making her way through the streets of San Salvador. All on her own.

She said a brief prayer for strength, took a deep breath, and set out on her first solo drive in a foreign country. Her first solo drive and her first Spanish class, all in one day. Taking classes at CIS had seemed the best option for Dara, as they were supposedly more practical, more immersive, more conversation-based than the grammar-intensive classes Pete had been taking at the Jesuit university. Plus, they were a lot cheaper. At CIS, students could pay by the week and there was little commitment involved.

Dara had liked all of these attributes, and when Jenny McGee offered to take classes with her, she was sold. David and Jenny had become some of the DeSoto's closest friends in San Salvador. Pete and David started surfing together in the mornings before work, and Dara loved exploring Jenny's art studio in her apartment and learning about the latest abstract paintings she was working on. Her recent exhibit had been called *Pixel Painting* and it was a lighthearted play on the way digital images become blurry when they are blown up to a larger format.

"When the picture gets super large, it breaks down into pixels," Jenny explained, "and if you're standing really close to it, all you can make out is a fuzzy schematic of squares."

Jenny was petite with dark brown hair and bangs cut straight across her forehead. She led Dara through a group of canvases filled with tiny, colorful dots.

"But as you walk away, it starts to come into focus," Jenny continued. "Like life, like reality. The truth of what we see every day becomes clearer when we're able to have a critical distance. A separation from it."

Dara thought about this as she followed the directions she had written out to Jenny's house. Perhaps, if she distanced herself from the idea of driving in San Salvador, it wouldn't seem as big and scary as it did right now. Maybe the same could be true for learning Spanish? For all of it?

She picked up Jenny and the two of them headed to their class at CIS. They walked up the cement steps and through the arched doorway of the converted home. The instructors were all former guerrilla fighters with the FMLN. They drank lots of coffee and told stories about the war. They passed out poems written by Argentinian freedom fighters and sang songs from the revolution. They showed gory videos of Salvadorans being massacred and told of how the American government was responsible. How Ronald Reagan was evil. Not a single word was translated into English, but the negative tone was easy to pick up.

"Did I hear them say the US government was involved?" Dara leaned over and asked Jenny in a whisper. "That Reagan was *malo?*"

Jenny nodded.

Dara's head began to throb, as though her heart had relocated itself to her skull. Pound. Pound. Pound. She tried to blink away the pain. To focus on the words instead of the images. But none of it was making sense. *Is any of this true?* she wondered. It seemed so awful, it was hard to wrap her brain around. The instructor continued to speak in lilting, rapid fire Spanish and Dara realized that in the last three hours, she had understood a total of maybe five words.

Five words in three hours.

Dara saw an image of her former high school English teacher peering at her from the front of the class.

"Why don't you understand what a noun is?" the teacher had asked.

"I, uh . . ." Dara had sputtered, feeling the eyes of all her classmates boring into her. "I think it's a . . ."

"A person. A place. Or a thing," the teacher said, impatience marking every syllable.

Dara felt her face redden as she stared down at her desk, wishing the floor of the classroom would open and swallow her up.

Later that afternoon, her mother had picked her up from school and whisked her away to Hollywood where Dara was one of the top five finalists for the *Teen Magazine* model search. After she had gone through hair and makeup and passed wardrobe check, she felt the hot lights of the cameras on her and did what she always did. She smiled, she posed, and she hid the growing sadness that all she had to offer was little more than a pretty face.

The pounding in Dara's head grew louder than the Spanish instructor who was speaking in front of her. She felt a tightness in her chest that spread into her lungs. She couldn't breathe. She needed to get out.

Dara pushed herself up from the desk and walked quickly to the bathroom. She shut the door behind her and gasped for air. Her heart banged against her chest like a drum gone haywire, her head throbbed, and she could barely breathe.

What is happening to me?

She leaned her back against the door and let her body slide to the floor. She sucked in erratic bursts of air and prayed to Jesus like never before.

There on the floor of the bathroom, Dara felt an unmistakable presence. A warmth wrapped around her, holding her close. She leaned into it. Further, and then further still. First, her heartbeat began to slow, and then her breath along with it. The air came more easily and she dared to open her eyes.

The pain in Dara's head was still present, but everything else seemed to have passed. She pushed herself up from the floor and opened the door.

Jenny was standing outside waiting.

"Are you OK?" she asked.

Dara just looked at her, unsure how to answer.

"I don't know what happened to me . . ."

"You looked kind of pale when you left class."

"I do get migraines. I have one right now. But I've never . . . I was hyperventilating, and my heart was pounding like it was going to beat right out of my chest."

"It sounds like you had a panic attack," Jenny said.

"Really?" Dara asked.

"Maybe. Those are the main symptoms, anyway."

Dara stared at the brick wall behind Jenny and allowed the words to sink in.

"You poor thing!" Jenny leaned toward Dara and wrapped her arms around her.

Dara let her head sink into Jenny's shoulder and realized that here in El Salvador, she had a friend. A real one.

———————————

Marlena Fernandez pressed her finger into the doorbell and let her hand fall beside her waist. She adjusted the strap of the book bag that carried all her teaching materials: an English to Spanish dictionary, a stack of magazine clippings for visual aids, and Nasy Levy's *First Year Spanish* textbook. With home tutoring sessions, it was always good to have options and backup plans, especially when it came to working with new clients.

When Carla Bolanos had asked Marlena to take on yet another student, the first thought Marlena had was an image of her crowded daily planner. She saw each day filled with her own handwriting. By day, she was a photo journalist for the local newspaper, *El Diario de Hoy*, and in the evenings she gave private Spanish lessons to whatever clients Carla drummed up. Generally, the spouses of Carla's coworkers at the American Embassy.

And then there was Gerardo. Marlena had only been dating him for a short period of time, but there was something about his kindness, his gentleness that made her hopeful she might be carving out more and more space for him as time went on.

Another client was the last thing Marlena needed.

But Carla's eyes were hopeful, pleading.

Marlena tucked her dark brown hair behind her ear and sighed. "Tell me who these people are," she mumbled.

"They're missionaries from California," Carla explained. "The husband works with Walter at ENLACE, and it's actually his wife who needs lessons the most. She's at home all day with her four children, the older two she home schools, and she's gotten little opportunity since they moved here to actually get out, interact with Salvadorans, and practice the language."

Marlena nodded. "I don't at all have time for this," she said.

Carla opened her mouth as if to protest and Marlena stopped her.

"But I'll do it," she said.

Her father would do it, that Marlena knew. Her father had taught her that time was something you get creative about inventing and procuring for things that really matter in life.

Marlena thought of her family when she was seven years old—when they were Salvadoran refugees living in Canada. She thought of her own mother and the challenges she had faced learning English, trying to raise Marlena and her sister in a foreign land.

This family, whoever they were, seemed like they might be worth inventing time for. Especially if Carla was this persistent.

Marlena reached up to ring the doorbell one more time when it suddenly swung open to reveal a tall, tan blonde woman. Her face was beautiful, even in the absence of any visible makeup.

"*Buena noches*," Marlena said, holding out her hand.

"*Buena noches*," the woman repeated, lines crinkling around her blue eyes as she smiled. "You must be Marlena. Come on in."

"*Sí, es verdad.*" Marlena said walking through the door. "*Mucho gusto.*"

The woman's smile faltered a bit. "I'm Dara," she said. "You speak English, right?"

Marlena laughed. "I most certainly do. But you hired me for a Spanish lesson, no?"

Dara let out a nervous laugh and looked to the floor. "Yes, of course. I just . . . I'm not very good at this. At speaking Spanish."

Marlena set her bag down and looked at Dara. "That's very interesting," she said. "Because in my experience, if someone doesn't speak a language, it's hard for them to tell whether they are good or bad at it."

Dara felt the giant knot in her stomach loosen just a bit. She laughed. "Well, you are right in that I have no idea about any of this—how I sound when I try to speak, if I'm at all on the right track. All I know is that when I tried to take Spanish classes around the city, I walked away with a splitting migraine."

"Ouch," Marlena said. Her face softened. "You know, my mother had a similar experience when she was forced to learn English."

"Oh yeah?" Dara asked.

Marlena nodded and pressed her back into the soft couch, settling in. This would be a long story, and perhaps she shouldn't be sharing it with a woman she had only just met. But something about Dara compelled her to tell it. Perhaps it was the concerned look in her eyes. The way she seemed so well intentioned, but lost.

Marlena took a deep breath and allowed her mind to drift back to El Salvador in 1984, exactly two years after the start of the civil war. When power and money and freedom were tangible items being fought over in a vicious tug of war. Never enough to go around, the entirety of each had to belong to one side and one side only.

The elite members of Salvadoran society, the government officials, the owners of coffee plantations and department stores and successful businesses had all grown accustomed to living lives of comfort and excess. This was nothing new, of course. This same story of divided wealth and of hierarchy had been playing out since the beginning of time, throughout centuries, civilizations, and all corners of the globe.

Marlena's father, Pablo Fernandez, cared little how commonplace such narratives were. In his eyes, every person was made in the image of Jesus, and therefore had immense value no matter what class he or she was born into. Pablo was a Baptist preacher at a small church in San Salvador. He was evangelical, to be sure, but in the 1970s as the Salvadoran government started to commit grosser, more frequent human rights violations against its own people, Pablo did something few other evangelical leaders dared to do. He began to align himself with the Catholic church.

In 1968, the Latin American Catholic church leaders held a regional meeting in Medellín, Colombia to discuss a potential move toward solidarity and defense of the lower class. It was a recommendation handed down from the Second Vatican Council who had been thinking and praying over what it might mean to forge a relationship between the Catholic church and the modern world. Bishops in Latin America took a good look around their modern world and noticed the current business model in much of Central and South America was inhumane and bordered on all-out slavery. The upper class had grown dependent upon it. This was a problem.

Whole groups of people were denied access to economic mobility and basic human rights. Perhaps this could change if these groups were first educated about their rights, and then taught how to mobilize and fight for them?

Governments were oppressing their own citizens, which meant political changes needed to occur, and social consciousness was nonexistent. Those with wealth and comfort showed little care or compassion for the plight of the poor. The same was true even of upper class citizens of faith. Their faith didn't seem to have any bearing on the way they conducted their lives and businesses. There was a massive disconnect and this, too, needed to change. Social consciousness needed to be awakened and justice restored in light of the gospel. This became the mission of the Latin American Catholic churches in 1968. In later years it would be given a name: *liberation theology.*

Throughout the 1970s, Marlena's father reflected on the implications of his faith in the context of poverty and violence. Pablo began to appreciate certain aspects of liberation theology, as he had a heart for the peasant farmers who didn't know how to read, who slaved away for little pay, who fed their families corn and beans and lived in houses they constructed themselves out of plastic trash bags and corn husks.

Although these families were not traditionally educated, the Jesuit missionaries were rising up throughout the 1970s in a unified effort to teach them about their rights as human beings. To show them they deserved more and it might be worth it to fight for it. Slowly, these peasant farmers began to envision themselves inching into a world they never imagined they could access. A world they always thought was built for everyone else.

From there, they began to mobilize and to plan. Quietly. In secret.

The years went by and they grew in strength and number. They prayed and trained and tested out one theory after the next, until a clear and logical course of action was solidified.

The night before the plantation workers planned to attack their employers, the employers found out about their plans and overtook them. Violence ensued and a twelve-year civil war was born. It grew bloodier and more desperate by the day, as both sides were recruiting. Neighbor pinned against neighbor. Bodies piling up on roadsides.

In 1977 the Catholic church had appointed a man named Oscar Romero to be Archbishop of San Salvador. When the civil war broke out in 1980, Bishop Romero boldly proclaimed his allegiance with the peasant fighters, which was tantamount to the Catholic church opposing the Salvadoran government. When the government ordered its troops to open fire on innocent civilians, Bishop Romero publicly challenged them to disobey orders.

The Salvadoran government didn't like this one bit. Neither were they thrilled that these pastors still had the audacity to preach of human rights on Sundays and to rally their congregations in support of the lower class.

Priests or not, they needed to be stopped. The solution was a group of armed, paramilitary groups called death squads, whose primary function was to make meddlesome priests, like Archbishop Romero, disappear.

On March 24, 1980, Romero was leading a congregation in mass when a military death squad stormed the church and opened fire on him. He was shot in the heart by a single bullet and died instantly.

The entire leftist movement was deeply grieved and saw fit to continue Romero's legacy. For Marlena's father, this meant doing everything possible to serve the victims of the war. As the army and air force took over entire Salvadoran villages, many families were displaced, like refugees in their own country. Children were displaced as well and were left orphaned because their parents were killed during the violent takeover. Some children were even kidnapped by military officers and sold on the black market to adoption agencies in the US.

Pablo and his church responded to this crisis by raising funds to build an orphanage for displaced children at risk. It was a refuge that would shield them from the fighting and the kidnapping. But as Pablo succeeded in protecting many of these children, he was unable to protect himself.

On October 28, 1984, the death squads came for Pablo Fernandez. He was walking some friends home from church on a Sunday afternoon when two vans pulled up beside him on the road. A group of men exited the vans wearing civilian clothing. They beat him with the butt of a rifle and he fell to the ground. From there, they shoved him inside the van and drove him to an undisclosed location.

He was held captive for a day and a half and physically tortured.

What the death squad wanted from him was information. They wrongly assumed that since Pablo aligned himself with the FMLN movement, he would know where the guerrilla leaders were hiding. This wasn't the case. As a pastor, his main role was to serve and to love the people in his midst. Fighting was something he left to others. He tried explaining this to his captors, but they didn't believe him.

After a day and a half, they took Pablo to the National Police Headquarters where he was questioned further. This time, they began to threaten his family. They knew he had a wife, a seven-year-old daughter named Marlena, and another daughter who was less than one month old.

Back at home, Marlena, her baby sister, and her mother were grieving and praying—enveloped in a circle of warmth by the strong matriarchy in their family. Marlena's grandmothers and aunt prayed constantly and cared for them while her father was held captive.

After several weeks, their prayers were answered through a barrage of phone calls and letters from Baptist churches all over the United States and Canada demanding that the Salvadoran government release Pablo. Support poured in from church leaders in Berkeley, San Francisco, Seattle, Toronto, and Winnipeg. Soon, it wasn't just the Baptist leaders putting pressure on the government. Presbyterian churches joined the cause and the United Church of Canada made a plea.

Finally, the government relented under one main condition: Pablo Fernandez could not stay in El Salvador. From the day of his release, he was given one week to leave the country. The Fernandez family applied for political asylum which was granted first by Mexico, and later by Canada where they ended up living until Marlena was twelve years old.

"And that is how I came to learn English," Marlena said, looking at Dara.

Dara sat across from her on the couch in wide-eyed silence. So, it was true. Everything she had learned during her week of Spanish classes at CIS—the video footage of massacres. It had been biased, of course, and terribly one sided. Dara saw that now. But she also recognized the ugly truth of it. Through Marlena's story, all the fragmented pieces of this foreign country were beginning to come together.

As Dara spent time with Marlena, she continued to learn about El Salvador's history. Their Spanish lessons varied from one week to the next. Sometimes they would pray together in Spanish, other times they would gab for hours in English because the moment they started sharing about their days, Marlena and Dara found they had so much to tell each other. Dara respected Marlena for her strength and tenacity.

She had been through more in her short lifetime than Dara could even comprehend.

Marlena respected both Dara and Pete for living out their faith so fully. Their faith was what brought them here, and that impressed Marlena to no end. As a pastor's kid, she had been around a lot of religious people who could preach all day long; yet, their actions and the way they lived their lives rarely seemed to match what came out of their mouths. But Dara and Pete weren't like that. They were genuine, they were bold, and they allowed their love for Jesus to guide them. It was both rare and beautiful.

In time, Marlena's in-home Spanish lessons transitioned into field trips around San Salvador where Dara could practice the language in real life situations. Marlena took her to produce markets and taught Dara how to buy papayas and barter for the best price. She taught her that most public restrooms don't have running water, and that she would need to fill a bucket with water and pour it down the toilet before flushing.

In early 2006, at the height of El Salvador's dry season, Marlena invited Dara on the mother of all field trips. They were to visit a remote village about four hours outside San Salvador, and Dara would need to drive, as Marlena didn't know how. Like many Salvadorans, Marlena hadn't bothered to learn. She simply took the bus around town, or walked.

Dara's driving experience in El Salvador had yet to venture outside the capital, but she agreed to do it anyway for two reasons. First, she knew she would be with Marlena who seemed ever capable of handling most anything. Second, Dara and Pete had a group of friends visiting from the US and they thought it might be fun to expose their visitors to a bonafide cultural experience.

The group woke with the sun and formed a caravan with a group of women from Marlena's father's church. These women had been teaching the female residents of the rural village how to weave baskets so they could sell them for money. In the US, we might call this a local mission trip. The goal is to marry resources with skills and knowledge so that less-resourced communities will be empowered to help themselves.

In Southern California, of course, there are nicely paved roadways connecting any and every community. In El Salvador, not so much.

When the caravan reached the city of Suchitoto, about an hour and a half northeast of San Salvador, they exited the main highway and turned onto an unmarked dirt road. A steep hill full of weeds without a path in sight. Just a narrow opening between straw-colored bushes.

Dara shifted the *microbús* into a lower gear and continued to follow the car in front of her. Her stomach churned a bit as she thought about all the passengers she was responsible for. There was Marlena, herself, plus five women and a man named Josh who were all visiting from the church she and Pete had attended back in Valencia. Dara was happy to show them anything and everything she could, but this? This was getting a little scary.

The *microbús* bumped and jittered and rocked its way over the dirt road. Thick layers of dust rose up with each turn of the wheel, making it difficult to see. Granted, they had entered the tail end of the dry season, but even in San Salvador the vegetation was still lush and green. This place they were heading felt parched and desolate.

"You guys OK back there?" Dara asked in a forced cheery tone. "No one's getting too car sick, I hope?"

Right as the words left her mouth, the front tire of the *microbús* lodged itself into a deep pothole. The engine revved and the wheels spun in place.

"I think we're stuck," Josh said. "Put the car in neutral, and I'll hop out and see if I can push us."

Panic welled inside Dara, threatening to take over. *Don't let it*, she told herself. She nodded to Josh and felt extreme gratitude for his presence.

With a quick bit of maneuvering and shoving, Josh managed to free the tire, and off they continued, crawling through the hot, dusty road at an average speed of five miles per hour. The *microbús* ended up stalling and getting stuck several other times. Before long, the whole crew got out and pushed together while Dara sat in the driver's seat trying to steer. The air outside was thick and humid, and everyone climbed back into the vehicle with sweat dripping down their faces.

It took about five hours to reach their destination, and when they did, they were greeted by a large group of curious children playing in the streets. The first thing Dara noticed was their swollen bellies, punctuated by skinny arms and legs. The hair on their heads was lighter than most Salvadorans she had met—a dishwater blonde. She found out later this was further evidence of malnutrition. The second thing Dara noticed was the lice. These children had lice crawling up their scalps and venturing down strands of their hair.

Dara attempted the intricate balance of absorbing what she was seeing without getting overwhelmed by it.

Marlena joined the other women from her father's church and began introducing everyone and giving a tour of their little village. She explained how there weren't any creeks nearby, which meant that water, both to bathe with and to drink, was always scarce. In these conditions, it was also hard to plant crops or create any sort of economy to support themselves.

That was why the church had committed to teaching these people some sort of trade. They brought in resources and materials so the women in the village could learn to craft. They hand wove blankets, baskets, and shirts, which the church members took with them back to San Salvador to sell, then brought the profits back to the villagers so they could feed their families.

In the midst of the most dire poverty Dara had ever witnessed, she noticed three pristine structures in the center of the village. The first was a basketball court that no one was using. The next appeared to be a newly-built school, and the third was a beautiful medical clinic. But again, no one was using them.

The classrooms were lined with chalkboards and desks, but as Dara peered through the windows, she noticed the shelves were totally empty. There were no textbooks or supplies in sight. The clinic, too, felt like a gorgeous shell of something that could be great, but had no real substance on the inside. No medicine, no staff, no moving human bodies bringing energy and purpose to an otherwise lifeless building.

"What is all of this?" Dara finally asked Marlena.

"Ah," Marlena said. "This is the work of a bunch of well-meaning nonprofits. Big ones. With names you have probably heard of and maybe even donated to."

"I figured as much," Dara said. "I mean somebody had to pay to build all of this. But I don't understand why it's not being used."

Marlena sighed. "Because you can't just spend a bunch of money to build a school and then leave without training any teachers. You can't just build a basketball hoop without teaching the children what the game is and how to play it. And you can't build a medical clinic without also giving the community a means to access medical supplies. To pay and attract capable doctors and nurses. These are the things that foreigners just don't understand."

Marlena threw her hands in the air in exasperation and continued. "I love the hearts of all the people who built this stuff, I really do. But the problem is that they came into this village, they saw all the poverty, and they said: 'We have all the answers for them! We'll give them what we think they need and then we will leave!' But that's not the way change works. Not meaningful change. It takes years and years of time and continued relationship. All of these beautiful structures come to nothing without that."

Dara listened to her words and thought of Pete.

Pete had been telling her this for years. Pete had spent all of college and his graduate work studying this very topic, and what he loved most about ENLACE was that they didn't build structures and leave. They committed to work with a community for a minimum of ten years, and not only that, they first approached the local pastors and community leaders with one single question. Not, *what can we do for you?* but *what is it that you need?* Rather than making assumptions about what was needed, ENLACE put the ball in the community's court and allowed them to guide the entire process.

That was why every community project Pete had worked with so far looked a bit different than the one before it. For example, one community decided they needed bridges built. So ENLACE provided building materials and structural engineers to help design them. But the community committed to doing all the manual labor to build the bridges. They determined the exact locations. It was an active partnership between them and ENLACE.

Another community might decide they needed a well. Another might want to build a medical clinic. It was ENLACE's job to empower them to carry out their vision by equipping them with the right experts and professionals who could supervise and implement everything.

Pete had explained all this to Dara several times. He said he'd never seen another nonprofit so committed to this model, and that was one of the many reasons he respected ENLACE and wanted to work with them so badly. Dara had always listened and nodded. It sounded good, she reasoned. It sounded logical.

But standing here in this remote village with Marlena was the first time she genuinely understood it. She looked at the children with their bellies and the older women who were their mothers—learning to weave, pulling out chairs for Dara and her American friends, offering up any token they could to make them feel comfortable in their homes—and her heart broke.

This is why I am here, she thought.

None of it had been her vision, none of it her dream. But she was here to support Pete because what he was doing was beautiful. These people were beautiful. And they deserved so much more than this.

Dara wanted to help them get it, even if it meant sacrificing a lot on her part, and most certainly it would. She imagined the *microbús* breaking down another half dozen times on the trip back home. She thought about the mosquitoes, the language barrier, the lengthy power outages that occurred every time a major storm hit. Every time she had just gone grocery shopping and stocked up her fridge.

This was Dara's life now. And for the first time since leaving California, she finally saw purpose in it.

PART THREE

TRAUMA

Trauma is an ugly shadow hard to shake. It can be tricky at times—wearing disguises, jumping out of hiding places, deforming reality.

When we run from trauma, it follows. When we deny it, it grows bigger. The only way to shrink it is to match its stride. To look trauma in the eye and say, "I'll walk with you."

CHAPTER 11

Is Something Wrong With Us?

San Salvador, 2006

The treadmill whirred underneath Dara's feet, emitting a calming, rhythmic hum. She wiped the sweat from her forehead and felt her heart thumping inside her chest. Her legs continued to carry her, mindlessly, as she pumped her arms harder, forcing her legs to follow suit. In little more than a month, Ron and Michelle Bueno would be moving back from their year-long hiatus in California and would be needing their Salvadoran home back. Where she and Pete would live once they returned still hadn't been determined. All Dara knew at this point was that she planned to make as much use as possible of Michelle's treadmill before they moved.

Especially since PJ and Isaac were in school now. Real school. The kind with teachers and recess and report cards. She and Pete had taken a major step in December by enrolling them in the International School of San Salvador. Home schooling had become more challenging as Dara came to realize that it, like everything else, was transformed into a completely different experience than it had been in the US. She could use all the same textbooks and materials, do everything exactly the same way that she had done back in California, but the fact remained: here in El Salvador, there weren't as many options to fill up the day once lessons were finished.

The boys would get antsy and rambunctious. After sitting them in front of the same *Power Rangers* DVD for the umpteenth time, Dara finally decided they needed a change. The International School had a great reputation and was modeled after the American educational system. Most classes were taught in English, and the students who attended hailed from all over the world. They were children of other missionaries, expats, or diplomats who worked at the US Embassy.

Most of Dara's fears were put to rest after she and Pete met with the principal who was both warm and supportive. The one element that continued to give her pause was the armed vigilantes who stood guard in front of the school's entrance. Every morning that she dropped off PJ and Issac, Dara had to battle the urge to speed past the men with massive rifles dangling from their hips and drive her boys straight back to the plazuela where she knew she could keep them safe.

Let ME keep them safe, she sensed God telling her.

There it was again. That invitation.

Each morning, she nodded in agreement, took a deep breath, squeezed her boys tightly, and sent them off, watching as their bright backpacks disappeared through the doorway. Fear and love battled for room in Dara's chest, but there was only so much the heart could hold at one time.

Sweat trickled down Dara's temples as she lowered the pace of the treadmill to a brisk walk. *Please provide a safe and comfortable new home for us here in El Salvador* she prayed. *Show us how to go about looking for one.* She felt her heartbeat getting slower with each step and began to meditate on all the ways God had always provided for her family. Even in the smallest of things. She thanked Him for their house back in Valencia, their stay at Torres del Bosque, and now this beautiful place at Ron and Michelle's. She thanked Him for the International School and for the Union Church of San Salvador, a church they had been attending that was run by and for American expats. Every element, from the worship music to the sermon, was in English, and going there on Sundays was like entering a safe refuge with wooden archways and bright windows.

As Dara thought about the Union Church, she remembered hearing about a couple who also went there—James and Ruth DeBorst. An intriguing couple who had no less than six children in tow. Dara had only spoken to them a handful of times, but she had heard from friends at church that the DeBorsts were going to be relocating to the United States for a while. And if that were true, they just might need someone to rent their home while they were away. Dara flipped off the switch on the treadmill and allowed it to roll to a complete stop.

That's what she would do. At church. On Sunday. She would talk to Ruth and James DeBorst and ask about renting their house.

"Do we know anything about where this house is?" Pete asked.

"Nope," Dara said.

Pete looked skeptical. "This seems kind of random."

"I know," Dara agreed. "It's totally random, but it came to me while I was praying and I really feel like it's from God. I think we should listen."

Pete laughed and walked across the room to give Dara a kiss. "Whatever you say."

Ruth and James DeBorst walked through the doorway of the Union Church, standing tall with a deliberate and focused gait. Ruth was slim and she wore long, dangling earrings. Her dark hair was pulled back at the nape of her neck with sprinklings of gray framing her face. James had a white goatee and dark rimmed glasses. Together they exuded an aura of power.

Dara sensed it first in their children. She had been volunteering to teach Sunday school classes, and the DeBorst kids—all six of them— were often present. Although they were a blended family, with half being from Ruth's first marriage and half from James', they all got along well and had a grounded maturity about them. In class, they were quiet and polite, never talking back to Dara or showing any hints of entitlement. She was also impressed by how they viewed everyone they met as equals, regardless of the color of their skin, or economic status.

Dara had been in awe of this family for quite some time, and it occurred to her that she would normally feel silly doing something like this. Approaching people she barely knew and being audacious enough to ask to rent their home. Yet something in her spirit felt peaceful as she said hello to Ruth. And that peace made her brave.

Ruth's eyes widened in excitement the moment Dara questioned her about their house and what they planned to do with it after moving to the US.

"This would be the biggest blessing!" Ruth said. "We have thirty days until we have to leave El Salvador and it's all been such a whirlwind. Can you and Pete come over for dinner this evening? We'd love to talk further."

The DeSotos and DeBorsts crammed together that evening, elbow to elbow, at Ruth's banquet-style dinner table, which was maxed at full capacity. Ruth was a native Argentinian and had decorated the house with South American designs and intricate woodworking. Their home was in a gated *plazuela* on a hill in the upper-class neighborhood of Escalón. It was the very last house on the street, shoved up against a painted cement wall that wrapped around the perimeter of the *plazuela*. On top of the wall sat rings of barbed wire and an electric fence, providing a barrier between its residents and the families with less resources who lived directly outside its walls.

The house was beige with white trim, framed by unruly bougainvillea climbing up the sides. The top floor had four main bedrooms, plus a palatial master bedroom and bath. The first floor had an office and a maid's quarters, bringing the grand total of rooms outside of the kitchen and living room to seven. Seven rooms. It was the largest home Pete and Dara had ever stepped foot in, let alone considered occupying.

As the two families ate and drank together, Pete and Dara shared their story of coming to El Salvador and Ruth and James explained why they were leaving in such a hurry for the United States—they had both been granted scholarships to attend graduate programs in Massachusetts. James at Harvard, and Ruth at Boston University.

Once the empty plates were cleared from the table and all ten of the collective DeSoto/DeBorst kids were excused, the adults brewed a pot of coffee and the conversation deepened. The couples found they had much in common and discussed everything from parenting to liberation theology. The one topic that didn't come up was the topic

Dara was most curious about: What *exactly* happened to Ruth's first husband?

She and Pete had heard brief versions of the story from friends at church. It was widely known that he had been murdered while doing missionary work in Ecuador, and some said Ruth had actually been there when it happened. That he had been shot right in front of her and their two young children.

What Dara wanted to ask Ruth was how she survived something like that. How she managed to get out of bed the next day, and how her kids managed to get out of bed, and how they all managed to be the strong, amazing individuals that she saw before her now.

Pete silently wondered about it too. He imagined having to own a story such as theirs. It seemed a heavy weight to carry.

That night, the DeSotos and DeBorsts agreed that the DeSoto family would move into the DeBorst home, paying rent while the DeBorsts were living in the US. For a moderate sum, Pete and Dara would also purchase everything inside the home, from the furniture to the dishes, as Pete and Dara had absolutely nothing to fill a house of this size.

They moved in May of 2006 and spent the summer having backyard barbecues, making popsicles, and playing baseball games on the lawn. Although the rainy season was in full swing, Pete grew to love the set of hammocks that hung in the DeBorsts' backyard. On days when the rain settled down—when it wasn't so flashy and loud, but fell like a quiet mist—Pete laid in the hammock and let the drops land on his closed eyelids. He listened and rocked slowly, back and forth, noting how there was something so calming and nourishing about quiet rain. Nature's reminder to slow down, to exhale, to rest.

And after the rain came the mosquitoe
Hovering in thick, black cloud
Above stagnant water
In a field behind the DeBorst house.
Searching for invisible blood vessels
Beneath human flesh.

August 2006

Dengue fever is a painful, flu-like virus found predominately in Latin America, Asia, and places with wet, tropical climates. In the world of mosquitoes, the primary culprit for passing this virus along is of the female variety. The proper Latin name for a female mosquito is *Aedes aegypti*. We'll call her *Ae*, for short.

When an *Ae* mosquito sinks her pointed, needle-like mouth into a person's skin, she immediately begins searching for a blood vessel. Once she finds it, she secretes a saliva which prevents the person's blood from clotting so that she may then drink to her heart's content.

If the person whose blood she drinks is infected with dengue fever, then *Ae* will contract dengue, too. Whether the virus is as painful for mosquitoes as it is for humans, we do not know. Either way, our friend *Ae*, the mosquitoess, goes into a 4-6 day incubation period. Once that's over, she resumes her search for blood, only this time she is a dengue carrier and any lucky soul she bites next will likely contract the virus. If that person notices *Ae* latched to his upper arm and decides to swat her away before she is satisfied, she will then leave his arm, having already infected him, land on the next unassuming person, and then the next one, until her little abdomen is full. Then she'll go off and lay eggs, potentially transmitting the dengue virus to her offspring.

A beautiful cycle.

Dengue is also known as "bone crusher disease," a term Pete DeSoto found to be accurate the moment he was formally diagnosed with it.

Pete laid in bed with a fever for upwards of ten days, sweating profusely and cradling a glass of scotch mixed with Diet Coke. As a pastor's kid and now a missionary, Pete had never been much of a drinker. But the pain he experienced during his dengue outbreak flowed in intense, throbbing waves. His body ached all the way down to his bones, and when it became more than he could bear (which was often) a bottle of Johnnie Walker Red stood proud and tall on his side table.

"You went through another one?" Dara asked, holding the empty glass bottle in her hand, a look of incredulity on her face.

Pete avoided eye contact. "You have no idea what this feels like," he mumbled.

PJ, now almost nine years old, walked down the stairs from his bedroom and took a seat next to his dad on the white couch.

"You're starting a new movie?" PJ asked as he glanced at the television screen.

Pete nodded.

"Can I watch with you?"

Pete nodded again.

They stared at the television as the previews came to an end and the copyright warnings filled the screens in neon green.

"What does *encarcelado* mean?" PJ asked, reading every word of the warning. Since attending the International School, his Spanish had improved by leaps and bounds. His accent sounded natural and he could read and write with an ease that both Pete and Dara envied.

"It means go to jail," Pete said.

"So, if you buy or watch a copied version of this DVD then you'll go to jail?" PJ asked.

Pete was silent.

"What does that mean? What's a copied DVD?"

Dara looked at Pete for assistance, but Pete just shut his eyelids.

"You know all those guys you see selling movies on the street corners?" Dara asked. "The ones that lay out blankets and put the DVDs on top of them?"

"The place where we buy all our movies here in El Salvador?" PJ asked.

Dara nodded hesitantly.

"So, the movies they sell aren't exactly legal. They're called pirated DVDs because they had to copy them, or steal them in order to get them."

"You guys buy stuff that's been stolen?"

"It supports the local Salvadoran economy," Pete mumbled.

PJ frowned. He grabbed the remote and rewound the DVD back to the warning and then hit pause. "It says right here you can go to jail for that."

"Yes, honey," Dara said, setting down the empty bottle of Johnnie Walker, "but in El Salvador everyone buys pirated DVDs."

"So it's legal in El Salvador?"

Pete winced. The pain was acting up again and his drink was running low. "Dara, please go get me another bottle."

Dara sighed.

"You guys are breaking the law," PJ insisted. "This says you're breaking the law."

He motioned to the TV screen for emphasis and then hit the play button. The warnings disappeared and gave way to the opening scenes of *Pride and Prejudice*.

PJ turned to his father in exasperation. "You're breaking the law *and* you're watching a girl's movie?"

It occurred to Pete that he was being a horrible father. A horrible missionary. A horrible human being. And on top of it all, his masculinity was perhaps now in question because he was viewing a film based on a Jane Austen novel. Again, something he wouldn't normally do, but it was at the bottom of the DVD pile and Pete hadn't seen it yet. If *Pride and Prejudice* could help him zone out and forget about this agonizing pain for a few hours, so be it.

"Never mind," PJ said. "I think I'll go play with Isaac instead."

Pete's whole body throbbed. He didn't have the energy to object as PJ got up from the couch and walked away.

The dengue ran its course and finally dissipated one week later. Pete returned to work with a new awareness of his body and a newfound gratitude for the absence of pain.

September 2006

The tennis ball made a thwacking sound as Ron Bueno smacked it with the underside of his racket, sending it across the net and over to Pete. Pete ran for it and swung, catching the edge of the ball just in time to prevent it from touching the ground. The two men rallied back and forth for hours, smacking the ball over the net, zigzagging around the court in fierce, but friendly competition. Pete loved to feel his heart pumping. Loved moving his body and addressing a challenge head on. Especially now that the dengue had passed and Pete was finally feeling like himself again.

Playing sports ignited the force of life inside him, and when he saw that green tennis ball falling several feet short of where he was standing, he ran with all his might and dove for it with fervor. The edge of Pete's racket missed the ball, just as he lost his footing and felt himself careening toward the ground, inertia pulling his body forward and dragging his leg across the bottom of the court. Pete yelled out in shock and glimpsed his knee which had been ripped wide open. Blood came gushing from the wound.

Ron tossed his racket to the floor and ran over to Pete.

"I think we better call it a day," he said. "You going to be alright?"

Pete let out an awkward laugh. "My ego's pretty bruised, but other than that . . ." He hobbled to the bathroom and assured Ron he'd be fine once he put a band aid on it.

The moment Dara saw Pete's wounded leg, her jaw dropped and she insisted that he get it checked out. She drove him straight to the emergency room at Diagnóstico, the cleanest and most advanced hospital in the whole country, which was thankfully just down the street from the DeBorsts' home. The doctors took one look and determined Pete would need stitches. They loaded him up with Novocain, sewed his leg back together, and ordered him to take it easy for the next several weeks.

First dengue and now a substantial leg injury.

"Let's hope I survive the last few months of 2006," Pete joked.

October 2006

Dara was playing with Isaac on a Saturday afternoon when the lights in the DeBorsts' living room began to flicker and snuff out. An eerie silence settled over the house, the street, the entire plazuela. With all the tropical storms during rainy season, power outages were par for the course. It was an inconvenient, yet expected part of their life here.

"Time to get the candles and flashlights!" Dara said, prompting Isaac, now almost seven years old, to trudge through the dim hallways and into the maids' quarters, which they had been using for storage.

It was only midday, but one never knew when the electricity would finally be restored. It could take hours, if not days, so it was best to be prepared before the sun set. Isaac emerged from the dark hallways with the flashlight turned on, a beam of light shooting from his hand. He walked toward Dara and moved the light in circles, as though he were drawing invisible shapes across the floor.

Dara smiled and watched him play. She was about to make a comment—something random, or silly, or trivial—when a terrified scream pierced through her walls.

Isaac froze. The beam of the flashlight suspended in midair. His eyes widened and he looked at Dara for answers.

Another scream rang out, this one longer and at a higher pitch. Dara felt her stomach harden in fear. She pushed herself up from the living room floor and walked with reluctance toward the front window.

"Mommy?" Isaac asked. Tears formed in the corners of his eyes.

"Come here, sweetie." Dara picked him up and held him close to her as she peered out the window in the direction of the scream.

It happened again. Two shrieks. Loud and painful, as though the people across the street were being tortured or terrorized.

Isaac began to cry and Dara's stomach grew queasy and hollow. Whatever was happening, she had to do something.

Pete was hours away, visiting a small village with a team of ENLACE volunteers. Calling him would do no good. Calling the police wouldn't help either because Dara feared she couldn't explain herself clearly enough in Spanish. Sure, her language skills had improved a bit, but this was an emergency situation. The pressure of it made her heart bang against her chest. What if she couldn't remember how to say something? What if she didn't understand the operator's response?

She picked up her cell phone and called Ron Bueno.

"Ron," she said, trying to maintain her composure. "There's something happening to our neighbors and I don't know what to do. The power is down in the whole *plazuela* and I keep hearing these horrible screams, like someone is being attacked. Can you call the police for me? Please?"

Ron agreed, and twenty minutes later, a band of eight *policía* stormed the *plazuela* wearing bulletproof vests and carrying M-16 machine guns. They had black masks over their faces to conceal their identities, as relations between the police and the gangs were getting increasingly hostile. If the gangs were responsible for whatever was going on here, the officers that succeeded in catching them would be in extreme danger. Hits would be put out on their lives if the other gang members discovered the officers' identities.

Dara watched the men tear down her street like a group of heavily armed ants scurrying in all directions. Their presence was even more disorienting than the screams had been, conjuring up more questions and delivering little in the way of answers and assurance. Fear seeped into Dara's veins and clenched inside her jaw. She kept waiting to hear more screaming, a burst of gunfire.

There was nothing.

The police left and the other homes in the *plazuela* remained motionless, as though no one was even living in them. Dara peered out her window and waited for signs of life. She wanted someone to come out, someone to come talk to her and explain what was going on.

But no one did.

Everyone stayed locked behind their doors. Blinds closed. Windows shut. Sealed tightly by those blood curdling screams.

Night came and went. The screams continued to replay themselves in Dara's mind until the following afternoon when she looked out her bedroom window and noticed something strange. A young Hispanic couple was walking in circles around the perimeter of the house across the street. The man's brow was furrowed in confusion, and the woman's eyes were large, frightened.

Someone to talk to, Dara thought. *Someone who might have answers.*

Language barriers aside, Dara's curiosity carried her down the stairs, out the front door, and across the street to where this couple appeared to be carrying on an investigation of sorts.

"*Hola*," Dara said, approaching the woman.

She held her hand out and introduced herself, explaining with gestures and broken Spanish that she lived across the street.

The man walked toward her and introduced himself. His name was Moses and his wife was Alba Barrientos. They explained to Dara that this was their house, and then led her to the backyard. Alba pointed her finger to the ground where a thick trail of blood was speckled across the concrete. She then pointed to the back window, which had been shattered. Tears formed in Alba's eyes and Dara began scanning their bodies for physical wounds. *They must have been hurt by this intruder,* she reasoned. *Was it them that had been screaming?*

Alba rubbed the back of her hand against her wet eyes, and began speaking quickly in Spanish. She pointed to the barbed wire and electric fence lining the *plazuela* walls and Dara understood the words *no función*, meaning, not functioning, or not working properly. She thought about the power outage and how someone could have easily climbed over that wall because the power was down.

Alba then pointed to her neighbors and she made a stabbing gesture as she spoke. She continued to narrate the key events and Dara used the physical evidence in front of her along with Alba's animated gesturing to try and piece it all together.

Years later, Dara still wouldn't know for sure what happened. But based on her conversation with Alba, she was able to infer the following:

Alba and Moses weren't home when the break-in occurred. They were gone for most of the weekend and returned to find a broken window and blood in the backyard. After speaking with the next door neighbors, they learned that their house was broken into as well, but unlike Moses and Alba, the neighbors had been present at the time. The vandals then pulled out a knife and began to fight with the residents. It became a bloody battle and the vandals jumped out the neighbor's window and into Moses and Alba's yard, fleeing through it and back over the fence. Hence the trail of blood on their patio.

Dara shared her side of the story as best she could, telling them about the screams she heard and about the power outage.

Alba's eyes looked distant and sorrowful. Dara wanted to reach out to her in some small way. She had never even met this woman before, and even hugging her right now seemed like it could be crossing a boundary.

An image of soup came to mind. A pot of boiling, warm soup. With hearty vegetables and shredded chicken. It was what Dara's mother would do. Debbie's favorite way of showing love for people was by feeding them, by nourishing them in their souls and in their bellies.

Dara said goodbye to Alba and Moses and walked back across the street. She got out her cutting board and began chopping zucchini, tomatoes, onion, and carrots. She set the broth on to boil, drizzled a few key herbs and seasonings across the top, and infused every ounce of comfort and hope she could into the pot.

When the soup finished cooking, Dara poured it into a large glass container and walked it across the street to Alba and Moses. Alba's face softened when Dara presented it to her on her front porch. That moment forged a lasting friendship between the two women. Though they could hardly speak each other's languages, they still enjoyed weekly dates of walking around the *plazuela* together and drinking coffee. Through their mottled conversations in Spanglish, Dara learned that Moses was a rep for a major pharmaceutical company and that Alba had grown up in Guatemala where her father owned a sugar cane plantation.

Each meeting with Alba was a bit of sweetness, a happy respite amidst a season of otherwise bizarre and traumatic events that had been plaguing them throughout September and October. But this was a new month, Dara reasoned. Perhaps November would be different.

November 2006

Pete and Dara's friends were visiting from the US and decided they wanted to make pancakes for breakfast one morning. They mixed the batter, set the table, and greased a griddle pan. All they needed now was to turn the stove on and get the pan preheating.

Except the pilot light didn't seem to be catching.

They had turned on the gas and ladled several spoonfuls of batter onto the grill, but no bubbles were forming. The pancakes weren't cooking.

At a loss, the friends went upstairs to grab Pete and see if he could help them. Pete followed them into the kitchen and crouched down to investigate. He noted that the pilot light wasn't catching, and flicked the switch on his butane lighter. The moment the flame made contact with the gas, Pete's world went into slow motion as a ball of fire came barreling toward his face. The whole kitchen began to shake and a massive banging sound sent pots and pans flying off their shelves, crashing to the floor.

Dara and the kids had been playing in the backyard, and thought for sure the sound was an earthquake. They came running into the kitchen to find their father with singed eyebrows and patches of hair missing on his legs and arms.

"Do I still have my face?" Pete asked, grabbing the nearest chair and trying to balance himself so he wouldn't fall over. His ears were ringing, his vision was blurred, and he looked like a disheveled mixture of Kramer from *Seinfeld* and Doc from *Back to the Future* after just returning from one of his time travels.

Dara grabbed Pete's arm and led him into the backyard to begin washing him down with the garden hose. When she finished, she turned off the water and rolled the hose back into a perfectly stacked circle. Pete stood above her, dripping and silent. Dara's eyes met his and a shared sense of fear passed between them.

Pete and Dara spent the rest of November treading cautiously, glancing over their shoulders before making any sudden moves. Worrying that something must be wrong with them. That their family was cursed. Or, at the very least that Pete might be cursed.

But then the month of December came and went and it was blessedly uneventful. They celebrated PJ's and Issac's birthdays and hosted Pete's parents for the holidays. Life was back on track, and with the turn of the new year, Pete began to reflect on all he had learned. He prayed and journaled and decided to write an update for his blog.

He had begun blogging back in July after finding a newer website called Squarespace. Pete had never heard of it. Few people had back in

2006. But Pete liked its clean design and the ease with which he could share parts of his life in El Salvador with friends, family and donors back in the States.

At first, he wasn't sure what to blog about, as he didn't know anyone else who had a blog, but over the last six months he had fallen into a rhythm of sharing whatever topics were on his mind and heart. Sometimes it was a collection of photos and stories of the villagers he worked with through ENLACE. Other times, it was a video of three-year-old Hannah singing a song, or a link to a news article about the gang violence in El Salvador.

On January 14, 2007, Pete sat at his computer, said a quiet, humble prayer, and then wrote the following:

> *If you looked in my office, you would find a list of books that I plan to read this year. You would also find a list of areas in which I plan to grow, academically, physically, spiritually, relationally, and professionally. Yet, I will not even come close to reaching all that I have set before me. As much as I want to, I cannot control how 2007 will turn out. I have no idea if one of my family members will get sick. I don't know if I will get hurt again (I got hurt 3x's last year). All I can do is lay these lists before the Lord, trusting that He has guided me to write them only as guideposts in my journey to live out a life that honors Him.*

CHAPTER 12

The Shooting

Los Abelines, January 18, 2007

Absalon Rivas placed his hand on the cold metal handle and pulled open the door to the backseat of the white Nissan Patrol. Inside his head was a mental list of all the camera equipment he and Pete had brought with them to Abelines that morning. Microphones, cameras, tripods—all of it safely tucked into the backseat. He and Pete had made certain of it. The interviews they had filmed that morning with pastors, doctors, and community members had gone extremely well. Combined with the footage of the medical clinic expansion in Abelines, everyone back at the ENLACE offices would be thrilled to see how this community was making such progress.

Absalon hoisted himself into the backseat and waited for Pete to finish talking to a woman named Hilda who was riding with another group of volunteers and workers that would caravan with them back to San Salvador.

"The road divides between the villages of Sirigual and Pajigua," Hilda explained to Pete in Spanish. "It's best to turn there."

"But I usually go straight at that point," Pete said. "If I'm going to lead, I should probably stick with what I'm used to so we don't get lost."

Hilda shrugged. "Whatever you want."

She hopped into the back of a Honda CRV and explained the route they would be taking to the driver, a young American woman named Amy who was working in El Salvador with a non-governmental organization (NGO).

Absalon watched Amy and Hilda talking from the backseat of the Nissan Patrol. It was going to be long ride no matter which way they took. This he had learned on the way up. Slowed by four-wheel-drive, the steep turns, and the rugged terrain, a car couldn't average much more than two miles per hour. He dug out his white ear buds from the front pouch of his backpack and began scrolling through his iPod. *What to listen to on this road trip?* His finger paused above the 'D' section of artists when he saw the band Dream Theater. Only a few month earlier, *Guitar World Magazine* had listed their album, *Metropolis Pt. 2 Scenes from a Memory*, as one of their "100 Greatest Guitar Albums of All Time."

As it should have been. The ninth song on the album, "The Dance of Eternity," contained 130 time signature changes in just over six minutes. As a drummer, the mere thought of anyone's fingers being quick enough to move like that along the guitar frets blew Absalon's mind. And it wasn't just that. It was the way Dream Theater played their music backwards. It was the rhythmic complexity. On a good day, he and his bandmates could perform maybe half those time changes. Maybe.

Pete got into the driver's seat of the Nissan Patrol and the other women who were riding with them, Patty, Doris, and Dr. Mireia, all piled in after him. Absalon sat in the backseat behind Pete. He hit the play button, closed his eyes, and allowed the music to drift over him. The notes from the electronic keyboard mixed with violins, sharp guitars, and drum beats that were quick and addictive. The song was purely instrumental, but the music was so full of energy, no words were necessary. The rhythm itself was an adrenaline rush, like a celebration, a roller coaster ride, a———

"*Bájate!*" Doris yelled, yanking the buds out of his ear. "Get down!"

Absalon opened his eyes to see that the driver's side window next to Pete had been shattered. All he could see was a distorted web of green jungle. But how? When? What on earth could have happened so quickly?

POP! POP! POP! POP! POP! A barrage of bullets pierced the door beside Absalon. He heard the ping of metal on metal and noticed Pete was holding his neck. Was that blood between his fingers?

"*Bájate!*" Doris said again, placing a firm grip around Absalon's arm and yanking him toward her. He felt the pressure of her insistent fingertips pressing into his flesh. At the same moment, the door beside him vibrated with the force of a bullet landing right below the window pane and forcing the glass to crack in one loud break.

The bullets seemed to only be coming from one side of the jungle, so if they got out of the car and crouched below on the right side of the vehicle, maybe it could shield them?

"Get out!" he told Doris and Patty. "Open the door and get down below on the ground."

Both women nodded and reached for the door handles. Absalon watched as Patty glanced over at Pete. Her eyes were all Absalon needed to confirm that yes, that was blood and yes, Pete had been shot. She jumped out of the vehicle and on to the ground as Pete crawled over the front seat, droplets of blood sprinkling across the gray interior.

Clouds of dust rose up from below. All four of them crouched in the midst of it next to the Nissan and Absalon could hear his heartbeat, almost as loudly as the gunshots.

Then came a moment of total silence.

The quiet continued, and felt like a vacuum sucking him in. He opened his eyes and they met Pete's. Pete was on his knees making deep, wheezing sounds and clutching his throat. His neck, shirt, and hands were all covered in crimson.

As the driver of the vehicle, Pete was fully alert when the shooting had begun. He remembered moving slowly around the sharp corner of the jungle, expecting to find little more than some stray branches creeping into the road. Instead, he was met by a shrill scream, like a wounded animal gone mad. The noise was coming from a male whose frame and height were small, like that of a teenager. His entire face was covered by a black mask and he was holding a .22 caliber rifle. After spotting their vehicle, he had jumped down from the hill above and landed near the driver's side, gun pointing squarely at Pete. He was close enough for Pete to see his muddy brown eyes. They bore into him from behind the ski mask and told a story Pete knew not how to translate.

As the bullet blew through the driver's side window, Pete felt a sharp burning sensation in his neck, like a glowing orange cattle prong had seared his flesh. The blood poured in a warm and steady trickle. Without even thinking, Pete's hand went straight for the wound. *Must stop the bleeding. Must stop the bleeding.*

Yet, even that, Pete couldn't control. The blood seeped past any barrier he tried to create, and his eyes widened as he tried to take a breath, but the air around him wasn't cooperating. His mind told him to breath deeper, to suck in more oxygen, just as it would if he were on a treadmill at the gym. But still the air evaded him. His chest tightened and he could feel his head growing dizzy.

So, this is it, Peter thought as he crouched on the ground beside the vehicle.

He had always wondered what this moment would be like. He closed his eyes and managed a raspy gulp of air. *Please help me,* he prayed. A calmness began to wash over him. The gut wrenching scream of that man, the brown eyes, the mask, the sound of the bullets blasting through the glass—all of it grew dim.

Several minutes behind the Nissan Patrol, Hilda sat in the backseat of the Honda CRV, alongside a teenage girl from Abelines named Dalila. Dalila had hitched a ride to Ciudad Barrios with them because she wanted to visit her boyfriend. The driver of the Honda was an American volunteer named Amy, and next to her, in the passenger seat was Lori Margaret. As this group rounded the corner, Amy and Lori were struck by the confusing scene that lay before them: The Nissan Patrol was completely stopped and its windows were shattered. All their friends were gathered together on one side of the vehicle and Pete was on his knees, bleeding and clutching his throat.

Amy and Lori looked at each other in shock.

As Pete continued to pray, he felt another body come beside him and a pair of hands lifting his own hand away from his wound.

"I've got it," said Dr. Mireia. The pads of her fingers felt considerably smaller than his own, but their intentions seemed surer, more deliberate.

Pete looked to his other side and noticed Doris. She was crouched into a ball, her back expanding and contracting with every sob. Patty was next to her with eyes that were locked in a frozen, empty gaze.

"We have to get out of here," Absalon said.

He wanted Doris to drive. Surely, Doris should drive, as she knew the place so much better than the rest of them. Doris continued to rock back and forth. Her dark brown hair hung around her shoulders and when she lifted her head, several strands stuck to her wet cheek. She didn't bother to brush them off.

Absalon surveyed the situation. Patty was visiting from the United States, and although she had been in El Salvador for several weeks working with ENLACE, today had been her first trip outside of the office buildings. She certainly couldn't drive. Dr. Mireia was attending to Pete. Pete was—*don't think about Pete.*

Absalon shut his brain down before it could take him any further and made the decision that he would drive. He had no idea where he was going or how he would get there, but he would. No other possibilities remained.

"In the car," he told them. "*Rápido!*"

Knowing how crowded the backseat had been, Doris made a split-second decision to switch cars and drive with the crew in the Honda, leaving more room for Pete and Dr. Mireia in the back. Patty nodded at Absalon and climbed back into the front seat, while Dr. Mireia guided Pete up to his feet and back inside the Nissan. Absalon swung himself into the driver's seat and slammed the car door, causing what was left of the window pane to shatter onto his bare arm. Tiny shards of glass burrowed into his skin as he turned the key and started the engine.

Absalon had never driven a 4x4 vehicle, and with little idea of what to expect, he pressed his foot on the gas pedal with all his might and the Nissan Patrol jumped to life. It bumped and roared down the narrow road, past one blind turn after the next, up a confounding hillside, back down again, and this time straight into a shallow river without a bridge. Absalon charged through, sending muddy water exploding outwards like a broken sprinkler hose.

Absalon glanced at the rear view mirror and spotted Dr Mireia. "I'm going to need you to tell me where to go. Can you do that?" he asked her.

She met his gaze in the mirror and nodded. "The closest medical clinic is in Ciudad Barrios," she said, her fingers still pressed firmly into Peter's wound. "They won't be able to remove the bullet, but they can at least take x-rays and stabilize him."

Pete laid his head against Mireia's shoulder and took another wheezing gasp of air. The pain in his neck and throat was growing more intense and all he could think about was Dara and the kids.

All four of his kids' birthdays were lined up like dominoes, and they had just finished celebrating them last month. The birthdays began with baby Kaya in October, who had turned two. After her was Hannah whose birthday was at the end of November, which meant it sometimes landed on Thanksgiving, and sometimes didn't. Next came PJ's birthday. He had turned nine last month, in December. Three days later, Isaac turned seven and that completed the birthday roundup. Just in time for Christmas. Pete could feel the sting of leaving them deep inside his stomach. It was an emptiness more painful than the searing wound in his throat.

Behind the Nissan Patrol, Amy was tailing closely in the Honda, her heart pounding with the realization that they were just about to the end. One more corner and they would be out of Abelines and on their way to Ciudad Barrios. *Please, God, please*, she prayed, gripping the wheel with all of her might.

Just as she rounded that final turn, the white Nissan came into view, only it wasn't moving.

"Why are they stopped?" Amy asked, tightness seizing her chest.

From the back seat, Doris began to wail. "*Pobre*, Peter! *Pobre*, Peter!" Her entire body convulsed, and her mind flooded with the knowledge that people in El Salvador didn't just get shot; they got shot and *killed*. It was only a matter of time until these gunmen came back to finish the job. Terror gripped her heart.

"*Ay*, no! *Ay*, no!" Doris screamed.

"*Why are they stopped?*" Amy asked again.

When the Nissan Patrol had come to a jolting halt, only minutes earlier, it caused Pete to open his eyes. Sure enough, they had made it out of Abelines and the paved highway leading to Ciudad Barrios lay before them. Absalon leaned forward and craned his neck in each direction to check for oncoming traffic. Just as he was about to pull out, Pete remembered something. *The wheel locks. The 4x4.*

"Wait!" Pete tried to yell. A trace of blood seeped from Pete's lips and the pain in his throat turned up a notch. He reached across the backseat and tapped Absalon on the shoulder.

"Don't move. The wheels. Stop the car," Pete said in a raspy whisper. "If I get out of this thing alive, I want my car in one piece."

Patty, Absalon, and Dr. Mireia all turned to look at Pete. *Was he seriously thinking of this right now? Was he making a joke?*

Absalon's lips broke into a nervous smile and he nodded. So this was why he had noticed Pete doing something strange to the wheels earlier that afternoon.

After the group had finished eating lunch at Pastor Victorio's house, Absalon had walked outside and noticed Pete crouching on the ground and fiddling with the axle on one of the Nissan's back tires.

"*Qué estás haciendo?*" he asked. "What are you doing?"

"I'm locking the wheels," Pete explained. "We can't make it down this road without using 4x4, and the car won't go into 4x4 unless we manually lock each wheel."

Absalon was fascinated. The technicality of anything, whether it was computer code or the arrangement of musical notes, called out to him. It asked him to pay attention, to learn, to file it away in the back of his brain for future reference.

Absalon's long, black hair was secured in a ponytail at the base of his neck and it fell to one side of his shoulder as he crouched next to Pete.

"See this lever?" Pete asked, pointing to a small metal switch in the middle of the tire. "Just click it up. It's that simple."

In the back of the Nissan, Pete looked at Dr. Mireia whose fingers were still pressing into his neck wound. Pete pointed to Absalon and then to the car door to indicate that he needed to get out and observe him.

Mireia looked incredulous, but knew this was smart. If the wheels were unlocked, it would save them time in the long run. They could get to the clinic a lot faster, and that was the most important thing. Not some stupid car. *Men,* she thought, shaking her head. She removed her hand from Pete's throat and allowed him to place his own hand where hers had been. Pete tried to match the exact point and amount of pressure Mireia had been using. *What a blessing it is to have a doctor here,* he thought.

His breathing was still labored, and it would take every inch of strength he had to climb out of that car. He opened the door handle with his one free hand and then used it to push his body down onto the ground. Neither Pete nor Absalon spoke, but merely gestured.

This lever?

Yes, that one, their hands said.

Up? Over there?

Yes, just like that.

Absalon repeated the process with all four of the wheels, working as quickly and efficiently as possible.

"They're moving again!" Amy announced. She watched as Pete and Absalon climbed back into the Nissan and made a quick turn onto the main highway.

Lori had just finished praying with Doris and Hilda in the back of the Honda. Doris sniffled and opened her eyes. "*Es verdad?*" she asked. "It's true?"

Lori nodded, and grabbed her hand. Amy placed a tentative foot on the gas pedal and tailed the Nissan as closely as possible. Once they had safely made it onto the highway, she remembered to breathe.

San Salvador, January 18, 2007

It was 5:00 a.m. and Dara DeSoto woke to her usual alarm clock of singing birds and honking buses. The morning sky was still a dark canvas waiting for the sun as Dara found herself wandering down the stairs and into the kitchen. She ran her hand along the wall in search of a light switch. A yellow haze flickered above and Dara walked straight toward her greatest friend and confidant: the coffee maker.

These quiet, coffee-filled mornings had carried her through the last eighteen months she and Pete had been living in El Salvador. As a woman of habit and ritual, Dara cherished everything about this time. The mug she used, morning after morning, the inviting smell, the way the cup felt warm and comforting across her palms. The time she spent meeting with God and reading her Bible before the kids awoke and breakfast needed to be made and the boys taken to the International School with their notebooks lined up and placed into the correct backpacks.

Today was slightly different than most because Pete would be joining her. He had to leave within the next hour to drive out to Abelines, and Dara was happy to invite him into her sacred space. She dug her metal scoop into the pungent coffee grounds and set the coffee maker on. It whistled and dribbled, releasing that glorious aroma.

"Morning," Pete said, emerging from the dark hallway and walking into the kitchen. His short hair was matted in front and pointing every which way. Dara could see he hadn't bothered to look in the mirror yet.

She cracked a few eggs into a bowl and began whisking them up. Pete poured himself a cup of coffee and took a seat at the kitchen table. Even half awake, his excitement was palpable, like the steam flowing up from his freshly poured mug.

"I really feel like we're going to make it here," he said.

Dara nodded, humoring him. She knew his peppy mood was the result of his former employer, Regency Lighting, agreeing to donate a considerable amount of money to build a medical clinic in Abelines. Construction had already started, and today Pete would be able to see it and report back to them on the progress. This was the type of thing Pete lived for, and she was thrilled about it, too. Of course she was. Why else had they come to El Salvador but to promote development such as this?

As for them making it in El Salvador, on the other hand? All the enthusiasm in the world couldn't fully convince Dara of that.

Last fall had been the toughest season of her life. So much had happened. Violent things. Terrible things. Yet, as the sun began to rise outside her kitchen window, she couldn't deny how beautiful the yard was in the DeBorst home. There was a garden out back, a mango tree, and space for the kids to run and play.

Dara poured the egg mixture into the frying pan atop the stove. It sizzled and popped as she began to stir it around with her spatula.

Pete smiled and looked down at his coffee mug. God always came through, and He wove things together in the most strange and surprising ways. In spite of that tough fall season, Pete felt extremely blessed to be living in El Salvador and working with ENLACE. After everything he and Dara had been through, he felt in this moment that it was all paying off. Today would be good. He knew it.

"I'm glad you get to go today," Dara told him.

"I know," Pete laughed. "It sucks that David broke his leg, but I'm glad I get to go."

The night prior, David McGee had called Pete to ask him to drive to Abelines with the ENLACE crew.

"You know that soccer injury from last weekend?" David asked. "It turns out it was a broken ankle, so there's no way I'll be able to make it in Abelines—hobbling around those uneven roads with crutches. I would just be in everybody's way. Would you mind going in my place?"

"I'd love to," Pete said.

Dara pulled three plates out of the cupboard and began dividing the scrambled eggs into even portions. She then opened the freezer and plopped a few ice cubes from the tray into a clear glass.

Their house guest, Patty LaVoie, came walking through the kitchen doorway, and wished them a sleepy good morning. Dara smiled and nodded toward the glass of ice. "It's all ready for you," she said.

Patty was visiting from the United States, doing IT work with ENLACE, and had been staying with Pete and Dara. The one thing she'd been missing most was ice. As someone well acquainted with homesickness, Dara understood how Patty felt and was happy to provide her with ice for her water whenever possible.

Sometimes it was the littlest things that meant the most.

Pete swallowed the last drop of coffee and rinsed his mug out in the sink. He exited the kitchen and noticed his reflection in the hallway mirror, stopping for a moment to straighten his messy hair.

"Bye, sweetie," he said, grabbing his car keys and pausing briefly to give Dara a kiss.

Dara watched the white Nissan Patrol pull out of the driveway and disappear around the corner as it exited the cul-de-sac and headed past the security guards that kept watch over their *plazuela*. She glanced at the clock ticking on the kitchen wall and noted that she had a few quick minutes to spare before the kids needed to be woken up for school.

She took a seat in the comfy leather armchair, folding her legs into a relaxed position with her Bible on her lap. Dara closed her eyes and invited the Holy Spirit to guide her as she read. Inside her Bible was a cloth bookmark, indicating the exact place where she stopped reading the Psalms yesterday morning. Psalm 52 was short, and as she finished reading the last few verses, her eyes caught on the word *mercy*. "But I am like a green olive tree in the house of God. I trust in the *mercy* of God forever and ever."

Dara's eyes traveled to the footnotes at the bottom of the page where it explained why the green olive tree was significant: "The Psalmist exults (through this simile) that the one who trusts in the mercy of God is productive and secure," it said.

But what does His mercy look like? Dara wondered.

As she closed her eyes, her mind was flooded with thoughts of that night back in April 2005 when they had first moved to San Salvador.

She remembered the rising sun making bright orange ribbons across the horizon line as their plane had landed. She remembered her eyes feeling swollen and tingly. How she struggled to keep them open while her seven-month-old daughter wiggled in her arms. Baby Kaya had let out a low whine and shoved a defiant little fist into Dara's chest. Next to her sat two-year-old Hannah, who had been sleeping throughout most of the flight, but was awoken by the pressure in the cabin as the plane dove downwards. Hannah began squirming and frowning intently. Dara knew that look, and could see that the five hour flight had extracted that last bit of patience straight out of her. It was only a matter of time before Hannah's tears started flowing.

Dara remembered making a mental list of the snacks she had left in her purse, and just as she was about to retrieve one, the "fasten seat belt" sign went dim and all the lights were turned on in the cabins. "*Bienvenidos* a San Salvador," the flight attendant announced over the speaker.

Jamie Huff, Pete's oldest friend from Ron Bueno's Anthropology class, leaned across the aisle and placed his hand on Dara's armrest.

"You ready for this?" he had asked.

No, she thought, fear welling up like a knot inside her stomach.

Please show me your mercy, Lord, Dara continued to pray, her mind floating back to her living room. *What does it look like? How will I know it?*

The doorbell rang and Dara's eyes blinked open. She set her Bible on the side table and went to unlock the door. Javier, their water delivery man, stood before her with a toothy grin.

"*Buenos días, señora!*"

His rust-colored skin was creased around the edges of his eyes, and he hobbled back and forth as he walked on two bowed legs, knees arching outward. He rolled the hefty water jug through the tiled living room, past the staircase, and around the corner into the kitchen.

Javier began to chat with Dara, as was his routine. "You look beautiful today, *señora.* And how are *los niños?*"

Dara noted with a small surge of pleasure that she was starting to understand him more and more. She thought for a moment how to conjugate her verbs and cobbled together an answer that actually said something more than a nod, and a generic "They're fine," as she used to respond when he first delivered their water.

"Ah yes, *los niños!*" she said. "I have to wake them now and get them ready for school. This morning went by *muy rápido.*"

Upon completing her sentence in Spanish, Dara felt an enormous sense of pride. It was a good sentence, and Dara was almost certain she had said it correctly. She would have to share this moment with her teacher, Marlena.

Javier rattled off a response but Dara was too distracted to try and listen. All she could focus on was a single thought that popped into her brain, seemingly from out of nowhere:

Pray for him.

Right now? She wondered.

Pray for him, and for my mercy.

Javier's support belt was fastened tightly around his waist, a large, black padded contraption that overtook most of his short torso. Dara watched as his small frame lifted the two monstrous jugs of water her family would drink for the next week. As he did so, she said a soft prayer for his safety, for his family, and that God would keep them safe today and provide for them.

As he made his way back to her front door and they said their goodbyes, Dara heard another thought:

Pray for your children. Pray for my mercy.

She felt puzzled, yet intrigued. Rarely had she sensed such strong directives throughout an ordinary morning such as this one.

Thank me for my mercy.

Dara smiled and furrowed her brow as she walked up the stairs to wake her children. "OK, Lord, I thank you for your mercy," she spoke aloud. "And for my children, and for Peter, and for all of your blessing and protection."

While Dara watched *The Wiggles* with her daughters that afternoon, played dolls, fixed their lunch, and sat Indian style on the floor with them, rolling balls of Playdough across her palm, the directives to pray would become stronger and stronger.

CHAPTER 13

Ciudad Barrios

January 18, 2007

The tires of the white Nissan Patrol rolled across the driveway of the wooden clinic painted sea foam green. To the left was a triage center with one nurse sitting at a folding table under a rusted metal roof held up by wooden pillars. Several children waited in line, pulling on the hem of their mother's skirt and peering around the premises for something interesting with which to entertain themselves.

They watched as the tires skidded to a stop, creating a cloud of dust. They watched as a man with a long black ponytail thrust the car door open and ran directly through the front doors of the clinic.

"We have a man who's been shot!" Absalon yelled.

Thanks to Dalila's phone calls, the clinic workers were ready for this man, this gringo from *El Norte*. They rolled out an old, rickety gurney and loaded Peter DeSoto's six-foot frame onto it as carefully as possible. His shins and ankles dangled off the bottom, as it was designed for the smaller residents of Ciudad Barrios, *mestizos* with a mixed ancestry who were part Salvadoran, part indigenous Pipil Indian tribe. What looked to be a teenager, clad in pale green scrubs, placed the elastic band of an oxygen mask around the back of Pete's head. The front portion was left over his mouth. The moment the mask made contact with his chin and cheekbones, Pete's eyes widened in panic. It felt like all the air in the room was being suctioned from his lungs.

Pete began choking. In desperation, he lifted his right hand in the air and slammed it against the gurney, making quick, loud thumping sounds. His whole body rocked back and forth, gasping for breath.

"What's happening?" Mireia asked. Her tone was brusque, insistent. "Is that oxygen mask broken?"

She hurried to Pete's side, pushing past the clinic workers who had crowded around him, whose eyes darted back and forth from Pete to each other, unsure how to proceed.

"This mask looks too small," Mireia observed, lifting it above Pete's mouth and pulling it off of his head.

Pete took large, wheezing gulps of air. He began coughing fresh droplets of blood on top of the dried blood stains already crusted into his blue plaid shirt.

Mireia examined the oxygen mask. It was sized for a child. There was no doubt about it. "*Dios mío,*" she said under her breath.

An older nurse entered the room with a clipboard and a pen. She had a kind smile and worked methodically to clean Pete's gunshot wound and wrap it in gauze.

"Can you move your legs for me?" she asked Pete in Spanish. As the words left her lips, the nurse silently prayed that he could. His ability to move them would prove he did not sustain serious spinal cord damage, as she feared might be the case based on the bullet's location.

Pete nodded, focused his intention, and slowly wiggled his toes for her. The nurse's eyes lit up.

"Can you bend your knees?" she asked.

Again, Pete complied, this time taking a large breath to give him strength enough to flex his quadriceps muscles, gliding his knee off the gurney and pointing it upward. The nurse's face softened in relief and she made notes on her clipboard.

Pete watched her pen travel across the page and tried to ignore the deep burning sensation that occurred every time he swallowed. His whole throat felt as though a match were being repeatedly lit inside it— the flames spreading in power, getting hotter with every spark. Every breath zapped him of energy.

Next, the nurses and clinic workers told Pete they needed to photograph his wounds and take X-rays. They rolled him into another room with a long metal slab in the middle of it. When Pete's body was lifted on top of it, the coldness of the metal shot through him and reminded him of the stone table where the character of Aslan was sacrificed in his favorite childhood series, *The Chronicles of Narnia.*

The nurses commanded Pete to move his head to the right. Sharp pain shot through the length of his spinal cord. They snapped a photo.

"To the left," they said.

Photo snap. Sharper pain.

"Move your torso to the right."

Oh, the burning! Snap, snap, went the camera.

"How about one more time to the right."

Burn, burn, burn. Snap, snap, snap.

Pete felt himself becoming one with the pain. He couldn't tell where it ended or where it began.

"Now, please stand for X-rays," a male clinic worker told him.

Pete stared at him in a daze. *Was he joking?* The objection was right there on the tip of Pete's tongue. He wanted to shake his head. Tell them no. Tell them they were asking too much. The pain was too much. His energy reserves had been used up.

You can do this.

A quiet thought inside his head, urging him on.

Pete lifted his head and noticed a figure standing in the doorway. It was a small man with a cowboy hat and square chunk of a mustache decorating his upper lip.

"Victorio," Pete whispered. An involuntary smile spread across his lips.

Victorio waved to Pete from the doorway. His kind eyes looked troubled yet hopeful. And his presence was enough to transfer invisible energy to Pete, who now felt that if he could stand long enough for the X-rays, his reward would be getting to talk with his dear friend.

Pete held his hand out for the nurses. "Help me up, please," he said.

In the waiting room, Lori, Amy, Absalon, Mireia, Doris, and Patty were all surrounded by nurses and clinic staff and engaged in a heated conversation about where to take Pete next.

"*Necesitamos un helicóptero*," the receptionist said. "We'll need a helicopter. It's the only way to transport him to a hospital that can do surgery."

"*Sí*," another agreed. "The distance is so far, it could take hours on the highway. And the traffic."

"But which hospital?" Doris asked. Her eyes were red from crying and the skin surrounding them was puffy. "How are we to get a helicopter? That alone could take just as long as driving him."

"San Miguel is the closest major hospital," the receptionist said. "I say we fly him there."

The doors to the clinic swung open and in walked several *policía*. They were here to examine the bullet holes in the Nissan Patrol, they explained, and to obtain individual testimonies from all parties involved. "We'll be calling you outside to talk, one by one," they said.

Absalon volunteered to go first, and Lori decided to check on Pete. As she exited the waiting room, the receptionist repeated the words "San Miguel Hospital." Everyone in the waiting room seemed to nod their heads in agreement.

Lori walked through the tiled walls of the clinic, past a painted mural and into the room where Victorio and Pete were gripping each other's hands, eyes closed in prayer. Lori considered joining them, but thought it best to let them have this moment. She closed her eyes in the doorway and joined them in prayer from afar.

When Victorio finished, she entered the room with a tight smile.

"How are you feeling?" she asked Pete.

Pete's face was pale and his neck was wrapped in white gauze.

"Better now that this guy's here," he rasped, motioning to Victorio. "I told him he was a crazy jackrabbit for getting down that hill from Abelines so quickly."

Lori laughed. She could feel the wetness building behind her eyes as she noted that Pete was joking and in good spirits, even now. He really was something.

"Dalila called him on her cell phone right after the shooting," Lori said, "and he somehow managed to get here within minutes of us. I think he knows some secret route we don't."

A secret route.

Lori's words struck Pete and brought him back to a conversation he had almost forgotten about.

"The road divides between the villages of Sirigual and Pajigua. It's best to turn there."

"I usually just go straight at that point. If I'm going to lead, I should probably stick with what I'm used to so we don't get lost."

"Whatever you want."

Hilda's words hung in Pete's ears as he saw an image of a small man dressed in black, wielding an over-sized gun, and materializing from the bushes as though he had been placed there by video game designers.

Another path out of Abelines had existed. A path without a gunman. Without a neck wound. Without this clinic and these crying friends gathered round him. A path that, had Pete taken it and listened to Hilda, would have meant he would be almost back to San Salvador by now—getting ready to have dinner with Dara and the kids.

The choice had been right there. Right in front of him, like a roll of the dice. Pete had been that flippant about it. That sure of himself. That foolish. But how could he have known? How could anyone have known that when Pete chose to take that route, and when he chose to go to Abelines in David McGee's place, those two decisions would change the course of his life in ways that could never be altered?

San Salvador

Ron Bueno's right foot angled downward, applying slight pressure to the brakes of his SUV. He noted the long line of vehicles in front of him on the highway, all of which were at a standstill. He stared out the window at the massive shopping complex to his left. It boasted a movie theater with stadium seating and state-of-the-art sound. There was a Benihana, a Starbucks with a scenic patio, and major department stores dotted with high end boutiques, like Gucci, Prada, and Louis Vuitton. It was the part of San Salvador where tourists flocked—tourists, and the small percentage of wealthy Salvadorans who either owned thriving businesses, or had affluent relatives sending them money from the United States.

Across the from the mall, were run-down shanties with cement walls and garage doors for roofs. This double existence, the clashing of two worlds, was evident everywhere in San Salvador.

Ron had grown accustomed to the tension of this double life. His parents had moved to El Salvador to do missionary work in 1961, and Ron and all three of his brothers were born and raised there. The double life began as a child, growing up in a working-class neighborhood of San Salvador where half his friends were kids from squatter villages, and the other half came from families of young professionals. The church his parents pastored was made up of families with little resources; yet, Ron also studied with the elite at the American School. His daily bus ride was a visual manifestation of the opposite worlds he straddled as the bus traveled from one side of town to the other. The contrast was stark, and Ron watched the terrain unfold from the windows of the bus, where he ultimately got out and was greeted by classmates whose parents owned coffee plantations and major department store chains.

A man on a scooter came whizzing past Ron's SUV, a blur of color and noise weaving in between cars and almost nicking the passenger side where his wife Michelle was sitting.

"Yikes," she said, looking at Ron and jumping a bit. "I swear, these drivers . . ." The melody of Ron's cell phone filled the car as Michelle watched with indignation as the scooter driver cut off another vehicle.

"What!?" she heard her husband say into the phone.

Michelle noted the concern in Ron's voice and turned to look at him. His eyes looked panicked, and though the car in front of him began to move, Ron sat with his foot firmly planted on the break. The gap between the two cars widened, and horns from behind began to blare.

"How? When? Is he okay?" Ron asked.

"What's going on?" Michelle mouthed.

The horns continued and a flustered Ron lifted his foot off the break, allowing them to inch forward at a slow pace. Ron collapsed his flip phone and began searching for an opening in the lane next to them.

"I need to pull over," he said.

"What happened?"

Ron's chest heaved. He paused and tried to process the phone call. Michelle's question hung in the air.

"Ron?"

His eyes scanned the highway until he found the break he was looking for and quickly darted the car across three lanes of traffic.

"Peter DeSoto was shot today," he said, turning off the engine and closing his eyes. "In Abelines."

Michelle looked confused. "But why?" she asked. "Abelines is the safest village you guys work in."

Ron grew flustered. "I have nothing in the way of answers right now. All I know is that he's still alive and at a clinic in Ciudad Barrios. They need to get him to a major hospital for surgery."

Tears burned the backs of Michelle's eyes. Without warning, they began to spill down her cheeks and she reached for Ron's hand.

"Does Dara know?"

Ron shook his head.

The tears kept flowing as Michelle closed her eyes and began to pray aloud. Ron bowed his head and the two of them sent pleas to Jesus that he would keep Pete safe, get him to a hospital, and give Dara strength.

Michelle opened her eyes and felt grounded. "We have to tell Dara."

"First, I have to make a phone call," Ron said.

If they were going to save Pete's life, they needed a helicopter. And if there was to be any hope of getting one, they would need all of their connections.

Ron flipped open his cell phone and searched his contacts for Carla Bolanos at the US Embassy.

It was May of 1984 when President Ronald Reagan gave his speech about the threat of communism based on the geographic relationship between Central America and the United States. When he stated,"San Salvador is closer to Houston, Texas, than Houston is to Washington, DC. Central America is America. It's at our doorstep, and it's become the stage for a bold attempt by the Soviet Union, Cuba, and Nicaragua, to install Communism by force throughout the hemisphere."

Perhaps it was that very speech that led the founders of Walmart, Sam and Helen Walton, on their their first trip through Central America less than one year later. It was 1985 when the couple toured the continent and learned that many students in that region of the world were being recruited by universities in the former Soviet Union. This troubled the Waltons deeply, as the US was still engaged in a Cold War with Russia, and the threat of communism seemed ever present.

It also troubled them on a personal level because it meant these students would likely never get exposed to the virtues of democracy and free enterprise—virtues that had clearly served the Walton's well. In 1985, Walmart's stock was readily growing, and *Forbes Magazine* had named Sam Walton "the wealthiest man in the United States."

Upon the couple's return from their trip, they decided to develop a scholarship program aimed specifically at bringing Central American students to the United States. The couple collaborated with three faith-based universities in their home state of Arkansas who agreed to admit these students and give them free tuition for four years. They developed a rigorous screening and application process, and began to spread the word throughout Belize, Panama, Guatemala, Honduras, Nicaragua, Ecuador, and El Salvador.

It happened that a pastor at the Assemblies of God church in San Salvador heard about this scholarship several years later and knew just who to recommend for it. A bright high school student in his congregation named Carla. She applied and was chosen to be a recipient of the Walton International Scholarship Fund. She attended University of the Ozarks and graduated with a degree in mass communication in 1995. While there, she met and fell in love with her husband, Walter Bolanos, who was also a scholarship recipient from El Salvador.

Upon graduation, the couple returned to their shared hometown of San Salvador, where Carla was later offered a job at the US Embassy. She began working as a medical administrative assistant in 1995 and is still there to this day, serving as a liaison between hospitals, doctors, and American expats living in El Salvador.

In 2001, her husband Walter was asked to join the staff of ENLACE, as they needed extra help after the two major earthquakes that occurred in January and February of that year. When the DeSotos moved to El Salvador four years later, Pete and Walter quickly became friends, working side-by-side to coordinate all the international mission teams who came out to build latrines, clinics and cinder block homes for the Salvadorans living in rural villages.

When Carla returned from her afternoon break on January 18, 2007, she sat down at her desk at the US Embassy just in time to receive a phone call from her husband's boss, Ron Bueno.

Ciudad Barrios

The x-ray technician walked through the hallway of the clinic lined with sea foam green tiles. In his hand dangled an x-ray of the interior view of his patient's neck. The .22 caliber bullet had somehow managed to miss the man's trachea and spinal cord by one centimeter before it lodged itself into his esophagus. But .22 caliber bullets had a reputation for shattering once they made contact with another surface, human flesh or otherwise. The fact that this bullet remained in one piece, that it stuck to the esophagus instead of blasting through the other side of Pete's neck, and that it neither paralyzed him nor killed him instantly by hitting major arteries or organs—all of it was puzzling if not downright miraculous.

Lori watched with curiosity as the x-ray technician made his way through the hallway. She lifted herself out of the waiting room chair and began trailing behind him. She cocked her neck to try to catch a glimpse of the x-ray as they walked. When he entered Pete's hospital room, Lori watched as he held it up to the light. The sun came streaming through the window next to Pete's bed and when the light hit the x-ray, Pete's spine came into view. Right next to his spine was the bullet. It looked as though he had swallowed it.

"It's still inside me?" Pete asked.

The technician nodded. "It will need to be surgically removed."

Pete was silent. The bullet's presence inside him felt invasive, volatile, frightening.

"They want to take you to the hospital in San Miguel," Lori said. "It's the closest."

Pete's expression changed from somber to determined. "I'm not going to San Miguel," he said. "If they're going to perform surgery, it has to be at Diagnóstico in San Salvador."

Pete had been a patient at Diagnóstico no less than three times over the last six months. From the dengue outbreak, to the tennis accident and the kitchen explosion, the hospital had become like a second home to Pete. Though, Lori and the others present didn't know it.

"I trust them at Diagnóstico," Pete said. "They're clean, they have good resources, and they know what they're doing."

Lori searched Pete's face and could see that his decision was a firm one. "OK," she said. "I"ll tell them that it has to be Diagnóstico."

"Thank you," Pete said.

He coughed and blood flew from his mouth, speckling the blue paper shirt the hospital had given him to wear. Even small amounts of verbal communication were growing increasingly difficult. He closed his eyes and leaned his head against the pillow.

"Whatever you have to do, just get me there."

―――――――――――

Getting a helicopter at the last minute was going to be complicated. That was the first thing Carla Bolanos discovered as she hung up the phone with American Citizen Services (ACS), a branch of the US Embassy dedicated to aiding Americans who encounter crisis while on foreign soil. ACS had just spoken with the Salvadoran military who said they could likely gain access to a military helicopter, but they would then need to find a pilot who was willing and able to fly at a moment's notice.

More complicated still was the question of where to land the thing.

"We need to find a large, flat, open surface," the man from ACS had told Carla. "The clinic in Ciudad Barrios is in a congested area of the city. The streets are narrow and filled with homes and storefronts, so we'll need to find somewhere else that's not too far from the clinic. A field of some sort. Then we'll have to find the same type of area in San Salvador—as close as possible to Diagnóstico."

Carla nodded, jotting all of this down with her pen. "I'll work on it," she said, thanking him and hanging up the phone.

There was little time for panicking, stalling, or even allowing thoughts like *this is never going to work* to enter her head. God knew those thoughts were threatening to invade with every breath she took, but she kept telling herself to remain calm and continue going.

Peter's life hung in the balance. She was not about to let him down.

San Salvador

Dara rolled over in bed as she heard her cell phone buzzing for the second time in a row. Hannah and Kaya were down for a nap, and Dara had decided to join them. She rarely ever got phone calls during the day except from Pete and she had the distinct feeling this wasn't him calling. She closed her eyes and hoped the ringing would go away. She really was not in the mood to chat.

Dara forced her eyelids open and glanced at her cell phone.

It was Michelle Bueno. *Why would Michelle be calling now?*

She hit the answer button and held the phone to her ear.

"Dara?" Michelle asked. "We're outside your door. Can we come in?"

Dara pushed herself up to a sitting position. The last lingering bits of sleep were still upon her and she was in that blurry middle ground between reality and dreams. *Did Michelle just say she was outside my door?*

"Um . . . yeah, of course," Dara said. "I'll be right down."

She tiptoed past her sleeping daughters and headed down the stairs. She clicked opened the lock and swung her front door open to find not only Michelle standing there, but also Ron, Jenny, and David McGee balanced on a pair of crutches. Both David and Jenny were staring straight at Dara with eyes that seemed downright terrified.

"Dara, where are the girls?" Michelle asked gently.

"Asleep," Dara said, a sense of anxiety creeping upon her.

Michelle nodded. "Do you mind if we come in? We have something to tell you, and you'll probably want to sit down for it."

Dara motioned for them to come inside and began mentally preparing herself for whatever news she was about to receive. She noted the staircase to the second floor, and decided to heed Michelle's advice. She grabbed the banister and lowered herself onto the bottom steps.

"We're not sure of the details yet . . ." Ron started.

Dara looked up at him and put her hand out in a stopping motion.

"Wait," she said. "I don't want to hear another word until we pray."

She recalled the inner directives she had been receiving all morning to pray for the people in her life and realized whatever Ron was going to tell her probably needed to be covered in prayer.

The McGees and Buenos looked at each other and then at Dara sitting on the stairs. They took tentative steps toward Dara and sat down on the floor beside her, as though any sudden movements might cause her to disintegrate. The five of them grabbed each other's hands, closed their eyes, and listened to Dara as she prayed.

She thanked God for his goodness and faithfulness. She asked that all immediate circumstances be placed in His hands. That He would guide, direct, and protect whoever was in trouble. She asked for His strength, for His love, and for His hope.

When Dara finished, she looked directly at Ron and said, "I'm ready now."

Ron nodded. "Pete's been in an accident," he said softly.

Dara saw an image of Pete's Nissan Patrol—smashed up and dented on the side of the road.

"How is everyone?" she asked? "Are they safe? Is the car okay?"

"Not that type of accident," Ron clarified. "He was shot."

Now she saw an image of Pete clutching his arm, blood gushing from it. *He'll be fine. He's strong*, she thought.

" . . . in the neck," Ron finished.

The image disappeared from Dara's mind. In its place, she saw nothing. The room in front of her began to blur.

"He's alive, though," she heard Ron say, but his words sounded muffled and distant. The next several moments ebbed and flowed like waves in the ocean. Dara's mind stopped and she stared ahead, unaware of what was going on around her. Through the haziness, she recognized her daughter's voice.

"Mommy, I'm hungry."

It was Hannah. She had woken from her nap and was standing behind Dara on the stairs.

Dara stood up in a trance. "Yes, baby, I'll make you something."

"Oh, no," Jenny said. "Dara, I've got it."

Dara watched a blurred version of her friend walk to the steps, grab Hannah's hand, and lead her into the kitchen.

"What would you like to eat?" she heard Jenny ask, although her voice sounded far away.

Dara grabbed the first thing she could find, a broom leaning against the wall in the kitchen. She picked it up and began sweeping. Her eyes focused in on each little crumb, every particle of dust. She collected them carefully into a small pile at the center of the floor and felt a sense of accomplishment. In the other room, she heard Ron and David making phone calls, their voices fading in and out.

A blue van pulled into the driveway. She watched Isaac and PJ jump out and run toward the house. Clearly, no one had told the boys yet because their little bodies were filled with energy and their faces carried a mixture of both elation and confusion. Dara could tell they were excited to see all these people at their home. Watching them broke Dara's trance and brought her back to the present moment.

"Come here, you guys," Dara said, forcing a smile and gesturing for PJ and Isaac to sit with her on the stairs. In the very place she had been told.

The boys dropped their backpacks on the floor and took their seats, staring up at Dara with bright, wide eyes.

The words came tumbling from Dara's mouth before she could think to stop them. "There's been an accident," she said. "Your daddy has been shot, but he's in God's hands and everything is going to be OK."

PJ's brown eyes switched from expectancy to anger. Then confusion. Then fear. He had witnessed a lot since moving to San Salvador, from the screaming neighbors who had been stabbed, to the police officers storming their *plazuela* and watching a stove blow up in his father's face. Each moment had made its mark on PJ, and this one seemed to be the tipping point. He ran out the front door, hopped on his bike, and began riding around the *plazuela* in furious circles.

Isaac looked from Dara to PJ and back again. His eyes filled with tears and they were pleading. Helpless. Dara sat down on the steps and wrapped her arms around Isaac. She felt his small breath on her shoulder and watched his back heave up and down as he cried. Together, they sat like that and held each other for what felt like a very long time.

Pete propped his head against the pillows placed behind his neck and let his eyes drift to the open-faced wooden cabinets in his room in the Ciudad Barrios clinic. The shelves were filled with little boxes wrapped in bright pink tissue and labeled with yellow construction paper. On them, someone had used their finest cursive to write out the words *mascaras* (masks) *para adultos*, or *mascaras para niños* in black, felt-tipped marker. A plastic flower was glued underneath the construction paper label on each box in a deliberate attempt at infusing cheeriness into an otherwise daunting atmosphere. It was just like the Salvadorans to do this. Disaster could strike, and still they would find a way to create beauty in the middle of it.

Pete was alone now, as Dr. Mireia was speaking with the police while Lori, Doris, and Victorio were all making phone calls in the waiting room. Pete felt the weight of each hour as it ticked by. He had been at this clinic, in this bed, for two full hours now. Simply waiting.

The closest they had come so far to getting him out was finding a helicopter pilot. That much had been accomplished, he was told, but the pilot couldn't take off yet because they hadn't secured a place to land.

Pete's eyes moved from the wooden shelves to the fluorescent panels of light in the ceiling. In his mind, he kept returning to the car ride from Abelines to the clinic:

The Lord is my shepherd, I shall not want.

Mireia's soft voice reciting Psalm 23 echoed in his head.

The jungle flashed by through the car windows in patches of green. *Ye, though I walk through the valley of the shadow of death, I will fear no evil.* The ride had been bumpy, yet a steadiness surrounded him. A steady sort of peace. It was big, heavy, pressing in on Pete's entire body to the point where he was not certain if it was the lumbering peacefulness blocking his breathing, or the bullet lodged in his neck. Both felt real and overwhelming in equal measure.

For Thou art with me.

Pete's head relaxed against the top of Mireia's shoulders, which felt thick and strong. Like towers. Her fingers continued to press into Pete's wounds, keeping the blood at bay. *Surely goodness and mercy will follow me all the days of my life, and I will dwell in the house of the Lord.*

Was that not where he was? Was the bumpy Nissan Patrol not being transformed into the house of the Lord? A swell of pressure began in Pete's chest and surged upward. He had sensed the Holy Spirit before, but never quite like this. In the past, it had been a guessing game of *I think, maybe, probably, this is the Holy Spirit.* On the ride to Abelines, there was no guessing. A vast, wide expanse of love was crushing his bones, bursting his eardrums, radiating from his skull. The car had been filled, and all Pete could do was allow it to wash over him.

Pete's memory was interrupted by the feeling of a hand on his lower arm. He opened his eyes and noted that the torso of an older woman standing at his hospital bedside was now blocking his view of the wooden shelves. Her head was adorned by a pale, blue-gray habit and a cross hung from a long silver chain on her neck. She clutched a strand of rosary beads in her palm and stared down at Pete with crinkled eyes that were calm, yet sorrowful. She began to pray over him in Spanish, first for God's healing and then for His forgiveness and grace.

How sweet, Pete thought. A woman he had never met before was coming in to pray for him.

Her brow furrowed in concentration and her voice took on a more insistent tone as she pleaded with God to save his soul, to rip it from the hands of the devil.

Pete bit his lower lip and forced back a smile. *She thinks I'm going to die. And she thinks I don't know Jesus. The clinic staff must have sent her in because they, too, think I am going to die . . .*

The nun continued to pray with fervency, and Pete tried even harder to subdue his lips, which were threatening to erupt into an inappropriate smile. The irony was too much.

The nun closed her eyes, made the sign of the cross above her heart, and exited the room.

Pete exhaled in relief and began to laugh, albeit painfully and in gasping breaths. If he'd made it this far, Pete reasoned, there was a strong chance he would live.

No matter what this nun and the rest of the clinic staff thought.

———————

"Yes?" Carla asked, picking up the phone at her Embassy desk.

"We've secured a place to land."

Carla exhaled long and slow. She felt instantly lighter.

"The helicopter is on its way and will be landing at the field inside the prison in Ciudad Barrios in about 45 minutes. The clinic staff have been briefed and they will be loading the patient into an ambulance that will drive him to the prison."

Did he just say prison?

Carla tried to speak, but the words stuck in her throat.

"Do you copy?" the ACS representative asked.

The prison?

THE PRISON??

"*Señora,* do you copy?"

"What about the field at the coffee plantation?" Carla sputtered. "We could land the helicopter there."

"We've already cleared everything with the prison wardens and they've agreed to go on lockdown. They're placing all inmates in custody as we speak."

"There's no other way?" she asked.

"There's no other way."

Carla thanked him and hung up the phone. In her head flashed images of the inmates with tattooed faces and inky black eyes. Inmates who were angry, fearsome, volatile. Inmates who had nothing left to lose.

The outer walls of the maximum security prison in Ciudad Barrios were painted an optimistic gold. A color that became brighter as it extended outward across the wall, like rays of the sun. The words "*yo cambio*" were painted on it in black letters. "I change," they said. A declaration and a promise. On each side of the words was a painted mural, which featured a man looking upwards. The man had wings like a bird and he stared at a variety of objects: a stack of books with a college diploma on top of them, a Red Cross sign, a beautiful woman who may or may not have been a nurse, and a pair of hands floating in front of a Bible. This mural told a story, to be sure. Whether or not it was accurate, was an entirely different question.

Behind these optimistic walls was a prison designed to house 900 inmates. But in 2009, *BBC News* would report that 1,800 inmates were being held in the Ciudad Barrios prison. Many without beds to sleep in. Instead, they slept side-by-side on the cement floor of the cells. Some even slept next to toilets because there wasn't room for them anywhere else.

The overcrowding of El Salvador's prisons began in 2003 and 2004 when the government, in response to all the gang violence plaguing their streets, passed a wave of *Mano Dura* (Iron Fist) laws. These tough crime laws gave police officers authority to arrest people for so much as affiliating with gang members, or looking like gang members because they were heavily tattooed, or wearing certain clothing.

By 2004, seventy MS-13 leaders had been thrown into jails across the country, and often they were held within close proximity of their rival, Barrio 18. In August of 2004, tensions were running high and a group of Barrio 18 members started a riot that killed thirty-two MS-13 members at the Mariona prison.

In response, the gangs demanded to be separated from each other and on September 2, 2004, the Salvadoran government conceded. They felt the inmates were out of their control and saw no other way to keep the peace. A public policy was signed stating that all gang members would be segregated into exclusive prisons designed for them and them alone. Over 1,100 inmates were shuffled around that morning, and the MS-13 members ended up in Penas Ciudad Barrios.

Over the next two and a half years, the inmates would band together and gain more and more control. They successfully bribed prison guards to smuggle cell phones to them so that they could arrange street killings, drug deals, and give orders to other members from behind bars.

Meanwhile, the prison food supply was dwindling and diseases were running rampant amidst the angry, restless, and overcrowded inmates.

Carla Bolanos considered all of this as she sat at her desk and imagined Pete's helicopter landing at the prison's soccer field. Yes, the inmates would be on lock down, but it still seemed far too risky. One wrong move and everything could go wrong.

At the clinic, Dr Mireia started raiding the shelves for supplies to bring with them on the helicopter ride. She grabbed bandages, gauze, gloves, and tissues.

Amy and Lori watched as Mireia opened each drawer in methodical fashion.

"Amy?" Pete asked. "Is your camera accessible?"

She nodded. "It's out in the waiting room with Hilda."

"Good," Pete said, placing a tissue in front of his lips and coughing up another mouthful of blood. "Assuming I get out of this alive, I want pictures of this clinic, the helicopter, everything."

"You got it," Amy said taking Pete's hand and blinking back tears.

It was 4:43 p.m. and the helicopter was scheduled to land at 5:00 p.m. These last twenty minutes felt excruciating, but Doris was the first to hear the chopper blades in the distance.

Everyone stood up, ready to spring into action, but the phone rang at the clinic and the receptionist announced that it would still be another ten minutes until they were ready for Pete.

"The pilot and medical assistants want to wait until the dust clears from the helicopter landing," she said. "That way they can get him in and out of the prison yard as quickly as possible."

Amy retrieved her camera and killed time by taking photos. She took photos of the x-ray, the nurses in blue scrubs and white lab coats, and of a shirtless Peter laying on the stretcher with his legs hanging off the edges as they finally loaded him into the ambulance that would take him to the prison.

Lori, Amy, and Hilda waited for the ambulance to leave before they piled into the Honda CRV. They raced through the narrow streets of Ciudad Barrios and up a hill where a large coffee plantation was located. From the plantation, they knew they would have a perfect view of both the prison and the helicopter as it took off. They drove past dozens of plantation workers sorting through coffee berries in preparation for them to be harvested, bagged, and delivered all over the world.

The sun was setting as Pete's body was finally loaded into a Huey helicopter painted brown and olive green. Pete thought it looked exactly like the helicopter from the TV show M*A*S*H with long, skinny chopper blades. The US government had donated several helicopters during El Salvador's civil war, and Pete shuddered to think of the stories this helicopter could tell were it able to speak. Stories of the infamous Colonel José Domingo Monterossa Barrios who fought for the Salvadoran government during the civil war.

Colonel Monterossa was first commander of a rapid response battalion funded and trained by the US called Atlacatl. He was also the mastermind behind the tragic massacre at El Mozote and several other human rights atrocities throughout the twelve year civil war.

Monterossa's vision was to eradicate the threat of communism by killing any and all supporters of the FMLN. The expression he used to describe this bloodshed was *La Limpieza*, which means,"The Cleanup."

Monterossa's tactics were ruthless and often effective. His battalion would hone in on a village they wanted to destroy by creating a blockade around one side, and forcing its citizens against any natural barriers that existed on the other side, such as mountains or rivers. First, the army and special forces would move in on foot, then the Huey helicopters would sweep down in an explosion of bombs and artillery.

During one particular battle in 1984, Monterossa's men had captured a group of FMLN fighters who were trying to escape with broadcasting equipment and the transmitter for Radio Venceramos. Radio Venceramos was a primary means of communication and hope for the FMLN. Their program aired every evening and it was a subversive, controversial force. Guerrilla supporters would tune in to hear songs of the freedom fighters, and satirical skits poking fun at all their key political opponents. The US Ambassador Deane Hinton often starred in these parodies, as did Colonel Monterossa himself, and neither were ever cast in a favorable light.

Monterossa despised Radio Venceramos and how they heckled him every time he lost a battle. He had long been wanting to destroy Radio Venceramos, as it would be tantamount to destroying the heart and soul of the FMLN. Monterossa celebrated upon hearing that his men had the Radio Venceramos transmitter in their possession. He called every major news outlet he could find and told them he wanted them in San Salvador, filming his Huey helicopter as it landed and he emerged from it in victory, the transmitter in hand.

The news outlets complied. Even a reporter from TIME Magazine was ready and waiting to capture this historic event. But what none of them predicted was that the guerrilla fighters had intended to be captured that day. They sensed that Colonel Monterossa's vanity would actually be his demise, and they strapped eight sticks of dynamite to the inside of their spare radio transmitter.

The dynamite had two detonators. One operated by remote control, and the other was activated by air pressure. If the radio transmitter reached a flying altitude of 300 meters, it would automatically explode.

As Colonel Monterossa's helicopter ascended into the skyline, long before it ever reached the bevy of reporters stationed in San Salvador, the dynamite inside it erupted into a giant ball of flame. Monterossa, his helicopter, and all the other men on board with him exploded into tiny pieces, falling from the sky and joining with the remains of the villagers they had murdered below.

From the top of the coffee plantation, Amy noticed the helicopter blades finally begin to spin and lift into the air. To everyone's relief, there were no inmates rushing the helicopter and no commotion of any kind. They safely transferred Pete inside and Dr. Mireia hopped in next to him.

Amy flipped on her digital camera and clicked several photos as the thunderous propeller punctuated the air. She kept snapping photos as it traveled higher into the sky, soaring over the coffee fields and heading toward the volcanic mountains that lay between Ciudad Barrios and San Salvador.

Inside the helicopter, Pete laid on his back and felt his body slipping with every turn. No one had bothered to strap him down. Even more frightening was the realization that Hueys were designed without doors so that fighters could hang out the sides of them during battle.

Not only was Pete not strapped down, but it seemed at any moment that he could slide out the open door and into the threatening patch of blue sky that lay outside it. The helicopter veered to the right and Pete's body veered with it. Dr. Mireia gripped his hand and held him steady as the wind and the chopper blades created a deafening roar.

Pete tensed every single muscle and felt himself slipping again. His foot brushed the edge of the door and he fought to hold on to Mireira's hand.

I've come so far, he prayed. *Please let it not be for nothing.*

At 6:00 p.m., the sky was dark. Carla Bolanos stayed close to her Embassy desk, although she would normally be heading home at this time. Her phone rang yet again, and she picked it up quickly, hoping ACS would have news that Pete had landed safely and was on his way to Diagnóstico.

Instead of hearing the voice of the ACS rep on the other line, she was greeted by the San Salvador police department.

"We hear there is a gringo on board this helicopter that will be landing at the Sheraton, yes?" he asked.

"Yes, that's right," Carla said.

"There's been a major traffic accident and some of streets are blocked off between Diagnóstico and the Sheraton. Not only will it be difficult for the ambulance to get him there, but the ER is also going to be flooded with car accident victims."

Carla's heart sank. What else could possibly go wrong?

"You need to get the gringo there first, ahead of them, so we will be escorting your ambulance driver."

"The police will be escorting him?" she asked.

"*Sí, señora.* Please contact the ambulance driver to let him know there will be a group of cars with sirens ready to accompany him through the streets of Escalón."

Carla's eyes grew wet with tears. "Thank you so much," she said.

CHAPTER 14

Diagnóstico

San Salvador, January 18, 2007

When the ambulance finally pulled into the hospital parking lot, the doors swung open and Pete gripped his IV tube as he was wheeled through a series of long white corridors underneath fluorescent lights. Dara was there to greet him along with Ron and several other members of ENLACE's staff. The nurses and doctors worked quickly to regulate his breathing and monitor his vitals. They placed tubes down Pete's neck and began prepping him for surgery. Dara listened helplessly as the nurses communicated with each other in rapid fire Spanish. As she stood at Pete's bedside clasping his hand, the lights in the hospital flickered and the entire room began to vibrate. It started with the shiny silver instruments laid out on a tray by Pete's bedside. They rattled noisily, as though being prompted by invisible hands.

Lori had arrived at the hospital and was sitting in the waiting room when the ground beneath her feet started to rattle. The shaking grew more fierce and persistent until it seeped into the walls, the furniture, and finally the roof itself began to sway. As the hospital employees ran for cover, Lori closed her eyes in disbelief.

Another earthquake.

Pete's hospital bed shook violently as his fingers gripped the thin blanket covering his legs. Being jolted around threw his body into further shock, and he felt the urge to cough moving from his chest to his lungs until a large spattering of blood flew from his mouth.

Dara began scanning the room for tissues or wipes. Something. Anything. The hospital staff was on alert, and Dara could see they were debating what to do with both themselves and the patients. If the whole building began to collapse, the entire waiting room and hospital staff could run for safety, but Pete could not. He would just be stuck, immobile, defenseless. Trapped in this bed as the ceiling fell on top of him.

Dara noted a paper towel dispenser hanging on the wall above the sink, and yanked out a thick stack of them as the dispenser shook. She handed half of them to Pete so he could cough into them. The other half she used to dab up the blood speckled all over his chest. A small consolation, but it was something.

Pete grabbed Dara's hand and held it still for a moment amidst the shaking and the chaos. His heavy eyes met hers and they said *Thank you*. They said *If you only know one thing, please know this: I'll love you always*.

In the waiting room, Lori ducked under a doorframe and held her breath. She had seen what earthquakes were capable of. She knew their power and her own powerlessness, but she also knew the same force that destroys can be capable of mercy. She prayed and hoped and asked for mercy to reign. Today, in this moment.

The 5.4 magnitude earthquake ceased its shaking just as quickly as it had started. Night fell in San Salvador, and little damage was reported.

It was about 7:00 p.m. when the hospital workers took tentative steps toward continuing the work they had begun. No one knew if there would be aftershocks, but they did decide that come what may, they would begin to operate on Pete at 9:00 p.m. that evening.

After nine long hours of lingering in Pete's esophagus, after tumultuous car rides through the jungle, a series of x-rays, a helicopter flight from a maximum security prison, a police escort through the streets of San Salvador, and a 5.4 earthquake, the .22 caliber bullet would finally be removed.

Upon hearing this news, Dara took a brisk walk to the waiting room and felt the adrenaline coursing through her veins. She was awake and jittery, like she could run a marathon. The first face she saw was that of her friend and neighbor, Alba Barrientos. Alba came running to her and threw her arms around Dara.

"*Pobrecita, pobrecita,*" she kept repeating. Dara could feel Alba's tears dampening the crease between her shoulder and the crook of her neck.

"*Comó puedo ayudarte?*" Alba asked Dara. "How can I help you?"

Dara felt a distinct prompting inside her to take Alba's help. She thought for a moment.

"Can you spend the night with my kids so that I can stay at the hospital?"

Alba agreed, and Dara introduced her to the McGees and Buenos. Together, they all devised a plan to ensure the DeSoto kids would be taken care of over the next few days and that Dara could easily go back and forth between the hospital and her home.

When they finished coordinating, David McGee received a text from Pete and Dara's former pastor back in Valencia, California.

"You're never going to believe this," David said, "but there are 600 people gathered together right now and praying for Pete back in California."

John and Lucia DeSoto arrived at Diagnóstico shortly after Pete was released from surgery. Weary from their last-minute, overnight flight from San Diego to San Salvador, they operated off pure adrenaline as Walter led them through the narrow hallways of the hospital and into the waiting room where a young woman with dark hair stood up and greeted them with a firm handshake.

"My name is Mireia," she said. "I'm a doctor as well, although not at this hospital."

"From what I hear, she's part of the reason why Pete survived," Walter added. "She held his wound closed so that he wouldn't bleed out."

Lucia's eyes widened at the visual image of her son's neck. Dr. Mireia could sense her discomfort and looked at her with tenderness.

"He's doing just fine now," she assured Lucia and then averted her eyes to John to ensure that he knew it as well. "But before we go in to see him, I do want to prepare you for the state he's in."

Mireia paused and John nodded for her to continue.

"Your son has tubes up his nose and throat and he's making loud, guttural breathing sounds. As I mentioned before, everything went well with the surgery, I just don't want you to be alarmed when you see him."

Mireia and Walter walked the DeSotos through the maze of beige colored hallways. When they entered Pete's room, he was wearing pale blue hospital pajamas and had multiple tubes taped to his body, snaking every which way. His mouth was wide open and his eyes were closed. Dara sat quietly at his bedside, watching Pete's chest as it rose and fell with every breath.

"Hi!" she whispered, her eyes brightening at the sight of them. She stood up and wrapped her arms tightly around Lucia. Pete's mother was like a beacon of peace and tranquility. Dara could feel it from her, even now, as she hugged her petite frame. A woman with a soft voice and a deep inner-strength.

As Dara looked at her, she thought back to that first phone conversation she and Pete had over a decade ago in college. The day Dara had attempted to call Pete's roommate Aaron, but ended up talking to Pete for hours instead. Pete had described his mom back then as a woman who lived for serving others. She ministered to children in the park, she counseled the homeless, she had read Pete bedtime stories of the saints who gave up everything to follow Jesus. It was all Dara could do to keep herself from picturing Lucia as Mother Theresa in a black habit.

Lucia turned toward her son and placed a soft hand on top of his lower arm. As she did, Pete's eyes began to flutter open.

"I've been thanking God every single minute that you're still alive," she said.

"Mom," Pete whispered.

John stood on the other side of Pete's bed, and Dara watched as he tried to remain calm and composed. She imagined what it might feel like to almost lose Isaac or PJ and tried to envision either of them at the age of 30, lying in hospital beds with long, grown legs and faces that had developed into mature men. But she couldn't because she knew it would never matter what age they were, how many decades had passed, how different they looked on the outside, they would always stay in her mind exactly as they were now. Always.

Dara shut the door quietly behind her and gave Pete's parents a moment of privacy with their son. She walked into the waiting room and was greeted by a weeping Marlena Fernandez who jumped out of her chair and walked quickly toward Dara.

Marlena held a damp, tattered Kleenex in her hand and flung her arms around Dara.

"I——, I——" Marlena stuttered, and broke down into sobs.

Dara held Marlena and let her cry, unsure if she should join her in this frenzy, or if her own tears would only make things worse. If they might further exacerbate Marlena.

Marlena lifted her head. The mascara she had been wearing had smeared into gray pools under her eyelids.

"Look at you," she said, cupping Dara's head in her hands. "You're like a pillar of strength."

Dara smiled "I don't know about that."

"You are," Marlena insisted. "I can feel it. And here I am. A mess."

"Thank you for coming so late at night," Dara said, noting that the clock behind her read 11:00 p.m. She picked up Marlena's hand and squeezed it tightly.

"Always," Marlena said. "But what can I do for you? How can I help?"

Dara thought about it. She would be sleeping at the hospital all night.

"I could really use a toothbrush?"

Marlena laughed. "A toothbrush?"

Dara laughed too and nodded.

"OK, *mi amor*. Let's get you a toothbrush!"

Marlena wiped her eyes and gathered her purse. The two women exited the electric sliding doors of the hospital and walked into the quiet streets of the Escalón neighborhood. The hills were steep and dimly lit by overhead lamps that provided just enough light to navigate them. Of all the neighborhoods in San Salvador, this was the safest, yet still Dara wondered if the two of them should be walking alone without any weapons or form of protection.

John DeSoto had always wanted to be a cop. He took criminal justice classes straight out of high school and deeply resonated with both the need to investigate, and the need to protect those around him by using whatever means necessary.

As a child, John had been the only male in a house full of women and felt a tremendous sense of responsibility to protect them. He lived with his mother, his two sisters, and two female cousins in a one bedroom house with a trailer out back. John's father had walked out of his life before John could remember him, his brother had gone to fight in Vietnam and never came back, and his mother had never remarried. All of which meant there had been no role models to guide John. What it meant to be a male and a leader were two questions he often wrestled with.

One night when his mother was working late and his sisters were at home, John thought he heard a rustling outside their front door. One of his sisters heard it too, and then they both saw the shadow of someone followed by the crunching of leaves underfoot.

John rushed to his room and removed the BB gun from under his bed. It was not much, and it certainly wouldn't kill the guy, but John hoped it would be enough to scare him off. He felt the weight of cold metal in his hand, and sneaked into the garage. He peered out the small window next to the door and saw the profile of a man in a navy blue sweatshirt, the hood pulled over his head. John's heart began to beat and his fingers took on a mind of their own. They worked quickly, clasping the trigger, feeling its pull and release. The BB shot out into the night, hitting the intruder in the foot.

The hooded figure let out a yelp and went running as John stood in the driveway, frightened and elated by what he had just done.

Ever since David McGee called to tell John about Pete's shooting, the question that had been repeating in his head on a continuous loop, was the question of why. *Why on earth would a masked gunman want to hurt his son? Who was this gunman? Where did he come from? And most importantly, was he trying to kill Peter?*

John's palms felt damp as he considered this last prospect. If the gunman had intended to kill him, and by all accounts it certainly seemed that way, then what would stop him from finishing the job?

John stepped outside Pete's room and examined the hallway. The signs on the walls were in Spanish. A group of women in scrubs walked toward him. Behind them, a man was limping with eyes that were dark and hollow. John looked away, half expecting a figure in a black mask to materialize.

He stepped back inside Pete's hospital room and took a quick inventory. There were machines measuring Pete's vitals, tubes connected to bags of liquid, and a small cot where John would be sleeping tonight. Nothing even remotely resembled a weapon. He swallowed hard and made a silent pact with himself. He would protect his son. No matter what it took.

Lucia padded around the corridors of the hospital looking for a quiet place to write. In her hand was her prayer journal with a ballpoint pen suspended in the spiraling wires of her notebook. Her favorite way to dialogue with God was by writing him her thoughts and then capturing the spirit of what she felt was his response.

Her brown eyes gravitated toward an empty bench. She sat down and took a minute to close her eyes and steady her mind.

Thanks. Today would be about giving thanks.

Lucia opened her eyes and began writing, a sense of giddiness overtaking her pen as she began to record every single miracle that worked to save her son's life.

First was the positioning of the bullet. She thanked God that it had missed his spinal cord, his trachea, and his esophagus. She thanked Him that Pete wasn't paralyzed. She thanked Him that there was a doctor present to attend to Pete's wound and keep him from bleeding out. She thanked God for Absalon's bravery as he drove the Nissan out of the jungle, for the clinic workers in Ciudad Barrios, the helicopter that flew him to San Salvador, the nurses and doctors that operated on him, and every other invisible part of this big crazy miracle God had conducted like an orchestra.

Words could not express the height and depth of her gratitude. For today, *thank you* was all she needed to write. All she needed to say. *Thank you* was everything.

Lucia closed her notebook and tucked her pen back inside the spooling wires that bound the pages together. She exhaled deeply and began a slow walk back to her son's room. Halfway down the hall, she noticed Dara coming toward her. The two women met in the middle of the hall and Lucia reached out to squeeze Dara's hand.

"How are you doing dear?" she asked, looking Dara straight in the eye.

Dara smiled and squeezed her hand back. The ever calming presence of Lucia was here to disarm her.

"I've been thinking," Dara answered. "There's so much going on up here," she said, swirling her hands around her head.

Lucia nodded. "I imagine you and Peter have some big decisions ahead of you."

Dara let out a long sigh. "I'm just not sure where we're supposed to go from here. Does this mean we leave El Salvador? Does it mean we stay? What's best for the kids? What's best for Peter? Are we meant to fulfill the commitment we already made to stay and work here for 3-5 years? Or do we go back on it? Do we walk away now and throw in the towel?"

"What are you feeling in your heart?" Lucia asked.

Dara smiled. A private smile.

Moments after she found out Pete was shot—when Ron was at her dining room table, David was making phone calls, and Jenny was watching the girls—Dara had picked up a broom and started sweeping the kitchen floor. Her hands and feet made slow, robotic movements detached from the rest of reality. They said nothing as they swept. They felt nothing as they swept. The feeling and the thinking were taking place in her brain where a single, solitary idea kept repeating itself over and over. *This is your golden ticket. This is your golden ticket. This is your golden ticket to get the hell out of this country.*

"I don't know yet," Dara said.

How could she explain it all to Lucia? Lucia wouldn't have thoughts like that, Dara reasoned, because Lucia wouldn't be looking for a golden ticket. She would simply trust. She would stockpile every single one of her cares and toss them at Jesus' feet. Then she would wipe her hands and walk away. Just like that.

Or, maybe not.

Maybe Lucia wasn't quite as superhuman as Dara always made her out to be in her mind. Maybe she had flaws and doubts like the rest of us. Maybe she did the wrong thing sometimes. Maybe she too, at one time, felt an outrageous longing, so deep and wide it would take an entire lifetime to climb through.

Dara stared at Lucia's petite frame, her softly wrinkled skin and silver-streaked hair, and everything inside Dara yearned to be on the other side of that longing. On the other side, where Lucia dwelt.

"Do you have any idea how strong you are?" Lucia asked.

Moisture filled the back of Dara's eyes. "No, I'm not," she said.

The longing was so strong that it materialized and began to leak out of her.

"A weak woman would not have left everything she had and agreed to move her entire family to another country."

Dara's tears kept falling.

"A weak woman would not have stood resolutely at her husband's bedside after he was gunned down in a jungle. A weak woman would not have taken the time to nourish her children in the midst of it all, tucking them in at night while her husband was in surgery."

"But none of that is me," Dara said. "It's all Jesus. I feel like He's giving me this supernatural strength and half the time it surprises the heck out of me."

"Exactly," Lucia said. "And He will continue to. You don't need to be anything or anyone special. You just keep being open and going to Him. That's it, that's all. And over time, it will become like a reflex. It will become a part of you, and that's when the fear starts to lessen just a bit."

"I want that so badly," Dara said.

"Give it time," Lucia said, pulling Dara toward her and embracing her in a hug.

Dara felt her body soften, the tension dissipating slow and steady.

"In the meanwhile, be good to yourself. Celebrate how far you've come. God longs to celebrate these things with us, I think."

Dara nodded and smiled. "Thank you," she said.

"Anytime."

The tangy smell of antiseptic filled the corridors of the hospital as the two women headed back to Pete's room. They opened the door to find Pastor Juan sitting on the edge of Pete's bed. He was wearing a baseball cap with the *Harry Potter* logo emblazoned across the top of it. He and Pete were laughing.

"Juan says he's going to sneak some Pollo Campero in here next time he comes," Pete told Dara to catch her up on the joke. His voice sounded stronger today. Not like before the shooting, as his rhythm of speech was slower and he couldn't project with quite the same enthusiasm. But the whisper, the raspiness, was subsiding.

Pollo Campero is a chain of fried chicken restaurants known and loved throughout El Salvador. Imagine a KFC with fresher chicken, actual servers, and laminated menus similar to the type you would find at Denny's and you've got Pollo Campero. Every time Pete and Dara drove out to San Martín to visit Juan and check up on the water project ENLACE was helping to coordinate, they would always stop first at Pollo Campero to pick up a bucket of fried chicken and french fries.

Juan's very presence emboldened Pete. Juan was both a fighter and a visionary. When teams of missionaries arrived in El Salvador from the US, one of the first places Pete would take them was to visit Pastor Juan and he would tell them all his stories. Stories Pete grew to know by heart. Juan would rattle them off in Spanish and Pete would translate for the American missionaries.

There was the time Juan was trying to build his church in San Martín, but he had little money or resources to do so. A small plot of land had been donated for the church, and someone else had given them cement to lay a foundation. But in San Martín, there wasn't any access to water. Without water, Juan couldn't mix the cement, and without cement, he couldn't lay the foundation.

Any other man may have simply chosen to wait. Wait until the dry season passed, as it inevitably would, until the rain poured down by the bucket loads. But, attempting to construct a church in the middle of the rainy season wouldn't be wise either.

Juan was in a quandary and the only thing he knew to do was pray. Like Elijah in the Bible, he prayed for rain. Rain in the middle of the dusty dry season. Rain, although it was nowhere in the forecast.

After several minutes, Juan lifted his head and noticed a small gray cloud forming in the distance. This encouraged him, so he bowed his head and prayed some more. "Let the cloud get bigger. Let it be carrying lots of water. Let it release that water right above us. Right where we need it most so we can build your church."

By the time he finished praying, the cloud was overhead, and it did indeed rain. Juan and his companions ran quickly to grab buckets to catch it. It rained and it rained, all afternoon until their buckets were overflowing and they had enough water to mix their cement.

"*Gloria a Dios*," Juan always said at the end of his tale. "Praise be to God."

———————————

John DeSoto lay on the sofa bed inside Pete's hospital room and re-positioned himself for what felt like the hundredth time. He had tried sleeping on his back, on his left side, and then his right. Always, the bed felt lumpy and he couldn't bring his mind to rest.

He had spent most of the day chatting with Doris, Absalon, Lori, and anyone else who could help give him clues as to what happened when Pete was shot. He had also conducted various Google searches in hopes of learning more about the gangs in El Salvador. If indeed, the shooting had been gang related, John wondered if the shooters were out looking for Pete right now. He imagined them searching the corridors of the hospital. Waiting until just the right moment to storm through the door and open fire.

John blinked his eyes open and peered at the shadows moving outside the hospital room door. A pair of footsteps approached slowly and came to a stop right in front of it. He held his breath and scanned the room for some form of weapon. There had to be something. He sensed the presence of whoever was on the other side of the door and watched the handle, waiting for it to turn.

John's heart began to pound. He felt the tension rising inside him, and suddenly the shadow outside the door moved again. He braced himself, anticipating the very worst, but then the footsteps walked away. The door never opened. Nothing happened.

From his research, John recalled how neither the MS-13 nor the Barrio 18 gangs ever wore masks. When they came after people, their faces were bare, save for the numerous tattoos covering most of their skin.

But if this masked gunman hadn't been a gang member, then who was he?

January 21, 2007

"Dara, could you bring me my laptop?" Pete asked.

Pete waved goodbye to two-year-old Kaya as Isaac helped her climb down from the hospital bed. Dara had been bringing all four of the kids to visit Pete every day after school. They squeezed together until all of them fit like one jumbled mass on top of his bed. Pete flipped the TV mounted in the corner to *Dora the Explorer* so together they would watch, hoping and pretending that the presence of this cartoon could help normalize an otherwise intense situation.

Every day, Pete noticed the fear and confusion in their faces as they stared at the bandage on his throat and the small tubes weaving in and out of his nose. He did his best to make jokes and lighten the mood for them, as his motto in life was to keep pressing forward. This shooting was merely an obstacle, and together they could all get past it.

Dara looked at Pete with hesitation. "What do you need your laptop for?"

"For work, obviously."

PJ, Isaac, and Hannah all looked from their mom to their dad and back again.

"You just had surgery three days ago. Don't you think work can wait a bit longer? Maybe take this time to rest up?"

Pete's expression changed from a light smile to a furrowed brow. "No, I don't think it can. And besides that, I'm going to go crazy for the next two weeks if I'm just sitting here in this hospital bed doing nothing."

"Pete . . ."

"Dara, I want my laptop. This isn't really a discussion."

Dara started. She looked at her kids and was unsure what to do or say. Should she hide her offense? Should she start an argument with him and tell him he had some nerve, like she wanted to?

The tension in the room expanded. Hannah looked scared. Kaya looked like she was about to start crying.

"Alright," Dara said. "I'll bring you your laptop tomorrow, but later on, we need to talk."

She asked the kids to say goodbye to daddy and then led them into the hall.

After they left, the nurse came to examine Pete's throat and administer another round of medications and vocal steroids. Then it was time for "dinner," which meant drinking chocolate flavored Ensure through a tube in his nose. Pete's throat was still healing, so ingesting food orally was off limits.

Before leaving, the nurse scheduled a gastrointestinal exam for the following morning and reminded Pete to give his voice a rest.

"I know you've been getting a lot of visitors, but remember to let *them* do most of the talking," she cautioned, giving Pete a stern look.

Pete nodded. "My voice sounds good, though, doesn't it?"

"Yes, but your speaking capacity might not stay at 95 percent if you don't allow your vocal cords to heal properly."

Pete smiled. Instead of saying anything, he gave the nurse a thumbs up. *See,* he thought, *I'm practicing already.*

Marlena Fernandez showed up the following afternoon and brought along her father, Pastor Pablo Fernandez. Pete got so excited to meet this man he had admired and heard so much about—from Pablo's humanitarian work, to his infamous capture by the death squads—that he soon forgot about the nurse's warning. The men prayed together, traded stories, and chatted for upwards of an hour.

Pete then typed up a blog post about his experience in the hospital, and made a phone call to one of ENLACE's donors he had been meaning to contact. His main presumption was that since his voice felt fine, it must be. Anything to prove to himself and the world that this shooting was just a speed bump, a momentary obstacle that he would soon be racing over.

The hospital released Pete on January 31. He had been at Diagnóstico for over fifteen days. The following day, he wrote an exuberant blog post to his friends and family:

> *I can't explain to you all how wonderful it felt yesterday to leave the hospital with Dara and my dad, knowing that I was returning to my home. I haven't stopped hugging Dara for the last 48 hours. I've never smiled more with my kids. Food has never tasted so good. Sleeping in my own bed, I felt like I was floating on clouds last night.*
>
> *It still is so much to take in. Just two weeks ago, I came as close as one can to leaving this world (see x-ray pic below of bullet in my neck). Over the last two weeks, I have watched God bring thousands of people together in prayer. I have seen him unify a community here in El Salvador to provide unbelievable support to our family. I have watched God use three doctors and a host of nurses to carry me through recovery. I have seen God slow a bullet, and safely land it in the only place in my neck that would not kill me. I have heard about a church in Abelines that now has even more resolve to serve its neighbors and pray through ways to make the community safer. Simply put, I have seen God actively engaged in my life and in the lives of others.*
>
> *I don't understand all that God is doing through this incident. I still struggle with understanding why God protected me, while there are other wonderful people whose lives have been cut short. Yet, it has been so evident to me that God is engaged in our lives, not just a passive bystander. Often, I think it's easy to believe in our heads that God is active, but then go about living as though He is on a coffee break, or maybe tending the garden around the pearly gates. These last two weeks*

have really demonstrated to me the radical involvement God has in our lives.

Life is so precious. It is so precious because, God gifts it to us. In His mercy, God has let me have more life to live.

CHAPTER 15

Who Did This?

The question of who shot Pete and why remained a puzzling, yet persistent one for nearly a decade after it happened. Ron Bueno and David McGee returned to Abelines several times to investigate the shooting, and uncovered multiple theories as to what exactly happened.

Theory number one involved a group of local teenage bandits who resided in the Abelines region and had a reputation for jumping out of hidden corners of the jungle—just as the men who shot Pete had—and robbing vehicles they deemed unrecognizable (i.e. cars not belonging to local residents and therefore transporting people that may have valuable possessions). These cars were routinely stopped by the group of juveniles, held at gunpoint, and allowed to proceed, unharmed, so long as the passengers complied and handed over the requested items.

This theory sounded plausible at first. Pete's white Nissan Patrol fit the profile of cars targeted by the bandits. It was possible they even knew that the Nissan was filled with expensive filming equipment because Pete and Absalon had been roving round the village that morning conducting interviews of the residents. In Lori Margaret's field journal account of what happened that day, she reported seeing large groups of World Vision volunteers handing out educational resources to residents that morning. If these bandits were looking to rob outsiders, it would have been the ideal time to do so, as multiple options were available, from the ENLACE workers to the World Vision ones.

But in all the robbery accounts on the road to Abelines, most have not been reported to include actual gunfire. If all the bandits had wanted that day was some loot, why start shooting at Pete's vehicle right away, without even giving the passengers the option of surrendering their valuables?

There were four bullet holes in the side of the Nissan, which meant the gun didn't misfire accidentally; those bullets were deliberate and were aimed to kill. In addition, Pete remembered the gunman shrieking at the top of his lungs. Whether or not he was in his right mind is another question, and one that will likely never be answered. One emotion that couldn't be denied was that the gunman was filled with rage.

But why?

To answer that question, Ron and David examined the second prevailing theory. This anecdote began with the tale of a general contractor who had been overseeing various building projects throughout Abelines in 2006/2007. The man was rumored to have been cheating his workers out of their wages and to have been caught in bed with another resident's sister. The combination of these two offenses was enough for some of the more wily villagers to put a hit out on him. In addition, this foreman also drove a white, 4x4 vehicle and loosely resembled Pete in stature.

If this theory was true, then Pete's shooting was merely a case of mistaken identity. Pete was in the wrong place at the wrong time, and perhaps the gunman realized he had the wrong man after he started shooting. Maybe that's why he didn't finish the job?

The fact that not a single person died in the Nissan Patrol is yet another mystery. As Lori Margaret explained, "In El Salvador, people don't just get shot; they get shot and killed."

Others speculate that the gunman may have recognized Dr. Mireia's face in the backseat and stopped shooting out of respect. She was a much-loved village doctor and had saved multiple lives. Another theory suggests that the gunman was unaware of the Honda CRV trailing only a minute behind the Nissan. Some believe it was the sound of the Honda's tires turning the corner that caught the gunman off guard and made him flee. Perhaps he feared the Honda's passengers might withdraw guns of their own and begin a wild west-style shoot out?

As for the identity of this shooter, that too, was mired in conjecture and hearsay. Those who suspected the gunman was part of the band of delinquent teenagers also believed that the kid who shot Pete died several years later in a fatal robbery attempt. After several successful hijinks, he finally met his match when the driver of the vehicle he was holding up pulled out a gun and killed him on the spot.

So, the gunman had died then?

Maybe. Or maybe not.

As American journalist and author Joan Didion found, facts in El Salvador are difficult to pin down. In 1982, Didion was sent to El Salvador to report on the civil war. She later compiled her accounts into a book called *Salvador*, and in it she wrote as an outsider who was trying to explain what she saw as accurately and candidly as possible. But she kept getting frustrated because nothing in El Salvador was quite as it seemed.

In one chapter, she tried reporting on a simple helicopter crash, but even that became complicated as all the news outlets and eye witnesses seemed to contradict each other. Some said the helicopter crashed in Honduras. Some said it crashed in Morazán, the region right near the Honduran border, where Abelines lies. What became of the four passengers in the helicopter was even more innocuous. All were reported dead at first, but days later, allegedly began to surface—as prisoners of war, or claiming to be prisoners of war, or turning up as patients in local hospitals, but "*incommunicado.*"

Finally, Didion was forced to concede, "In the absence of information (and the presence, often, of disinformation) even the most apparently straightforward events take on, in El Salvador, elusive shadows, like a fragment of retrieved legend."

In a country where neighbors, friends, and family members were recruited for both sides of the civil war, where dead and mutilated bodies popped up daily on random street corners, it was not always clear who was with you and who was against you. Keeping secrets became paramount and has since forged itself into the culture. Especially in small villages like Los Abelines.

CHAPTER 16

Home From the Hospital

February 2007

In honor of Pete's first weekend home, Dara thought it would be fun to have a barbecue to celebrate. John and Lucia had flown back to California, and life was slowly returning to normal. The kids gathered in the backyard, proudly sucking on popsicles they had helped to make the night before by pouring fresh guava juice into plastic molds.

Pete manned the barbecue, smoke wafting up from the grill as small drips of fat fell from the hamburger patties and into the flames. Dara fiddled with the iPod dock, finally selecting an album by Amos Lee.

It was beautiful to have Pete home, standing in front of her, alive and doing something as simple as barbecuing hamburgers. She glanced at him over her shoulder and what she saw meant the entire world. Her heart felt large and full. This moment was precious and it was rare and she wanted to freeze it in her mind and come back to it often.

"Mom, what are they doing?" PJ asked.

He stood at her side and pointed up to a tree several feet outside their yard. In it was a trio of young boys climbing their way to the top branches, one right after the other. They were chatting loudly in Spanish as each of their necks angled downward and their eyes landed on the DeSoto's yard. Dara watched as the boys glanced at the yard and then at each other, silent thoughts of mischief dancing back and forth.

"It looks like they're just playing in the tree," she said.

PJ frowned. "But they're staring at me."

"Just try to ignore them, honey," she said, smiling.

The initial sound of the boys' feet touching the tree branches had startled Pete. His whole body shuddered when he heard it and a cold shock of fear surged through his neck and shoulders. *It's just some stupid kids*, he told himself, and tried to redirect his focus to the sizzling grill.

The kids in the tree began to laugh. Pete heard them and looked up. Their dark eyes seemed sinister and were boring directly into him, poking holes in the top of his head. Pete felt his neck begin to burn where his bullet wound was still healing.

These kids were encroaching on his privacy. They were peering into his yard at his family and they sure as hell had better not be plotting anything.

One of the young boys cackled and Pete looked up at the tree. His eyes met the boy's and Pete gave him a stern look. The boy, about twelve years old, frowned back at Pete, and Pete sensed a challenge in them. The boy poked his friend, whispered something to him, and the other boy nodded.

Pete's breath began to quicken and he his fingers gripped tightly around the spatula he was holding.

The two boys laughed and then tossed a metal vice grip into the yard. It made a thud in the grass, landing about a foot away from Isaac, who was just finishing the last bite of his popsicle.

Pete slammed the metal spatula down on the plate he had been reserving for the cooked hamburger patties. "What the f—— do you think you're doing!" he shouted.

Dara's eyes widened. The husband she knew never spoke like this. Especially not to a group of children. Especially not in front of his own children.

Isaac looked up at Dara and started to cry. She held him against her as Pete walked away from the barbecue and headed straight for the fence line in their backyard, as close as he could get to the kids in the tree.

"Get out!" he shouted. "*Ándele!*" He held the spatula in the air and gestured wildly, as though it were about to fling from his fingertips at any moment and fly toward the trouble making kids.

The kids scrambled down the tree branches and Pete felt his heart pounding. He turned back around to see Isaac crying, Dara looking shell shocked, the hamburger patties burning, and Hannah, Kaya, and PJ sitting perfectly still, as though they were afraid to move.

He felt shame. Confusion. Anger.

"I'm sorry," he muttered.

Pete looked to the ground, afraid to make eye contact. He glanced one more time at the empty tree and then went back to the barbecue.

Maybe I can still rescue these burgers, he thought.

———————

As the days went by after Pete's initial surgery, his throat became weaker. By the end of the first week, he felt a noticeable difference in his ability to breathe, as though some passageway were being blocked. But the doctors couldn't find anything wrong. They stuck a twelve-inch metal rod down Pete's throat with a camera on the end of it and noted that his vocal cords seemed paralyzed. When he tried to speak, there wasn't any movement at all.

"Can't Daddy read to us?" Hannah asked, pulling the covers up to her chin.

Dara knelt down to eye-level with her four-year-old daughter who was anxiously awaiting her bedtime story.

"Remember how we talked about this? Daddy's whole throat is hurting a lot right now, so it's really hard for him to read or to talk."

Hannah nodded, and Dara could see the little wheels turning inside her head as she tried to process this information.

"How about this? I'll read you a story and afterwards we'll pray and ask Jesus to watch over Daddy and make his throat feel better."

Hannah smiled. "OK," she said.

Pete had been watching this exchange from the hallway and could feel the backs of his eyes growing moist. *This had to change. He couldn't go through life like this. Without a voice.* He thought of the blog post he had written after coming home from the hospital. Pete had meant every word, yet here he was one week later, listening to his daughter's pain and fearing that prayer might not work this time. Pete wished more than anything to go back to that moment when he first came home, to the elation he had felt because his voice seemed to be healing and life itself was an outrageous gift.

Pete tried to breathe and began to choke. The air trapped in his lungs and agitated his throat. He coughed and coughed until everything felt raw, and when he lifted his palm away from his mouth, he noticed it was speckled in blood. Pete dropped his hand to his side and then lifted it back again, hoping the blood would disappear.

It didn't.

The walls of the house felt imposing. He need to get out. Without telling Dara, Pete walked out the front door and into the night. Rather than finding comfort and freedom, he was greeted by the barbed wire and the tall green wall surrounding the *plazuela*. For all he knew, and for all he tried not to think about it, danger was lurking on the other side. Several months earlier, all this so-called security hadn't kept it out.

Visions of faceless men dressed in black invaded Pete's thoughts. They crawled over the walls en mass, armed with machetes and filling the backyard of the neighbor's house across the street. He tried to imagine what Dara had witnessed that night. When she was home alone with the kids and heard their neighbors screaming.

The thought of both Dara and the neighbors having to endure that break-in caused Pete's fists to clench. A surge of anger traveled up his neck and shoulders, and he was frightened by its intensity.

It's okay to be angry, the gentle voice inside him said. *It's okay to hurt.*

Pete dismissed both thoughts immediately. He didn't want to hurt. What good would it do?

In the past, there had been moments where he had climbed into the pain with Jesus, leaning on Him, calling out to Him, and processing with that same gentle voice that was speaking to him just now. But this time felt different. This time, Pete wasn't sure he wanted to listen. He wasn't sure he could trust it fully, even if the force behind that voice was the same force he had been depending upon all his life, growing in intimacy with, and learning to both test and lean into.

Especially that day in the rainstorm.

That day, four years earlier, when Pete felt God asking him to trust and to walk in faith. Pete had listened. He had trusted with all his heart and with all his life. He had come here, sold everything, given up everything. He had put his family in danger, himself in danger. And for what, exactly?

So that God could carry him long enough to drop him. One January day, right at the very moment Pete needed Him most.

The 25 kilogram barbell hit the rubber mats lining the floor of the gym with a heavy thud. Pete could feel a pulling and tightening across the scar on his neck. His skin engaged in a tug of war. He wiped the back of his hand across his sweaty forehead and glanced at himself in the mirror. The scar had not ripped open. Everything was good.

He scanned the rows of weighted plates and boosted the volume up several notches on his iPod. The opening chords for Pearl Jam's song, "Alive" blared through the tiny speakers.

He could go heavier.

Eddie Vedder crooned in a lilting, scratchy voice. *"Have I got a little story for you."*

"Go easy," the doctor had told Pete only a few days earlier. "You can walk briskly, but don't run."

"Ohhhhhhh . . . I'm still alive!" Vedder wailed, as the electric guitars amped up their pace.

In college, Pete and his friends had listened to this album on repeat. They had thrown surfboards in the back of his forest green pickup and belted out the chorus as they headed to the beach. Windows down, carefree smiles, sun baking into the lower half of their arms dangling outside the truck.

"Don't carry or lift anything above 10 kilograms for another several weeks," the doctor had said, pencil in hand, glancing over Pete's chart.

The music softened as Vedder practically whispered,

"But do I deserve to be?
Is that the question?
And if so, who answers?
WHO ANSWERS???"

I DO, Pete thought as he grabbed five more kilograms and added them to his barbell. He braced himself, latched his aching fingers around the steel bar, and utilized every muscle in his legs, abdomen, and back to lift the bar upright.

The tug of war across his throat intensified. He ignored it. A flash of weariness traveled over his body and everything felt sore. He ignored it. In his headphones, the pounding of the drums and electric guitars alternated, creating a perfect rhythm for lifting.

One, Pete breathed, fighting to suck in more air, fighting the pain that was invading every inch of him. *Two.* The black mask and brown eyes. *THREE.* The sight of Doris rocking back and forth on the ground. *FOUR, FIVE, SIX!* The wailing pitch of the electric guitars combined with an angry beat of the drums and his body screamed and everything inside him screamed and his clenched up fingers released, sending the bar to the ground in surrender. Pete gasped for air and felt that all the screaming in all the world would never ever be enough.

February 10, 2007

Pete sat at the kitchen and Dara watched his face grow pink as he tried to swallow more air, forcing it down his throat by opening his mouth wider and arching his neck forward. His eyes looked desperate.

Dara walked over and placed a hand on his back and shoulders. A small gesture of comfort. Cindi Lombardo sat across the table and watched this couple she loved so very much. Cindi had flown out shortly after Pete was released from the hospital and had been staying with the DeSotos ever since, supporting them in whatever way she could. She spent her mornings singing songs and playing with Hannah and Kaya. She picked up the boys in the afternoon from school, and helped Dara prepare dinner in the evenings, the two women slicing and chatting, side by side.

April would mark three full years since Butch and the boys died. Three full years since Dara had flown out to Kansas to comfort Cindi and mourn with her. The memory of it remained between them as they chopped and stirred. Sometimes, Dara would watch Cindi in awe, noting the contrast between the woman Cindi had been three years ago—so struck with grief that she couldn't even brush her teeth—to the woman who stood next to her now, an international speaker and advocate.

Over the last three years, Cindi had grown in prominence as a pastor and mentor of young women. After her husband and sons died, she turned their empty house into a discipleship home for girls. She decided to call it My Sister's House, and some of the girls Cindi mentored were invited to travel with her in the coming months. They would be speaking at a conference in South Africa in April and May. Then volunteering at an orphanage in Zimbabwe come June. As they traveled the globe, the goal was to spread the message of Jesus by whatever means possible.

Dara marveled at Cindi's strength and ability to carry grief and contentment in tandem. Yes, Cindi missed her family. Of course she did. Always. But even without them, she had found so much to continue living for. She had found a purpose and a mission that yanked her out of bed in the morning and provided razor-like focus. Cindi wasn't about throwing pity parties. She was about serving others. That attitude seemed to be the driving force that brought her to this place of peacefulness as she sat across from Dara and Pete, serving them.

"You need to go back to the doctor," Cindi told Pete. "There's something still wrong and I can feel it."

"I have an appointment Monday," Pete said in a raspy whisper.

"He's gone in for check-ups twice a week since they released him," Dara said. "If there's something wrong, I don't know why they haven't found it."

"I don't know either," Cindi said. "But I'm praying they will find it on Monday."

Monday's exam with the ear, nose, and throat doctor began as they all did. With Pete trying not to gag as the metal rod with a microscopic camera on the end of it was inserted into his throat. The doctor told him his vocal cords were loosening up a tiny bit, yet there appeared to be a small object underneath them. It was trapped right inside his trachea and looked like a piece of glass.

The surgical extraction of this mysterious object was scheduled for the following day, when the doctors found that it wasn't glass at all. It was a piece of blue plaid fabric, roughly half the size of Pete's fingernail.

When the doctors showed it to Pete, he recognized it immediately. This was the material of the same shirt he had been wearing on the day he was shot. When the bullet ripped through his neck, it had apparently taken a tiny portion of the collar along with it.

"Your body has been working to get rid of the fabric," the doctor said. "It's been moving through your system and inhibiting your breathing in the process."

Pete was stunned, but hopeful. "Do you think my voice will go back to normal now?" he whispered, his vocal cords still weak.

The doctor's face went blank. He paused and searched for his words carefully. "Only time will tell."

February 14, 2007

Pete's Blog Update:

I'm on pretty strict orders to not do much talking. This is probably the hardest part of the recovery because I'm pretty limited in what I can do until I get my voice back. God is teaching me patience through it all. I have felt some pretty strong emotions of frustration, anger, and depression over the last week. Yet, I'm watching the Lord walk me through each moment. Whenever I start feeling overwhelmed, He encourages me either through his Word, through an email, or a phone call. It is so amazing to watch God speak in such creative and beautiful ways into my heart. He is our great comforter and friend.

Thank you for all the prayers that went out yesterday. God responded with great faithfulness. I feel good about the procedure and hopeful that I'm on the right path to recovery. Please continue to pray for my voice. If it doesn't return, I will have to truly pray through some life choices in the coming months. But, I feel confi-

dent that God wants to restore my voice. I'm willing to accept either
direction. But I'd really prefer the ability to gab again.

March 27, 2007

It was 9:00 p.m. and the kids were finally in bed. The dishes were
done, Dara was upstairs, turning out the lights in the boys' room, and
Pete seized the moment to sit in silence for once.

He had been battling his thoughts all day long. Warding off
visions of the masked gunman while trying to drive to work. Fear about
his voice not coming back had begun to taunt him at every moment.
Listening to himself speak these days was like being in a dream, the
equivalent of glancing in a mirror and finding another person's face
staring back. He no longer recognized the sound of his own voice, and
with that came a loneliness he could barely stand to think about.

Pete sat on the white leather couch in the empty living room. It
was dark and he didn't bother to turn a light on.

Please heal me, he prayed. *Show Your power, Lord. I'll give You all*
the glory, I promise.

Earlier that afternoon, Pete had been leading a team of volunteers
to help with the water project in Las Delicias. A group of fifteen people
had flown in from Visalia First Assembly Church. Most had never been
on the mission field before, and some had never even left the United
States. They had needed clear directions and someone who could easily
assign roles. That was Pete's job after all. With his usual fervor and
energy, he opened his mouth to speak.

His words came out veiled and raspy. He tried again.

The crew of volunteers frowned.

"Can you say that one more time?" a woman asked.

Pete's throat was raw. A prickly sensation began at the top of his
mouth and led into the back of his throat where he swallowed.
Swallowing was painful.

He tried one more time, repeating the same directive with all the
volume he could muster. And then he began to cough.

He noted the people's faces staring back at him. They looked at him confused. They looked at him with pity. Pete was a cripple in their eyes, a verbal cripple. And he didn't want their pity. It angered him. He would show them he could do this. He would get them to listen. There had to be a way.

God will fix this, he thought, *if I just keep praying. He'll fix it and restore my voice back to normal. He gave me this job. Obviously, He wants me to do it and do it well. God wants me to thrive. There's absolutely no reason why He wouldn't.*

Ever since Pete was a teenager, his voice had been strong. When he spoke, it was commanding. He got attention, and more than anything, he enjoyed talking with people, being a mouthpiece, connecting with those around him through words and conversations. As he got older, Pete excelled at telling jokes, giving talks, explaining himself in a direct and accessible way.

In retrospect, he had taken it all for granted. Assumed it would forever be a part of him—that expressing himself verbally would always be fun, challenging, effortless, even.

All of it was a way of defining who he was. He had rooted his identity in his charisma, his dynamism. Pete was a salesman. A leader. A man of the people. When Scott Anderson offered him the job at Regency Lighting all those years ago, he sensed Pete would be good at it. Scott had been right. Pete was not only good at it, he was competitive and daring and surging with confidence.

And then he got shot.

The word handicapped fluttered through his mind and it made Pete bristle. He didn't want to be handicapped, he didn't want any of this, and damn that man who shot him! *How could he have taken this from me?* Pete wondered. *How could God have allowed him to? And how could God then not restore my voice?*

I saved your life.

Pete was silenced. He felt a rush of humility.

And then the tears came. Not tears of gratitude. Tears of fear.

I'm scared it will be this way forever, he whispered.

He placed his head in his hands and leaned forward, elbows on his knees, back heaving up and down as he sobbed in the dark living room.

He had no idea who he was anymore. Inside, there was a deep emptiness, a vacuumed out hole. The vastness made him shudder.

From the top of the stairs, Dara looked down at her husband, the shadow of his arched back moving up and down against the dimly lit wall. A few quiet tears fell from her own eyes. She had been married to Peter for nearly a decade, and never once had she seen him like this.

Can't I do anything to help him? she prayed.

But even as the words left her lips, she knew the answer was no. How could she help when she had no idea what he was going through?

I've got him.

It's okay.

Let go.

Dara nodded. Wishing she could run down the stairs and hold him. Wishing for words that could erase the pain. But there were no words. No formulas, no quick fix. Dara did the only thing she had learned how to do over the past two years in El Salvador, the thing she had been practicing, though it rarely came easily or naturally.

She listened to the voice.

She came into agreement with it, trusting that it was real and true and not a figment of her imagination. She would let go. She would believe that God was holding him, that He would heal Pete's heart, if not his voice, and that together, she and Pete and their children would find happiness again. Someday.

When this would ever happen, she had no clue. How God would do it, she couldn't figure either. But she chose to believe, and this time she took it one step further.

She said *thank you.*

March 2007

"Can you tell me about your first husband getting shot?" Dara asked.

She and Ruth DeBorst were sitting across from each other in the backyard of Ruth's El Salvador home. The one Dara and Pete had been renting for nearly a year now.

Ruth took a sip of her iced tea and looked Dara in the eye. Ruth and James were visiting El Salvador from Boston, and Ruth had come by to check on the house and see how Dara was doing. Especially after what happened to Pete.

"We were living as missionaries in Ecuador," Ruth said. "And we were working in a rural village. Just like Pete when he was shot."

Dara sat quietly and continued to listen.

"I remember we were parked on this remote dirt road, waiting for my husband to get back from taking pictures of the villagers. My two kids were in the car and I was pregnant with my third at the time. We were all just waiting there when a group of bandits approached the car and tried to rob us. My husband got back just in time to try and stop them, but they freaked out . . . They shot him."

Dara's eyes widened.

"I don't think I realized you were pregnant at the time."

Ruth nodded and she blinked back tears.

"I haven't cried about this in so long," she said.

Dara leaned forward and took Ruth's hand.

"There are certain things in life that never make sense," Ruth continued. "You can search for answers and explanations, but there really is no explaining senseless violence like that."

Dara felt her own eyes getting wet. She used her free hand to wipe her cheek and continued listening.

"There's no explaining why God would allow my husband to be shot and killed right in front of me and my kids, but He did. And in the middle of it, all I knew for sure was that He was with me. Throughout the whole experience and all through the aftermath when I was mourning, Jesus was with me every second of every day."

"It's hard to explain, isn't it?" Dara said. "If anything, you'd think I would stop trusting because of what happened to Pete, but actually it's the opposite. It's like He's more real now than ever."

Ruth nodded. "He is close to the brokenhearted. I think that's the most exciting thing I realized—that if I could experience him then, so could other people who are hurting."

"So, what did you do after it happened?" Dara asked. "Did you move back home to Argentina?"

Ruth shook her head. "Actually, we stayed in Ecuador."

Dara bit her lip and stared off into the corner of the yard. "But, why?" she asked. "Why stay?"

Ruth smiled. "Because there's always more to the story."

———————————

Dara and Pete sat beneath the night sky feeling a warm breeze brush against their skin. The stars above clustered around a semi-full moon and created mysterious patterns against the blackness.

Since Ruth left that afternoon, Dara had been praying and reflecting on their conversation. Ruth hadn't wanted her children to leave Ecuador thinking it was an evil place. That it was incapable of having any other sort of narrative. She wanted to teach them of redemption and that Jesus was still worth following, even after He allowed tragedy to strike.

It occurred to Dara that if she and Pete moved back to California, the act of leaving might color their children's view of El Salvador even more than the shooting. It would send the message that the country was done for. Scary. Not worth their time.

It would feel like they were running as opposed to standing their ground and fighting.

Dara thought about her own childhood. How every time something got hard, she had been allowed to quit.

"I don't want our children to be quitters," she told Pete.

"Neither do I," he said.

They both grew quiet and allowed the idea to expand.

"Let's show them what it means to keep fighting," Pete finally said. "Let's show them what it means to actually trust God and follow him because I'm afraid if we leave, the kids and everyone else are just going to look at us coming over here as one big, tragic mistake."

"Do you think it was a tragic mistake?" Dara asked.

Pete was quiet.

"On my good days, no," he said softly. "But on my bad days, I have no idea how to fully trust God again. Other than by staying. Staying feels like we would actually be stepping out in faith again, demonstrating that we still know He's good no matter what. We're still following and we're still giving him everything. Leaving feels like we'd be slamming a final nail in the coffin and saying we can't trust God as much as we thought."

"Want to know the first thing I thought right after you were shot?" Dara asked, "Right after I found out you'd be okay?"

Pete waited.

"I thought to myself: This is it. This is my first class ticket out of here. We can go back to California and no one will think any less of us.

"But then you went through surgery," Dara continued. "And our friends and family filled the hospital room and I saw so much fear in our kids' eyes, and it was like everything changed. I literally felt like God was telling me, *See, this shooting isn't why you leave. It's why you stay.*"

"We did say we'd commit to about five years here," Pete said.

"I know."

"Should we keep that commitment? Should we stay even though our friends and family just might kill us for it?"

Dara smiled an ironic, bewildered sort of smile. "I think that's what He's asking us to do."

Pete leaned toward her and took her hand in his. Their knees were touching and they bent their foreheads, low, resting against each other, feeling each other's fear and love and hope and heaviness, carrying the weight of these things in unison.

"Alright," Pete said. "So, we'll stay."

PART FOUR

SURRENDER

Surrender is a practice,
a way of seeing,
a mantra,
and above all, a choice,
That's made daily and nightly
and every moment in between.

There's no 3-step-guide,
No ironclad action plan or blue print.
Surrender looks different for everyone.

You'll know you're doing it right because it's uncomfortable and it costs you
everything.
But it results in a sense of peace, deeper and more real than anything you
could have imagined.

CHAPTER 17

Project Milagro

San Martín, El Salvador, 2005

Oscar held a stick of dynamite in the palm of his hand. The brown, paper cylinder felt light in comparison with what it was capable of. He said a prayer, as always, gripped it tightly between his thumb and forefinger, and struck a match. The fuse began to sizzle and crackle and Oscar knew that he had only a matter of seconds. He tossed it into the ever-deepening hole in the ground behind his house and ran as swiftly as his legs would carry him.

The explosion was quick and muffled, like a gunshot. Oscar's heartbeat always jumped at the sound of it. He turned back around to see the thick plumes of smoke rising up from the hole he had been digging for the last ten years. The hole that one day, God willing, would bring fresh water to him and his family.

Oscar had heard fantastical tales of people who dug deep enough beneath the surface of the earth and tapped into a fresh water source. An underground aquifer. A stroke of magic.

In all these years and after all this time—from shoveling by hand, to tossing one stick of dynamite after the next—Oscar still had not struck water. His hole was now 200 feet into the ground. It was deep to the point that oxygen was scarce, and when he was lowered down to the very bottom to continue with the digging, he needed to take a plastic hose along with him in order to suck fresh air from it.

No one ever said digging a well would be easy.

And so Oscar continued, month after month, year after year. What else could he do? His only other option in the Las Delicias region where he and his family resided was to continue paying 25 dollars per month, nearly one third of his monthly income, to buy jugs of water from the local water truck.

Even at that price, the water wasn't exactly clean. It was drawn from one of the most contaminated rivers in the whole country; yet, he and his family needed it to bathe and to drink and to cook. Contaminated or not, it was their only choice. Which was why Oscar spent the last decade digging, sometimes in sweltering heat, and sometimes knee deep in mud after a torrential rainstorm. He dug and he dug because somehow, some way, he sensed that eventually the land would have mercy on him. That it would give him this gift.

Pastor Juan lived one village over from Oscar and had been helping with the well. Miguel's village didn't have access to fresh water either. In fact, there were three villages in the Las Delicias region with a total of 6,100 people residing in them, and every single one of them had been forced to survive off jugs of contaminated water from the local water trucks. It was both a financial burden and a serious health risk, as everything from typhoid and cholera to gastrointestinal parasites were transmitted through this water.

In Juan's heart, he had been dreaming of the day when these communities could finally have access to their own fresh water supply. He began praying in 1994. Right around the time Oscar started digging. It wasn't until 2005 that the idea started to gain a bit of traction. With the aid of ENLACE, Pastor Juan's church was able to partner with a nonprofit called Living Water International (LWI). Representatives from LWI came to Juan's neighborhood of San Martin and ran a series of tests on the soil. They deduced that there was spot on top of a hill that would be their best bet at finding water.

Juan's church did a fundraising campaign and contacted the local mayor's office, who was willing to contribute as well. In total, they raised $20,000. Enough to pay Living Water International to drill one well that could serve one community. It wasn't everything, but it was a start.

The stars were aligning, the equipment was sent out, the water experts arrived, and Juan's heart was filled with multitudes of praise and thanks as his dream of fresh water would finally be realized.

Then drilling day came.

Everything went exactly as planned, but after a full week of drilling, they came up dry. The words "geologically impossible" were uttered. Upon hearing them, Pastor Juan walked to the back of his house, stared out upon the land which had betrayed him, and collapsed into a ball on the ground. He rocked back and forth, the pressure in his chest hard to bear. Tears spilled from his eyelids and rolled down his cheeks. He thought of all the work that had been put into this. All the plans, all the dreams, all the financial sacrifices made by families who gave out of what little they could muster.

No matter how hopeless and unrealistic it had seemed, Pastor Juan had never given up on his water project. He had held onto that day in the rainstorm when God had parted the clouds and given him water to mix his cement. With the same blind, unrelenting faith, Juan had dared to believe his all-powerful, all-loving God would show up again this week and do the miraculous.

He watched in defeat as the drilling team packed up their tools. There would be no fresh water for their community. Not today, and maybe not ever. Juan let out a sob so deep he thought it might break his body in two.

Where are you, God? he cried. *Where are you?*

In every endeavor lies a delicate balance. From digging a well, to running a marathon, or writing a symphony, a tension exists between what we can control and what we cannot.

What we can control is the amount of work we put in. The effort, the discipline, the willingness to continue experimenting and learning. At any given moment, these choices are ours. The outcome, however? Now, that's a different story.

Success and failure are gifts from another realm. Call it fate. Call it the Universe. Call it God. Whatever you believe in, the nobler the endeavor, the more painful it is when things go awry. When the "whys" have nothing to point to. You weren't doing this to be selfish, or to earn money or fame. You were doing it for the sake of justice. You were following a deep calling or passion. A quiet drumbeat beckoning inside.

Even worse is that you weren't lazy. You didn't take shortcuts, didn't stop when the going got tough. You pressed into it. You moved forward—got creative, even—trying a new angle or a different technique. You studied, you practiced, you asked questions and solicited advice. You tried anything and everything you could, but still Joe Schmo managed to dig a proper well only two villages over, but you came up dry. The door opened for him, while it slammed shut for you.

The temptation is to give up. To say, "Screw this," to take your battered, war-torn heart and bury it in ambivalence. But as psychologist and author Brene Brown reminds us, "The question is not, 'What would you do if you knew you couldn't fail?' But, 'What would you do even *if* you failed?'"

What would you do and continue doing every day for the rest of your life, even if nothing came of it? What would you do because you know it's important? Because you, maybe even the world, can't live without it?

Those were some of the questions Juan wrestled with in the months after the well-digging fiasco in Las Delicias. Through the wrestling, he recognized something underneath mere personal desire. That thing was obedience.

At the root of it all, he felt God calling him to build a well and bring water to the people. It seemed impossible and downright foolish. It seemed a dream rife for disappointment. But if Juan were to continue with this water project, he recognized that this time it would need to be different. He could no longer assume he knew what the outcome would be, or when it would take place. He would need to let go of his preconceived time line, his expectations, and maybe even parts of his vision.

If you really want me to continue with this Lord, Pastor Juan prayed, *I will. But you'll have to tell me what to do and what to pray for. I'm done thinking that I have all the answers.*

In 2005, the leaders of the two surrounding communities of Las Animas and El Rosario approached Pastor Juan with an idea. What if they all worked together on this water project? Their communities also longed to have their own wells and were willing to contribute financially in whatever way they could. If water was found in either of their backyards, perhaps it could be piped into San Martín somehow?

It was worth a try.

Suddenly, what began as a water project that would benefit one small community, transformed into a massive experiment that, if successful, would benefit an entire region of more than 10,000. With those figures, it would be enough to go to the local Salvadoran water board and ask for help.

The water board agreed and instead of surveying only San Martín, they expanded their scope between all three communities and discovered a river bed, about three and a half miles away. San Martín was at the top of a steep hill, about one thousand feet in elevation from where this shallow river bed lay. In order to get water from the river all the way up the hill, they would need to build a master reservoir and an elaborate set of piping that could pump water up a steep hillside.

ENLACE began referring to it as Project *Milagro* (Project Miracle). It was ambitious, illogical, and almost bordered on the point of insanity. But they went for it. The local water authorities agreed to provide equipment for drilling, and in 2006, they successfully drilled not one, but three wells.

It would take another two decades worth of building, dreaming, strategizing and fundraising for Project Milagro to finally come to fruition. But in early 2016, the people of Las Delicias, Las Animas, and El Rosario would finally get their water. And Pastor Juan could finally rest.

CHAPTER 18

Gethsemane

March - April 2007

A chorus of staccato squawks peppered the sapphire backdrop of the Southern California sky. The pair of seagulls quieted their nimble wings in preparation for landing. Their golden webbed feet hit the sand right in front of the trash can laying at the base of a narrow staircase built into the side of a mountain. It was lined with palm trees and bougainvilla and it was rumored to have one thousand cement steps.

What it actually had was a mere 230 steps, but that never stopped anyone from referring to this gorgeous strip of Laguna Beach as Thousand Steps Beach. It certainly felt like a thousand steps as visitors made their steep descent from the top of South Coast Highway to the white sand below. The salty marine air seeping through the cracks of the green canopy around the staircase, accompanied by the sounds of rushing waves, laughing children, and screeching seagulls. Always, screeching seagulls.

The pair of birds plunged their golden beaks into the sand, hunting and exploring until they heard a familiar squawk beckoning them elsewhere. They fluttered their gray wings and lifted off, past the enchanting rock caves hugging the cliff side. Past the tide of water rushing in and out of the cave, licking its walls. They flew past the "No Trespassing" warnings and toward a small wooden cottage with a painted sign above the door that read "John Wayne Beach House." Indeed, the actor John Wayne and his wife did live in this home from the late 1950s until 1973 when it was sold to a documentary and IMAX filmmaker named Greg MacGillivray.

On January 18, 2007, MacGillivray was checking his email and noticed a prayer request chain that had been forwarded to him about an American missionary who was shot in El Salvador. And he was moved by it. So moved that he reached out to Pete DeSoto directly and offered to let him, Dara, and the kids come stay for one week at his beach house in Laguna.

For free.

MacGillivray had a soft spot for El Salvador ever since the late seventies when he had spent seven full weeks there shooting scenes for his surf film, *Big Wednesday*. This wouldn't be the first time he had offered up his home to strangers. He and his wife Barbara were ocean conservationists and had donated a stay at their beach house as a prize to be auctioned off for charities. Allowing the DeSoto family to stay there after all they had been through seemed as good a cause as any.

It was one of the kindest offers Pete had ever gotten from a complete stranger, and difficult to pass up. And it arrived at a fortuitous time because a voice specialist from USC Medical Center had also offered Pete a consultation if he could get himself to Los Angeles somehow. When his mother Lucia got wind of all this, she realized that Easter was right around the corner and had visions of grandchildren running around her yard in search of colorful Easter eggs.

And then there was Brian Howard, the DeSoto's former pastor from Copperhill, the church they attended back in Valencia. Brian and the people of Copperhill had been supporting Pete and Dara since they moved to El Salvador through finances, prayer, and friendship. When Pete told Brian about the voice specialist at USC, the people of Copperhill unanimously decided to pay for the entire DeSoto family to fly to California two months after the shooting. The family would be staying in the United States for four weeks.

Pete's bare feet left imprints in the sand of Thousand Steps Beach as he led PJ and Isaac on a short walk from the beach house to the tide pools. They were on a hunt for sea creatures living in the crevices between the wet rocks. Isaac was so excited his legs burst forth into a run. PJ took off after him with Pete trailing behind. The love he had for his boys and their sheer enthusiasm for life brought a smile to his lips.

He watched as Isaac jumped onto the first rock he could find and began scrambling up it. There really wasn't much to climb. An adult could have reached the top in two quick steps, but Pete felt his heartbeat quicken at the site of Isaac moving along them. The scar in his neck began to ache as he imagined Isaac's foot slipping, his small body crashing against the rough stone.

"Be careful!" Pete shouted.

He felt the air closing in around him. Like he couldn't get to his son fast enough. Couldn't protect him, couldn't save him.

Pete glanced at the idyllic palm trees framing the cliff sides. He watched the white foam chasing the shoreline, watched as Dara and the girls were playing in the shallow water, giggling and screaming with delight as they jumped over the tiny waves.

Tonight would be another outrageous sunset. Black palm tree silhouettes set against layers of violet, gold, and dusty pink. Pete imagined Isaac slipping and falling amidst the dramatic backdrop. His eyes grew moist at the prospect, noting that in one breath he wanted to cry out to God in thanks for such beauty. In the other breath, it was all he could do not to break down in despair.

Pete was in the most beautiful place imaginable, but the threat of danger clung to him. Even here. In wealthy Orange County where the streets were devoid of gangs. Where the tap water was drinkable, the mosquitoes weren't carrying diseases, and the weather was almost always perfect. Even here, his son could still slip and fall. His daughter could be carried out by a rip tide. Everything could still be taken away.

Pete tried to bury the thought, as usual, and focus on the positive. But it wasn't working. Without the distractions—the hustle and bustle of San Salvador—Pete began to recognize that it wasn't just his neck that was aching. Something inside pierced him at his core. Not a physical ache, but something deeper. Something no medicine could cure.

As a missionary, Pete had been asked several times to get up and speak at Copperhill Church. Most recently, Brian Howard had asked if Pete would give them an account of his experience being shot and what God was teaching him through it.

What was *God teaching him through it?*

Pete shifted his gaze to the stack of biblical commentaries Brian had given him. At the top of the stack was a manual on how to preach, written by an old-school theologian named Haddon Robinson.

"As a missionary, you'll be needing these," Brian had said. "First, so you can learn the Bible more in depth. For yourself. And second, so you can relay everything you're experiencing on the mission field. Tie it to biblical concepts, tell compelling stories of how God's working. Give mini-sermons, essentially."

Pete had lugged the heavy stack of books across the ocean and through customs. When he finally opened them in San Salvador and began reading his Bible with this new lens, the words he had been reading since childhood came to life anew.

"I get the sense that you know a lot *about* the Bible," Brian had said to Pete, "plot-wise and intellectually. But have you ever studied it to the point that you *know* it—deeply, personally, experientially?"

As a pastor's kid, no one had ever bothered to ask Pete that question. The common assumption was that pastor's kids just knew the Bible—through osmosis, if nothing else.

But this type of Bible reading was different. It was slower and more deliberate, with the added responsibility of having to march on stage and explain the text to a group of people who expected him to know it. This forced Pete to ask questions he wouldn't normally have asked. It led him down roads he may have otherwise skipped over. It garnered a rich, abiding curiosity that ultimately led him to love it.

Pete sat in silence at the John Wayne Beach House, listening to the quiet push and pull of the ocean and allowing any memories of the shooting to join him for once. He couldn't keep pushing them away if he was going to speak about them honestly. If there was any chance his story could help someone else through the telling of it.

But what had he learned?

Pete sat first with his fear. He picked it up in his mind, holding it at arms length, and examining it from multiple sides, as though it were a moving, breathing organism.

He had known moving to El Salvador wasn't going to be easy. He had expected to make sacrifices and endure trials. Power outages, culture shock, petty theft, the jarring site of dead bodies lying on the side of the road—as had been reported throughout the civil war. Stuff that would be uncomfortable and unsettling in varying degrees. But never. Never. Would Pete have imagined getting shot by a renegade gunman whose community he had poured his heart into improving.

He had loved Abelines. From the first lunch with Pastor Victorio, to the rainstorm in 2003 and the laying of the foundation for the clinic walls. Getting shot could not be the final memory Pete ever had there. It simply couldn't. The gunman could take his voice and his pride and any remaining shards of innocence he may have had left from his childhood, but he wasn't going to take Abelines and the relationships Pete cherished with that beautiful community.

But going back would mean facing the fear head on. It would mean pulling himself deep inside it and walking directly through. It would mean calling on Jesus to accompany him at every step.

As a child, Pete had viewed Jesus as being more sympathetic than God. Yes, he had read in the Bible about how Jesus was the exact representation of God, and that they were mysteriously connected. Both separate and the same. It was confusing, to say the least.

In the Gospels, Pete read of Jesus interacting with people. Having two-way conversations, telling stories, dispensing wisdom and advice. He healed some and got angry at others. Through reading the accounts of His life in Matthew, Mark, Luke, and John, Pete felt he could at least get a clear picture of what Jesus cared about most.

Jesus himself could be confounding and elusive at times—His stories, His thought process, the mystery of what exactly He did for his first thirty years on earth—but what He cared about *wasn't*. If nothing else, Jesus cared deeply when people around him suffered. Sometimes that suffering was physical, sometimes mental, other times spiritual. Either way, He cared enough to do something tangible to alleviate it. Jesus carried himself humbly, and more than anything, He loved and prioritized spending time with God, his father. All of that was relatable for Pete. It made Jesus feel trustworthy. Not predictable, as He was rarely that, but trustworthy.

God was a different story.

While we never read of a single instance when Jesus deliberate-
ly harmed anybody, we do read of accounts where God does. Unlike
God, we don't read of Jesus killing people, calling for plagues, or
enacting vengeance. When Jesus controls the weather, it's not to flood
the entire planet. He doesn't create crackling fires that burn entire cities
to ash. Instead, He's calming oceans so the disciples won't be
frightened on their boat.

Jesus dispelled fear. God, sometimes, incited it.

Pete sat with that thought for a moment.

He got a vision of a gold ticking alarm clock from the 1972 film, *A
Thief in the Night.* It was the first in a three part series about what
Christians like to call the "end times." Based on images laid out in the
book of Revelation, *A Thief in the Night* was about a young woman
named Patty Duncan who woke up one morning to find her husband
(a man of impeccable faith) had been swooped up to heaven, while she
(of lesser faith) was left sleeping in her bed.

The drama unfolded quickly, as people throughout the world
reportedly vanished, while poor Patty had little choice but to join the
throngs of others left behind on earth to endure all manner of horrors.
The film featured heads being chopped off, military tanks rolling
through the streets, and a series of close-ups of Patty Duncan's mouth
arched open in a constant scream.

Subtlety was not an art the directors had mastered.

In addition, the movie was shot in 35 millimeter, and when Pete's
father hosted screenings of *A Thief in the Night* for his church
members, he had to lug in a big projector which clicked and jumped
throughout the showing, adding an additional layer of spookiness.

As a kid, Pete sat rigid in his seat, taking in the graphic scenes that
were prophesied in the Bible. When the screening ended, he walked
out with eyes that were wide and trance-like, internally chanting the
mantra, *I can't sin. I can't sin. I can't sin.*

Shortly after the screening, Pete was eating breakfast one morning
at his parents' house in Mira Mesa. He was nine years old at the time.
He poured himself a bowl of Cinnamon Toast Crunch and watched as
the milk turned from opaque white to a pale shade of brown, swirled
with specks of cinnamon. He savored each bite, spooning the

cinnamon squares into his mouth. Once they were all gone, Pete tipped the bowl to his lips and slurped up the remaining bits of sugary milk, wiping his mouth with the back of his hand. His mom ordinarily wouldn't let him get away with such manners, but she was busy vacuuming at the moment and not paying attention.

As Pete got up from the table, he heard the steady hum of the vacuum cleaner in the living room. Usually the sound came in and out, growing louder and fainter with each push and pull as his mom moved around the house. Yet, right now that didn't seem to be happening. From what Pete could tell, the vacuum cleaner sounded like one loud roar. Like it wasn't moving at all. This was strange, so Pete went to investigate.

He padded his bare feet into the living room to find a lone vacuum cleaner. Still running, yet abandoned.

Where was his mother?

Pete's head darted from one corner of the room to the next. A feeling of terror crept upon him and he thought of Patty Duncan. Her yellow alarm clock. The ticking, the suspense, the way she woke up in anguish to find her husband had been taken in the Rapture.

Is that what happened to his mother? Right here? Right now? In the middle of vacuuming? *Had Christ really come back . . . Like a thief in the night?*

Pete's mind began to race. He needed to find his mom—to make sure she hadn't been taken. He left the vacuum cleaner running and burst through the front door, heading down the street and toward the yard of his neighbor's house, several doors down. Maybe she was there. She was often at the Newberry's.

His short legs carried him like fire, over the cement sidewalks and past the manicured lawns. He hammered his fist against their wooden front door. Pete waited a moment until the knob began to turn and the door opened to reveal Mr. Newberry standing on the other side.

"Hey, Pete," Mr. Newberry said, warmly.

Pete's chest was heaving up and down. He was out of breath from running, but managed to blurt out the words, "Is my mom here?"

Hearing her son's voice, Lucia turned in her seat at the kitchen table and angled her neck toward the front door. "Hi, sweetie!" she said.

Relief s settled into Pete's bones. It calmed his heartbeat, softened his knees. He steadied himself on the door frame and felt a wave of gratitude for having escaped being left behind.

At least this time, anyway.

In church, in youth group, and throughout the rest of Pete's adolescence, he thought a lot about the nature of God. In the Old Testament, God seemed fickle. Moody and angry and difficult to please. At times, Pete noted that he was making decisions in his life completely out of fear of how God might react. He made decisions out of rote obedience. He tried to earn God's love and prove he was worthy of it. Yet, Pete sensed there was something wrong with this transactional way of relating to God. This gritting his teeth in submission, as opposed to surrendering to a loving father because he trusted Him.

In college, Pete began testing the waters of his faith. He took more risks, trusting that God would catch him before he fell. And God always did. So Pete's faith grew. He risked and trusted, risked and trusted, all the way up until the day he was shot. That was when his faith became muddy and he reverted back to his nine-year-old self, running through the streets of a San Diego suburb, desperate for something stable to cling to.

If Jesus was that stability, and Jesus really did exemplify God, then what was he missing?

Pete sat on the porch of the John Wayne Beach House and noted the glassy surface of the water this morning. The waves were calm, rolling in and out in tiny, foamless bumps, like the ocean was tired and taking a rest. After speaking at Copperhill, Pete's dad had asked if he would share his story of the shooting at his church on Easter Sunday.

Pete pulled out his journal and began to write about Easter. About the cross and that heartfelt moment when Jesus was praying in the Garden of Gethsemane. Pete opened his Bible to Matthew 26 and read through the whole chapter, prayerfully. As he read, he circled back to this idea of *knowing*. Jesus *knew* full well that his mission on earth was to die a humiliating and painful death on the cross. In the Garden of Gethsemane, He knelt before God and begged to have "this cup of suffering" taken away from Him.

What exactly the cup of sorrow represents has been debated by scholars and theologians throughout history. Many assume it represents dying on the cross and that Jesus is saying, "Please don't make me go through with this. Is there any other way?" Thus, signifying how human He actually was. Especially as He tells the disciples in His very next breath, "The spirit is willing, but the flesh is weak." In other words, Jesus knows sacrificing himself on the cross is God's will. That it's necessary and beautiful and the most important thing He will ever do, but the difficulty of it, the actuality of it, is more than Jesus can fathom in His human form. In a state of desperation He concedes, "Not my will, but yours be done."

Others argue Jesus would never have been tempted to that extent—to want to abort His very mission and purpose of being on earth. They refer to the verse in Matthew 16 where a well-intentioned disciple, Peter, suggests that Jesus shouldn't have to die or suffer, and Jesus responds by saying, "Get behind me, Satan." In other words, He's warning Peter that that type of thinking is from Satan, and Jesus isn't willing to engage with it for even a moment.

Scholars in this camp argue instead that the cup of sorrow Jesus asks to avoid is permanent death and separation from God, which is a prayer that God answers because he does raise Jesus from the dead and brings him back to life. Yet, in debating what it was the cup of sorrow represented, perhaps it places the focus on the wrong question.

What if a more telling question is this: How did God respond?

When Jesus knew He would be betrayed at any moment and dragged off to be crucified, what did God say to get Him to go through with it? What made an anxious, indecisive Jesus suddenly become so resolute?

Did God respond callously by saying, "Nope. Sorry. There's no getting out of this one." Did he threaten Jesus with punishment if He didn't comply? Did God guilt-trip Him and say, "I guess you can back out, but you know I'll be really disappointed if you do . . ."

Or is it more likely that God responded to Jesus in love?

It says twice in I John 4 that "God is love." Not that He has it or feels it, but that He embodies it to the point there is no distinction between Him and love. They are one in spirit and essence. In I Corinthians 13:4-7 it says that love is never demanding, but is always patient and kind, which means we can presume that is also who God is and how He would have responded. So it was love that gave Jesus strength and renewed sense of purpose. It was love that brought Him to a place of peaceful, confident surrender.

Pete pulled out his notebook and frantically scribbled, capturing each thought before it escaped. His pen moved in a steady wave across the page and when he finally looked up, he smiled in victory. He had his sermon.

Both times Pete told his story, at Copperhill and then at Mira Mesa First Assembly, he walked off stage and started coughing. Speaking for forty minutes straight had been just as taxing on his vocal cords as he imagined it would be. And Pete would do it again many times over. It was that worth it.

In a blog post, Pete described what it was like to get on stage and try his hand at preaching:

> I loved preaching at my dad's church on Easter Sunday. The Lord really ministered to all of us through the story of Christ agonizing in the garden before His death, and the way He identifies with the pain we experience. I felt privileged to be able to proclaim the gospel after going through the trials of the last few months. I shared openly about the evident miracles that occurred to save my life, but I also shared about the struggle I've had to understand the tremendous suffering in this world.
>
> I shared about the way God has comforted me with the message of the gospel, the message that Christ has promised to always be with those who love Him. I'm beginning to believe that the core of the gospel is this notion of Jesus' actual presence in our lives, the amazing phenomena that occurs when we trust Him and fall in love with Him. This is a gospel that promises He will walk us through any trial

and that He will celebrate with us during times of joy. To trust in Jesus is a decision to never be alone.

As I shared this, a number of people approached me who have endured tough trials in their lives. They were encouraged by this message. They, like me, struggled with the "why" question regarding pain, tragedy, and God's decision to rescue some and not others. The only comfort they felt during their tragedies was the real, tangible peace they encountered through their relationship with Jesus. Their stories encouraged me to continue to trust deeper, and to follow Him further.

Los Abelines, August 2007

When Scott Anderson agreed to fly out to San Salvador to visit the DeSotos, he hadn't accounted for the fact that Pete would then get inspired to make a return trip to Abelines while he was there.

His wife Shawna would be furious if she knew. "You better promise me you won't do anything unsafe while you're over there," she had said while hugging Scott goodbye at the airport.

Scott nodded feebly, with every intention of keeping that promise.

Next thing he knew, Pete was picking him up at the airport in his white Nissan Patrol, bullet holes scattered throughout the side door. It had been one thing to hear about the shooting from three thousand miles away and then to witness Pete when he came to California with a faint scar across his neck and a gravely voice. That was rough enough. But this? This brazen evidence of violence—this graphic, taunting reminder that something terrible happened and could potentially happen again—made Scott question how likely it was he would be keeping his promise to Shawna after all.

Scott flew out with another college buddy, Jamie Huff. Several days into their trip, Pete suggested they all make the return journey to Abelines together.

"I can't think of two other people I'd rather have with me," Pete said.

At 6:00 a.m. sharp on August 19, 2007, the three friends made their way from San Salvador to the unmarked road leading up the hill to Abelines. Halfway through, they came to the meeting point where Nelson, one of Pastor Victorio's sons, was supposed to be meeting them to caravan and stand guard in case something crazy happened, but it was taking Nelson an awfully long time to get there.

Pete kept glancing at his watch and trying not to focus too intently on the stinging sensation he felt in the place where the bullet had pierced him. It was the same psychosomatic feeling he got every time he encountered danger. Anything from an angry dog barking, to the site of this man heading toward their parked vehicle.

Scott saw the man, too. He was wearing a faded brown cowboy hat and was followed by an entire herd of cattle. Against the lush green backdrop, he looked like a page straight out of *National Geographic*.

The color in Pete's face began to drain and he turned to Jamie. "If this guy pulls out a cell phone, we're out of here."

Jamie bobbed his head in agreement.

"What's going on?" Scott asked.

Pete's mouth felt dry. He could barely muster the words. "He might be a scout. Looking for people to rob. Calling in to let the others know."

Scott felt his heart rate kick up and considered making a nervous joke about scouts. *I guess we're not talking about Boy Scouts then, right?* he was about to say when a pickup truck came ambling down a narrow dirt road that looked more like a hiking trail. The truck pulled up right next to them and Nelson jumped out of the driver's seat, followed by another guy who had been riding in the back with one hand on the grip bar and another wielding a machete.

Scott stared at the arched blade of the man's weapon, uncertain whether this should make him feel safer, or less so. Nelson and Pete exchanged quick hugs, and then the man with the machete assumed his position as they followed them the rest of the way to Abelines.

In a blog post describing that day, Pete wrote the following:

We made it to the top of a hill that overlooked the entire eastern valley of El Salvador. We could see the base of volcanoes that lined the valley floor and felt a wonderful breeze that cooled the mountainside. For a moment, I forgot I was in El Salvador. It was no longer the country that had challenged me to my core, the country ravaged by war, poverty, corruption, and death. Instead, it was a majestic landscape, a place to experience the presence of God.

Jaime, Scott, and I had all studied anthropology together in college. We read fascinating books about development work, argued vehemently over theory, made bold statements about the way we felt things should be. Fourteen years and a few war wounds later, we stood together on the hill and we were quiet.

Ideas were far less important then the friendship that has endured.

Standing beside them, I felt such joy. They had traveled all this way to walk beside me through my healing. As the breeze blew, we soaked it in. Nelson climbed a tree and offered us mangoes.

We inspected a new tank that was to be part of a new water system for hundreds of families below. The water came from a natural spring miles away, connected by a single run of pipe. The tank was overflowing from the abundance of water, and it was clean—even cold. To me, it represented hope. I thought about the opportunities that people would have as fresh water flowed into their homes, and again, I smiled.

We spent the rest of the day visiting projects in Abelines. The new medical clinic was complete and stood an amazing testament to the ongoing work of the church. We also spoke to a number of residents who were friendly, yet reserved. It felt like nothing had changed because of the shooting. Life continues, I guess, but it did feel strange.

On our drive back to San Salvador, we discussed the response, or lack thereof, to my return to Abelines. Both Scott and Jaime had expected much more emotion from people. Maybe even a display of gratitude that I had returned. As for me, I came in with little expectation and found myself not wanting to engage much. My attitude was more about overcoming my fears and getting it over with.

But, I did reflect on how people in Abelines interpret violence.

They expressed much remorse the day I was shot, and they prayed for me diligently. Yet, because this is a part of the world where mothers have seen their babies murdered, men have been ripped from families by the army or by guerrillas to fight a war that only resulted in pain and death, these are families who have struggled each day to survive as they watch countless neighbors flee to the US to earn an honest wage. They must maintain a life resigned to the daunting fact that struggle and death are inevitable. Problems persist, regardless of the countless attempts they make to stop them.

What I realized in going back is that my shooting could actually be a gift. Yes, a gift. Because it's led me closer to understanding what people feel in El Salvador every day. Understanding the vulnerability one feels when climbing on a city bus, walking down a dirt road, or returning home after pay day. It has challenged my faith, causing me to question God's goodness. It has tested my belief that Christ is the only answer to heal a suffering world. But it is also producing in me a confidence that I did not have before. A confidence in the goodness of a Father that loves me and those around me. He called my family to serve Him in El Salvador. He asked me to trust Him, and through this trial, I'm learning that trust is only authentic when tested by struggle.

I have often asked myself why I remain in El Salvador. At times I've wanted to retreat, wanted to run home. But God continues to confirm that His work in me and in our family is not complete. As I trust Him, I feel victory. We defeat Satan with every act of authentic faith. He is powerless against those who have surrendered their entire lives to Christ, and placed their livelihood in His sole care.

If we choose to control our lives, we will never be content and will never experience the kind of life promised in Scripture. We may avoid pain temporarily, may even experience incredible heights of short lived pleasure, but our souls will be restless.

My hope is to go back to Abelines as many times as I can, to be a part of the work going on there, and to continue praying that day-by-day, I will step into the life of courage and freedom that He desires for me. I hope we can all aspire for this together.

CHAPTER 19

Antigua

June 2007

The average American school bus spends about ten years of its life carting children to and from school. Once it has reached that decade mark, or reached 150,000 miles (whichever comes first), the gold and black bus gets sold at auction and driven across several borders, through the whole of Mexico and into Guatemala, its final destination. From there, it will undergo a massive makeover. There's welding and sanding. Hub caps and blinking lights. The exterior is tricked out with luggage racks and bold, colorful murals. When the transformation is complete, this retired school bus will launch a new career as a *camioneta*, otherwise known by English speaking tourists as a chicken bus.

Dara stared up at the chicken bus painted teal with swirling red stripes and a grumbling diesel engine. She followed her friend Carolina through the front doors and down the narrow aisle. They found an empty seat towards the back, and Dara noted how its cover was made of faded brown cloth with a large hole worn across the rounded corner of the seat back.

The driver sped through the Guatemalan streets as the painted exteriors of the restaurants and shops whirred by through the windows. First in gold, then neon green, then faded purple. The relentless beat of *reggaeton* blasted from the bus speakers, serving as background noise for the wild, bumpy ride. Without warning, the bus lurched to a halt and Dara grabbed onto her bag to keep it from sliding across the floor.

The front doors sprung open and a young girl stepped on board, followed by two adults who were likely her mother and father. Before the man could even finish lifting his foot onto the platform, the driver slammed his foot on the accelerator. Dara held her breath as the man calmly lifted himself from the outer step and into the actual bus even as it was moving. He hardly seemed fazed, as though this brash lack of consideration from the bus driver happened every day.

The driver rolled to a stop in front of the majestic white fountain in Antigua's central park and Carolina's lips spread wide into a smile.

"We have arrived," she said in a thick Spanish accent.

Dara's heart quickened at the thought of getting off the bus, of actually stepping foot in this brand new country where she would be living and studying Spanish for the next four weeks. All by herself. Without Peter, or the kids.

It was a decision she and Pete had come to by way of necessity.

When they had returned from their trip to California, there was a freshness in their steps. A confidence that this time, as they landed in San Salvador, they weren't completely clueless. They knew what to say to the customs official and even gave him their address *en español*. From there, they drove to a home that had already been established. A home that was welcoming and familiar and felt like their own.

Yet, there was still one obstacle that remained persistent, and it was a big one: Dara's Spanish was extremely limited.

When PJ or Isaac tried to introduce her to their friend's parents at school, she could barely understand anything beyond "hello" or "nice to meet you." Rather than engaging in conversation, she was left to nod meekly and force a smile. The loneliness and shame would churn inside her, and now that she was back in El Salvador after spending an entire month in the US, the loneliness and shame were stronger than ever.

In California, she had wanted to leap and dance; she was so thrilled to be able to joke with her old friends and express herself freely without the invisible wall between her and nearly every Salvadoran she encountered.

Dara had forgotten how good it felt to verbally communicate everywhere she went. She had forgotten she was actually quite good at it.

Over the past two years, Pete's Spanish had shown steady improvement, as he practiced and spoke it for most of the day at the ENLACE offices and out in the communities he visited. But even after seeing a specialist, his vocal cords still hadn't recovered from the shooting. Every word he spoke sounded raspy and muffled.

"*Cómo?*" their neighbor, Moses Barrientos, had asked when Pete tried to summarize their trip to California.

Moses' face looked strained as he tried to make sense of the conversation, and Dara could feel Pete's eyes fixing themselves upon her. He needed her to communicate for him—to fill in the gaps of this floundering conversation. Since the shooting, Dara also found herself needing to order for him at restaurants and become the mouthpiece of the family that Pete always used to be.

She watched and listened as Pete's mouth formed the words in Spanish and then she tried to imitate them as best she could, never quite sure what it was she was saying. If it was accurate or made sense to anyone.

By the end of their first week back, Dara came to a decision.

"If we're going to stay here, I need to go to language school," she told Pete. "Something has to change."

Pete looked at her skeptically. He had been waiting and hoping for this day for the last two years, as every effort made to coerce Dara into learning Spanish had failed miserably. First, there had been the morning classes she signed up for at the Centro de Intercambio y Solidaridad in downtown San Salvador. A few weeks into it, Dara was getting migraines and wanting to quit. Then, they had hired Marlena to be her private Spanish tutor at the house, but she and Dara hit it off so well they ended up chatting in English for the majority of their time together. Whenever Pete tried to encourage her to practice more and take initiative, Dara got angry and defensive. *She couldn't do it*, she had said. *She hated learning Spanish.*

With each attempt, Pete silently wished she could just apply herself more. If he could learn the language, so could she. There was no reason why that wasn't true.

Dara sensed his judgment and got even more defensive. "If we're only going to be here a few more years, then who cares if I learn Spanish?" she retorted, knowing how much this would annoy Pete.

The din of their previous arguments faded from his mind as her head rested on his chest and the smell of her orange scented shampoo filled his nose. The thought of being apart from her made his chest tighten, but the reality was that El Salvador didn't have very good language schools. If Dara was to do this—to really learn Spanish, be immersed in it and devote herself fully to studying—she would need to be free from distraction. No kids, no cooking, no responsibilities. Just studying and practicing Spanish at a school that would teach her well.

"I've heard good things about Christian Spanish Academy in Antigua, Guatemala," Pete said.

Dara lifted her head, her piercing green eyes staring directly into Pete's. "I'm thinking I'll have to go for several weeks. Maybe a month."

The edges of Pete's smile crept downward and he tried to sail past the loneliness that was threatening even now, even at the very thought of her going, to wedge its way in and make him worried and fearful. He willed up an imaginary wall against it with a mock sense of stoicism that was knocked down immediately as Dara pulled him closer and said, "I'm going to miss you like crazy."

Pete laughed. "Just thinking about it right now is freaking me out," he admitted. "It's been a decade."

"Eleven years," Dara corrected with smile. "We've been married eleven years next month."

"Eleven years," Pete repeated. "Eleven years of you letting me drag you all over the darn place."

They both laughed and more than ever, Pete felt the reality of all she had given up for him.

The original plan was for Alba Barrientos to accompany Dara on the seven hour bus ride from San Salvador to Antigua. As native Guatemalans, Alba and her husband Moses had made this trek dozens of times. They knew exactly where and how to transfer at the major bus station in Guatemala City, and which of the elaborately painted chicken buses would be headed for Parque Central at the heart of Antigua.

Ever since the stabbing incident in the *plazuela*, Dara's friendship with Alba Barrientos continued to grow. The two women met weekly to take walks and drink coffee and soon, Alba's friend Carolina was joining them as well. Carolina also lived in the *plazuela*, several houses down, and she spoke a bit of English because her sister lived in San Francisco and she had gone to visit her several times.

When Dara told them she would be going to language school in Antigua for three whole weeks, Alba and Carolina both looked at each other and smiled.

"Will anyone be going with you on the bus to Guatemala?" Alba asked.

Dara shook her head.

"I guess that means we'll have to do it," Carolina said.

The three women giggled in excitement. It would be a grand adventure.

But the night before they were set to leave, Dara got a phone call from Alba saying that her mother in Guatemala was dying and she needed to leave immediately to go see her. The following day, Dara and Carolina traveled to Guatemala without Alba.

When the chicken bus came to a stop at Parque Central, Carolina gave Dara a big hug and the women said their goodbyes.

She was on her own now.

Dara watched a small bird with lime green feathers land on the edge of the white fountain at the center of Parque Central. The bird dipped its beak into the water to grab a quick drink. She had never seen this type of bird before in El Salvador, and it seemed a good omen that perhaps other things in Guatemala might be different too. In a good way.

Dara hoisted her duffle bag atop her shoulder, heavy with the weight of one full month's worth of clothing, toiletry, and books. Her legs seemed to magically carry her through the aisle of the bus, down its narrow steps and onto the cobblestone street below. The air was fresher here. Still humid, but not quite as suffocating. She glanced at the streets of this quiet, ancient town. There were children chasing each other through the grass, an elderly couple walking, arm-in-arm, and a woman with tan wrinkled skin and silvery black hair sitting on the sidewalk, selling brightly woven blankets and baskets. She looked to be part of a Mayan tribe, like she had been making and selling these items since the beginning of time. Dara's searching eyes met those of the woman who looked up at her from the sidewalk with a gap-toothed grin.

Dara could feel the usual tension floating away from the top of her neck, just the same as it had several months ago when she and Pete and the kids flew back to California. There had been a definite release the moment they exited the plane at LAX. There was something that shifted inside her every time she left El Salvador.

It was the absence of dread.

Dara continued down the street in search of the address she had handwritten onto a yellow post-it note and placed in the front pocket of her purse. The address was for the residence where she would be living for the next month with a host family called the Mendozas.

Señora Mendoza was a kind woman with short brown hair that crowded itself atop her head in a group of tight ringlets, none of which fell below her chin. She wore cotton skirts and roomy t-shirts, the excess skin of her upper arms dangling low and loose. The arms of a matriarch. Arms that held babies and patted cornmeal into tortillas and always gave the tightest, most comforting hugs. She and her husband, Señor Mendoza, would be celebrating their sixtieth wedding anniversary next month. Their years together culminating in the birth of five beautiful children and fourteen grandchildren.

When Dara showed up on their doorstep in Antigua she was shy, like a high school girl venturing away from home. What would she do in a stranger's house for the next month? Would she need to ask permission to grab a glass of water? Dara envisioned herself needing to use the restroom in the middle of the night, tip-toeing through a dark hallway trying desperately not to wake anyone up.

"*Bienvenidos!*" Señora Mendoza said, greeting Dara with eyes that crinkled as she smiled. She pulled Dara through the front door as Señor Mendoza grabbed the suitcase from Dara's hand, offering to set it down for her in the *sala*.

"*Siéntate, siéntate,*" he said, gesturing to the couch.

Dara sat down and said thank you in Spanish, the one vocabulary word she could always rely upon if she got stuck.

Señora Mendoza emerged from the kitchen with a brightly colored tray filled with *cafe con leche* and thin round wafer cookies Dara soon learned were called *champurradas*. Señora Mendoza showed her how to dip them in the cup of coffee and then take a soggy bite. Dara smiled as the sweetness of the cookie mingled with the bitterness of the coffee and seemed to disintegrate as she ate it.

Both Mendozas sat across from her in wooden chairs that looked like they had been carved by hand. They smiled at her expectantly and began to tell her how much they hoped she would feel welcome in their home.

"We're here to answer any questions you may have about the language or about the culture. We're delighted to have you as our guest," Señora Mendoza said.

Dara was touched. Although the Christian Spanish Academy had insisted that most all students stay with host families, Dara had been resistant. What she wanted most was to be alone here in Guatemala. To have a space to herself where she would be free to come and go as she pleased. Never would she have imagined this beautiful, elderly couple sitting before her and offering such genuine hospitality.

During the first half of every day, Dara attended Spanish classes at the Christian Spanish Academy. The heart of each class was learning to converse, so that Dara could listen and recognize words. So that she could gain the vocabulary necessary to introduce herself and tell her story to the people she met in El Salvador. Each week, she was assigned a new Spanish teacher. The beauty of this, she found, was that she was able to tell the story of Pete getting shot over and over again.

"My husband was shot in the neck," she told her instructors in Spanish. Each time Dara said it, it felt different somehow. Like it needed to be stated and restated a hundred times.

"*My husband* was shot in the neck."

"My husband *was shot* in the neck."

"My husband was shot *in the neck*."

"*My husband was shot in the neck!*"

How could that one small sentence convey all the emotion it carried?

Dara knew it couldn't and so she uttered those words as often as possible. Even in coffee shops, she found herself resisting the urge to pull each barista aside and say, "Did you know that my husband was shot in the neck?"

Every utterance a form of release, her shoulders falling lower as the weight they carried lessened.

When talking with her Spanish teachers, the words she used were few and basic. Dara's Spanish was like that of a toddler and for the first time, she felt freedom in this fact. There was no need to provide grave details to the stranger sitting across from her. Short sentences, peppered with new vocabulary words like *pistola* (gun) and *ladrones* (criminals) would suffice.

"I feel very sad. It was very scary," she would explain in Spanish, and the patient souls that were her teachers would sit quietly and nod as she butchered their beautiful language.

It was a gift, unlike any other.

But when Dara was asked to describe El Salvador, the country she currently called home, her face darkened and only two words floated to the top of her lips: *Feo y peligroso* (ugly and dangerous).

As the weeks progressed, Dara learned more of the Mendoza's story as they shared meals together of grilled pork with rice and beans. One night after dinner, Señora Mendoza felt it was time to "introduce" Dara to her family. She led Dara into the hallway and pointed to the framed photographs lining the wall. In this way she introduced each of her children, giving their names, ages, and occupations. When she came to the last photograph of a young man, Señora Mendoza paused and Dara watched as the smile faded from her eyes.

"This is my eldest son, Antonio. He was a doctor," she said.

Dara recognized her sudden switch from verbs in the present tense to the past. "He worked so hard, my boy did. Studying and riding the bus everyday to university. He always dreamed of a day when he could be successful enough to buy his own car, and sure enough, that day came. At 25 years old, he graduated from medical school and I will never forget how proud I was."

Señora Mendoza looked away from the photograph and off into the hallway. Dara felt the story turning. At any moment she would find out what happened to this firstborn son and that it probably wouldn't be pretty. She thought of her own oldest son, PJ, and felt her stomach dance with nervousness.

"He practiced medicine for four years and even managed to buy the car he always wanted. But when he was 29, he got into a car accident," Señora Mendoza paused. "He didn't survive."

"I'm so sorry," Dara whispered.

"He was in the Lord's hands," she said, looking Dara directly in the eye. "As are we all."

Dara's time in Guatemala was a re-learning of sorts. It was a reminder about life and the simple fact that death and trials are woven into the fabric of it. Not a single person was exempt. Not her own family, not the Mendozas, and not even Kathleen, a fellow student at CSA who was in her fifties and was also assigned to stay at the Mendoza's house shortly after Dara arrived. Kathleen was diagnosed with cancer at the age of twenty, right at the tail end of obtaining her bachelor's degree in sociology. In order to graduate, Kathleen had to cram for exams and endure rounds of chemotherapy simultaneously.

Ultimately, she was successful in both regards and emerged both cancer free and with a Bachelor of Science. Yet, physical ailments had continued to plague Kathleen's life for the next twenty-five years. First, the doctors told her they would need to remove a set of muscles in her shoulders. Muscles that she needed to hold up her neck. In their absence, she was forced to change careers and endure a painful process of learning how to activate different muscle groups to keep her head from drooping awkwardly to the front or side.

Decades later, after going back to school, studying to become an airplane engineer, and working in the field twenty-five years, Kathleen fell on the job and shattered both of her kneecaps.

Again, Dara found herself blinking back tears as Kathleen shared this story with her. They had just finished climbing the Pacaya Volcano with a group of their classmates. The air smelled of sulfur and the ground beneath them felt as though it might burn through their tennis shoes as lava swelled and surged beneath the surface.

Neither Dara nor Kathleen had ever climbed a volcano before. When CSA offered it as a cultural excursion, they both jumped at the chance, as though it were a calling. Their "tour guide," if you could call him that, had essentially dropped them off at the base of the volcano and said, "There you go! Now walk."

The climb was suspiciously void of any barriers or guardrails to keep them from falling. Kathleen and Dara clung to each other as they climbed, one step after the next, looking only ahead at the translucent puffs of smoke wafting from the top. Dara brushed the layer of sweat from her forehead and took a large swig from her water bottle. This woman standing next to her was not only brave, but deeply compassionate. Rather than worrying about herself, Kathleen had been watching over Dara ever since they met each other two weeks prior. She had sensed Dara's sorrow, identified with her woundedness.

Every afternoon, the two women had walked home from Spanish class together, often getting rained on in the process. The blue-gray skies would open up on top of them and rather than fighting the downpour and running for cover, Kathleen urged Dara to slow down, to feel the drops of water as they spilled down the back of her shirt.

"Close your eyes," Kathleen said.

And Dara did.

She closed them and smiled as the warm water drenched her face, her tank top, her long cotton skirt. Dara's long hair becoming tangled and stuck to her back. She listened to the way it bounced off the cobblestone and formed small puddles.

I want to stop fighting, she prayed quietly. *I want to feel alive and free and to stop being scared. To trust You with my family and with my entire life.*

A roll of thunder peeled across the sky and Dara felt Kathleen grab her hand.

"Are you ready to run for it?" she asked.

Dara laughed and felt Kathleen pull her down the street until they arrived at the Mendoza's looking like two drowned cats.

Dara thought about that moment as they stood on top of the Pacaya Volcano. Kathleen was one of the most compassionate people she had ever met. She was youthful, she was free, and she had been through hell and back to become this way.

"I can't believe how well you can walk now," Dara marveled, "And run, even." Her eyes traveled to Kathleen's covered kneecaps, searching for evidence of their once immobile state.

Kathleen nodded. "It's been a long journey. But if there's one thing I know, it's this: We are capable of withstanding so much more than we imagined."

On Dara's last day in Antigua, she said goodbye to Kathleen, to the Mendozas, and to her language school. She picked up her suitcase and ascended the steps of the chicken bus that would take her on the reverse trip from Antigua to Guatemala City, and then from Guatemala City back to El Salvador. This time Dara made the trip alone, which gave her plenty of time to think.

Upon leaving the city, the ride became even more unsettling. The bus began its ascension up a narrow, winding hillside. The brakes squeaked around every turn and the oncoming vehicles traveled so close, they practically brushed the sides of the bus.

Dara looked out the window at the massive cliff they were hugging. The grass below was wild and unkempt. It stretched for miles, over hillsides and deep valleys dotted with trees.

She leaned her head against the window of the bus and marveled at how much her Spanish had improved in only three weeks. She wasn't fluent by any means, but she did have a working vocabulary now. She had a context she could place certain words within. She had a framework for putting together sentences, and none of it had been obtained through reading textbooks or taking quizzes. Rather than forcing one way of learning on her—as had always been the case from elementary school through college—the Christian Spanish Academy had actually adapted to Dara's learning style. They let her learn through praying with her teachers. She had also learned by interacting with her host family. By watching Señora Mendoza sweep the floor and then asking her what the Spanish words were for broom and for floor and for sweeping. She learned by having to order for herself at restaurants because there was no one else around to translate for her.

As the chicken bus crossed over the Guatemalan border and rounded its way through the familiar sections of highway on the outskirts of San Salvador, Dara's stomach began to churn.

She was back.

Back in the country where her husband was shot.

The thought was like swallowing poison. Dara's insides felt rotten and her stomach muscles began to contract in violent pulses. She tried to ignore it, but the dread was liquid, spreading from her heart and her head, through her shoulders, arms, legs, and feet. Every inch of her body drenched in it.

I can't do this. I can't do this. I can't do this. I can't do this I can't do this echoed in her brain like a pounding chorus.

The bus came to an abrupt stop inside the depot and the engine went silent. The front doors swung open and a rush of humid, sticky air filled the small corridor of the bus. Dara's stomach contracted again, and she knew she needed to throw up.

Just hold it in. Just hold it in. Just hold it in. Just another minute. Please God, let me not throw up here.

The passengers in front of her moved slowly, rounding up their children, gathering their belongings, making their way down the aisle and out the front door in lethargic fashion. Finally, it was Dara's turn to exit, and she grabbed the handles of her duffle bag, dragging it and herself through the cramped bus.

She knew from the trip out to Guatemala exactly where the restrooms were located, and she ran to them with desperate urgency. She tossed her bag inside an open stall, locked the door and held her head over the toilet. Her body convulsed as she threw up three times, gasping for air, eyes watering with the intensity of it.

Dara wiped her mouth and leaned her back against the door of the bathroom stall. She was exhausted. Like she had been fighting a war.

It was confusing that just a few days earlier she had started to feel better, stronger, more hopeful, like a part of her heart had begun to heal in Guatemala. And it had.

But the juxtaposition of today was hard to reconcile. Dara wondered if maybe she had been wrong about turning a corner. Maybe she had only turned it because she was in Guatemala, and now that she was back in El Salvador, healing would be impossible.

She didn't have a therapist or trauma counselor to walk with her and tell her it's okay because healing can be like a Yo-yo sometimes. Yanking you up and down and until the grief loses its momentum and begins to stabilize.

When will I ever feel safe? she prayed.

It felt like an impossible question to answer. She had been asking it all her life.

Her childhood home hadn't felt safe because her parents were always fighting. Always breaking up, moving out, moving back in. While Dara knew they loved her very much, their love was hard to cling to amidst the spinning orbit of arguments and tears and being shuttled from one residence to the next.

There was little safety to be found in her career as a young starlet and beauty pageant contestant. Though Dara often won, she battled the underlying fear that next time she wouldn't. Despite all of her practicing, come competition time when she needed to open her mouth and sing, her vocal cords could freeze, or she might miss a note or two.

Then there was her physical appearance, which Dara feared would betray her eventually, even if her voice didn't. Physical beauty was the most precocious and elusive attribute of all. Yet, her entire career hinged on it.

When she secretly tried out for the tennis team in high school and was granted a spot, Dara's mother was quick to warn her that playing tennis was out of the question.

"Please," Dara had begged. "I'm sure I can squeeze it in between auditions. I can do both."

"This isn't about time," Debbie insisted. "This is about keeping you in one piece. What if you slip and fall? What if you hurt yourself?"

"But I won't. I'll be careful."

Debbie smiled and shook her head. "It's not worth it, sweetie. You're a model. Models don't have scars."

The young Hollywood scene of the late 1980s hadn't felt safe either. Whenever Dara opened her mailbox and received a hand drawn invitation to Alphy's Soda Pop Club, an underage dance club for child stars, her heart dropped because she knew her mother would want her to make an appearance.

"It's good for your career," Debbie insisted.

Dara nodded and resigned herself to an evening of standing in the corner and drinking flavored seltzer water as her peers eagerly greeted each other on the dance floor of the Roosevelt Hotel. Her peers being well known actors such as, Soleil Moon Frye, Alyssa Milano, Christina Applegate, River Phoenix, and both Coreys—Haim and Feldman.

The attendees of Alphy's Soda Pop Club ranged in age from 12-17, and most had been emancipated from their parents. They were adolescents making mountains of money and calling all the shots in their lives. In this world they inhabited with agents and complicated filming schedules, their parents had long stopped instilling curfews or any sort of traditional structure in their lives. As a result, the air at Alphy's was that of unadulterated freedom.

Excessive. Unsettling. Inappropriate freedom.

Decades later—after Corey Haim's drug addiction and premature death, after Corey Feldman's public disclosure that they both had been molested by people in the film industry—Feldman would write in his tell-all memoir:

"People always ask me about life after childhood stardom. What would I say to parents of children in the industry? My only advice, honestly, is to get these kids out of Hollywood and let them lead normal lives."

Words that weighed heavily on Dara's heart, but didn't surprise her in the least.

The day Dara decided she was leaving the industry for good, she drove home from college and began sifting through her pageant trophies and crowns, electing to donate all of them to the Special Olympics.

Debbie watched her daughter in a state of helpless disbelief.

"Don't you want to keep at least something?" she asked, selecting a bejeweled crown from the pile.

"Nope," Dara said.

Debbie held it in her hand, watched it glisten against the light. "But we worked so hard for these . . ."

"Oh, well," Dara said, resolute in her desire to start over. To create a new life, a safer one.

Dara lifted her head up from the toilet in the San Salvador bus depot. The memories settled around her feet like dust, and all she could think was, *Here I am. Back in the country with the highest homicide rate in the whole world.*

So much for safety.

Hot tears filled the corner of her eyes, and she pleaded with God to help her.

"I can't do this without you," she said, wishing she could stay forever inside this bathroom stall.

You've never had to.

The thought made her pause for a moment.

Dara sat on top of the toilet seat and closed her eyes. She saw an image of herself as a little girl. She was in her bedroom, covering her eyes to drown out the sound of her parents shouting on the other side of the door.

I was with you. I was there.

She saw herself as a teenager, auditioning for a music scholarship at Pepperdine University. The faculty sat in a straight line wearing matching navy blue suit coats. Dara felt their eyes boring into her as she stood in front of them. She sensed the panic welling inside her as she opened her mouth to sing the operetta she had been practicing with her vocal coach for the past several months.

I was with you. I was there.

She saw her entire family at the San Salvador airport on the morning they had first landed. Twenty-seven bags and all.

I was with you. I was there.

Philippians 4:7 came to her mind. It was a verse about God's peace which surpasses all understanding.

Dara opened her eyes.

What if safety had been with her all along?

Not the type of safety that prevented her husband from getting shot, or prevented her children from getting sick. Not the type of safety that came with protective bubbles or guarantees from harm or pain. This type of safety was different. It wasn't rooted in circumstance or in sentimental optimism. It was rooted in her knowledge and understanding of who God was.

Even when Dara was at her worst, God still seemed to reach out to her. Unconditionally. When she fumbled and failed, He loved her in the trying and the learning. He loved her when she ignored Him and forgot Him. When she avoided Him and was scared of Him. God loved her in her anger at Him. When she felt hopeless and confused and let fear win. Still, He loved her. He welcomed her back with arms open wide and said, "Let's try again. I have a better way, if you're interested in learning about it."

Why He cared so much and how he found the patience was beyond Dara. But because of this love, she knew that God always had her best interest at heart and would help her work toward it. In spite of whatever adversity life brought.

That was her safety. That was her promise.

Dara walked out of the bathroom stall and felt that it was truly okay to let go. If she stayed close to Him, she knew He would hold her steady. She didn't need to control so much. She could follow . . . and release.

CHAPTER 20

Punta Mango

Playa El Espino, 2009

The country of El Salvador has a long horizontal shape, lying east to west. On the west, it borders Guatemala and on the east, Honduras. If one were to draw a line down the center of the country, San Salvador would fall on the western side. As the country's capital, it is home to major banks and an international airport. Big business is conducted in the west. Money flows more freely and in greater abundance. During the civil war, it was the west, not surprisingly, who aligned themselves with the Salvadoran government.

The east, on the other hand . . . The east was called the *Wild East*. Think cowboys, outlaws, and guerrilla resistance fighters. Think farmers and native tribes whose villages did not have access to water or electricity. Think people who lived in huts, who believed in superstition and bits of magic in the universe. Think towns that were so forgotten or ignored, they weren't included on any maps.

Abelines is one of these towns. It lies northeast, in the mountains. Below it, if you were to keep driving south from Abelines—all the way through the gang-infested territory of San Martín, where Pastor Juan was conducting his water project—you would eventually hit the Pacific Ocean. You would hit a small beach community called Playa El Espino.

In another lifetime, Playa El Espino could have easily been a thriving tourist destination. The beaches have clay-like sand and the ocean glitters like a handful of diamonds tossed across the surface. Hidden along its shores is a secret surf break called Punta Mango. For the international surfing community, Punta Mango is arguably the second best wave in the country. *Punta* means point in Spanish, referencing the fact that it is a point break. Which means the waves create beautiful barrels as they break toward the shore, allowing for long, intense rides. As in the popular Keanu Reeves film, *Point Break*, these waves are the holy grail of surfing experiences. Surfers dream about them, make pilgrimages to them, and spend their lives aspiring to be good enough to one day conquer them.

Yet, Punta Mango remains a secret that few surf magazines have bothered to report. The few magazines who have run stories on it often reference the local legend that one can only access Punta Mango via boat.

This isn't true.

Punta Mango can be accessed by car, albeit it is a windy, bumpy drive. But the legend started because driving through the eastern part of the country, both during and after the civil war, was considered frightening and dangerous. The owners of a big hotel called Las Flores decided to use boats to safely transport fearful westerners to Punta Mango. Nowadays, they charge $50 for this ride and have worked hard to perpetuate the legend that their business is the only direct access point for Punta Mango.

When Pete visited Punta Mango, he did not take a boat to get to it. He drove, slow and steady, over the unpaved road. Stopping first to buy a coconut popsicle at the gas station in Playa El Espino. This would later became a favorite tradition of his, en route to Mango.

One particular afternoon in 2009, Pete viewed Punta Mango from a distance. He was far enough away to observe the empty plot of land hovering above it. A mound of dirt cluttered with overgrown trees. The land wasn't much to look at from afar. Up close, it got even worse. The weeds were monstrous and thorny. They required a machete just to hack through them.

Pete and his friend Mike Peterson sliced their way into the nasty mob of brush until they came to the end of it and were both staring out at a gorgeous expanse of Pacific Ocean. Barrel waves crashing along the shore of the gray-brown sand.

"I think we could do something with this," Pete said to Mike.

Pete had known the land above Punta Mango was for sale because a buddy of his from college had been all set to buy it only one year earlier. Pete had gone with this friend to meet the owner who was a lawyer from San Salvador. A lawyer whose roots were firmly planted in the west and who hadn't ventured to the Wild East since before the civil war. There were too many awful memories. Such violence, such fear wrapped up in everything involving the East—including this beach front property overlooking Punta Mango. The owner hadn't stepped foot on it for over 25 years.

It was time for him to sell it. To put that part of his past to rest.

In the recesses of Pete's heart, he had been harboring the great expat dream of one day buying a beach house all his own. An affordable beach house that could only be acquired on international soil.

It was a quiet dream. Pete was a missionary, after all. His funds were rather limited, and they had literally been cut in half two years earlier in the stock market crash of 2008. But the asking price for this plot of land above Punta Mango was only $25,000, and Pete's friend had backed out of the deal. It was now available for anyone to buy, and if Pete could just split that price with Mike . . .

Mike was also a surfer. Also, from Southern California, and also an alumnus of a small Christian college where he had met and fallen in love with his wife Brittney. When Mike and Pete first became friends at the Union Church of San Salvador, it was obvious they had loads in common. Even their wives got along famously. Dara and Brittney were quick to bond over the perils of learning Spanish, and the intense loneliness of life abroad.

Mike and Brittney Peterson were partial expats who lived in El Salvador three to six months out of the year. The rest of the time they resided on the outskirts of San Diego where Mike ran a thriving business selling fried food at county fairs all over California. The Petersons spent their summers peddling bacon dipped in chocolate and deep fried portobello mushrooms stuffed with Gouda. Their food stand was called Bacon-A-Fair and was frequently praised by the *Orange County Register*, and other regional publications.

After a long, sweaty summer of standing over deep fryers amongst throngs of hungry fair-goers, Mike and Brittney packed it all up and took a well-earned vacation at their beach house in El Zonte. About 30 miles southwest of San Salvador.

"Do you think we could do something with this?" Pete asked Mike.

The two friends stood at the cliff's edge and looked down below. Blue on blue. Where the ocean met the sky.

Mike already owned one beach house in El Salvador, and didn't technically need to own another one . . . unless this property he purchased with Pete could be used for something bigger. Something with purpose.

"What if we dedicated this land to God?" Mike asked Pete.

Ever since meeting the DeSotos and hearing their story—learning of all the difficulties Pete and Dara had faced, both trying to assimilate to El Salvador and trying to heal after Pete had been shot—Mike had been praying about some way he and Brittney could potentially help. Not just the DeSotos, but others who were like them. Missionaries who were doing important work in El Salvador, but were struggling both mentally and spiritually.

As they became acquainted with more expat families, Mike and Brittney noticed certain patterns developing. A web of similarities that began with missionary families living behind barbed wire and advanced levels of security. The families felt like prisoners in their own homes and would give anything to have a safe place where their kids could run free and where they could simply unwind and recharge. A place where they could be served, instead of doing all the serving. Where they could speak English and unload whatever stories, thoughts, and feelings they may have been bottling inside.

These missionaries needed support, Mike concluded. They needed guidance and community in an environment that was safe, beautiful, healing. A place like this Punta Mango property. If Mike and Pete were to buy it and develop it.

Pete listened as Mike explained all of this to him. He took in every word and was deeply moved. Here, Pete had been thinking only of himself and the fantasy vacation home he could build. Not that there was anything wrong with that, or in dreaming of something nice for himself and his family.

But what Mike was inviting him into was so much bigger. And so much better.

"I just have one thing to add," Pete said, turning toward Mike with a childlike grin. "Surf camps. In between missionary stays, we run surf camps. Teach kids, adults, and whoever's interested how to conquer Mango."

"Done," Mike said, reaching his hand out for Pete to shake it.

CHAPTER 21

Saying Goodbye

San Salvador, 2009-2010

When Jenny McGee got the first inkling that something was going wrong inside her body, she called the nearest doctor and made an appointment. They examined her breasts, conducted a needle biopsy, and concluded that the test was negative. The needle had hit a lump, yes, but it was only a fibroadenoma. A naturally occurring lump that happens sometimes when women are breast feeding. And Jenny had been breast feeding her one-year-old daughter Emma. All the bodily shifts, the abnormalities, and now the lumps even were being attributed to that. Many women had fibroadenomas while breast feeding, she was assured. It was nothing to be alarmed about.

Jenny went home from the hospital feeling grateful and light. But for the next three months, she got the strangest sense every time she sat down to pray. If she didn't know any better, it would seem that God was urging her to go back to the doctor and get a second opinion. But why? The test results had been negative and cancer was the last thing Jenny wanted to be obsessing over. It was time to move on and give thanks for another day.

Just go back to the hospital one more time.

Jenny sighed.

After she and David started having children, they had relocated to a small home in the mountains outside San Salvador. Where the traffic was slower, the crime rates were lower, and peace played a more prominent role in their day-to-day life. The only down side was that things like hospitals weren't quite as easy to access. Getting to the hospital meant traversing the usual unpaved roads and planning the entire day around a single trip so that she could arrive safely back home before dark.

Fine, she relented, *I'll go.*

This time her appointment was for a mammogram, and this time it came back with conclusive results. Jenny was diagnosed with an aggressive form of stage 3 breast cancer and it had already spread to her lymph nodes. She needed to start chemotherapy immediately, they said, and have a double mastectomy once chemo was over, followed by radiation treatments and a follow-up drug for the next year and a half. The majority of this would need to be done in the United States, and at best, she was given a fifty percent chance of living.

The night before Jenny flew back to the US to get a second opinion, Dara and Pete came over to the McGee's house to pray. They joined with David to lay hands over Jenny and cry out to God. Through love and tears, hope and sorrow, their words fell on Jenny like a peaceful rain. She gathered each of their prayers and held them close to her heart.

She would fight this, she vowed. No matter what it took.

Back in her hometown of Columbia, Missouri, Jenny received confirmation from the doctors that her cancer diagnosis was accurate. In response, she and David launched plans to move permanently back to the US. After eight years of living abroad, their El Salvador chapter was coming to a close.

When Dara heard the McGees were moving back to the US, she couldn't help but wonder when her own El Salvador chapter would come to a close. Dara and Pete were nearing their five year mark, which meant the original commitment they had talked about would be over.

Dara walked into the backyard of Union Church and sat down on the grass underneath the shade of the winding, mysterious tree in the backyard. The thought of Jenny and David leaving filled her with heaviness. Jenny would be on another continent undergoing cancer treatments and Dara wouldn't be there to comfort her. It was hard to fathom, especially because so many other expats she had grown to know and love in El Salvador had left as well. The faces at Union

Church were constantly shifting, and every time PJ and Isaac made a new friend, his or her parents seemed to get relocated within six months to a year for new job opportunities and various other reasons.

The expat life was one of transience. After five years, Dara had had enough. She was ready to move back to California, but had no idea how to talk to Pete about it. He was happy here. Not only with ENLACE, but also in his latest role—as pastor of the Union Church. The church leadership had asked Pete to take on this new role after the previous pastor had moved away. Through it, Pete had been able to meet and partner with some of his greatest social justice heroes.

Millard Fuller, the creator of Habitat for Humanity came to speak at Union Church. Pete helped coordinate wheelchair deliveries to physically disabled children in El Salvador alongside a quadriplegic woman named Joni Eareckson Tada. Gary Wilkerson, the creator of World Challenge, had agreed to fly out and lead a pastor's conference. It was all Pete had dreamed of and more. But Dara was lonely. And just as the day she arrived, she longed for the freedom to do meager activities, like strolling in the park without fear of being mugged.

It was time.

Dara shared all of this with Pete later that evening after the kids were tucked into bed. They sat in the backyard in the cool of the evening, drinking Malbec under a sky of blinking stars. As Dara spoke, Pete listened quietly. The thought of leaving El Salvador felt like a break up to Pete. A beautiful relationship he wanted to cling to but was being asked to let go of.

"We did say five years, didn't we?" Pete said, lifting the glass of wine to his lips, absorbing its rich, earthy aroma.

"We did," Dara agreed. "And now that we're nearing that five year mark, I don't really know what leaving will look like, for us, or for the places and people we'll be leaving behind here."

"You mean Union Church?" Pete asked. "Like who's going to be the new pastor if I leave?"

"Yeah, for starters."

Pete was quiet. "Guess we've got a lot of praying to do."

In certain schools of thought, the act of creation is less about breathing something new into existence than it is about discovering the contours of a buried object. Like archaeologists digging into the earth, whatever they are trying to uncover already exists, but its details, its intricacies, are heaped in layers of mud and mystery. So they break out their brushes and picks and tools—chipping and polishing, inch by inch—until the object reveals itself in its fullness.

Some artists believe that's what their job is, too. As painters and poets and songwriters. Their vocation is to discover the song they want to write or the painting they want to paint with the knowledge that it already exists, even if it is just in their subconscious. They don't need to create it, so much as they need to uncover it.

Perhaps our lives can be viewed in a similar fashion? Like archaeologists on a dig, Pete and Dara got to work each evening for months on end, praying, dreaming, and chipping away at the contours of their blurry future. In time, the answers revealed themselves.

Pete would go back to school. Not for anthropology this time, but for a Masters Degree in Executive Leadership at the University of San Diego. While Pete was in school, he, Dara, and the kids would live with John and Lucia in their modest, two story home outside San Diego.

There won't be enough rooms to accommodate Pete's family of six, plus John and Lucia, so Dara's father Dan will use his experience as a general contractor to remodel John's three car garage. Dan will use plywood and 2x4s to convert the space into two separate bedrooms. One for PJ and Isaac, the other for Hannah and Kaya. Dan will buy carpet at Home Depot and install electricity for each room. Pete and Dara will order bunk beds and dressers online. Upon delivery, Lucia will team up with Dara's mother Debbie to decorate. They will stuff pillows into shams, place lamps on top of dressers, and get everything set up so that when the DeSoto kids walk off the airplane, they will have beautiful bedrooms to welcome them.

Pete will find a new pastor for the Union Church. A man named Gary Powell who will take the reigns from Pete in 2010 and continue to run with them until the time of this writing in 2017.

For nearly a year after leaving El Salvador, Pete will remain in his position at ENLACE, overseeing their fundraising efforts, and coordinating church mission teams from San Diego. He will travel back to San Salvador several times, and there he will meet up with David McGee who will also be working for ENLACE remotely, as he and Jenny plant roots in Missouri.

Jenny will continue painting and will eventually be declared cancer free. She will commemorate her battle with the disease by creating a piece of art titled "Hate Cancer, Love the Cure." It will hang in the offices of the Missouri Cancer Associates and it will feature a *papier mâché* hand formed out of shredded pamphlets given to Jenny upon diagnosis. The hand will be propped on top of the word CANCER in capital letters, and surrounded by brightly colored flowers, signifying hope. The middle finger of the hand will be pointed upward—in stubborn, hard won victory.

After moving back to California, Dara will find a calling of her own as a doula/birthing coach for expectant mothers. The roots of this passion traveling all the way back to Dara's own experience of giving birth for the first time. She'll remember the loneliness she felt at the birthing center in Bethesda, Maryland, and how wonderful it was to have Scott Anderson show up and teach her how to care for her newborn. Dara will become that friend for other new moms. And she will absolutely love it.

Little Kaya will be five years old when the DeSoto's begin their new life in California. Having grown up in El Salvador from the age of seven months, Kaya will be unaccustomed to first world conveniences. She will giggle with delight in public restrooms when the dispenser magically spits out paper towels at her. Most of all, Kaya will love the freedom of being able to open her mouth while she is taking a shower in California. Awestruck, she will close her eyes and let the warm drops of water fall upon her tongue. Because there the water is clean and will not hurt her if she swallows it.

Hannah will be seven and will be thrilled by the smorgasbord of activities available to her in the US. She'll try ballet and then guitar. She'll get her very own library card and will enter every reading contest they offer, keeping score of her daily reading points with precision.

From books to ballet, Hannah will find it all intriguing. Nothing short of a luxury.

PJ, age 12, will step off the plane from San Salvador to LAX and he will try to imagine what his new life will look like. Based on his limited knowledge of Southern California culture, he will envision himself eating lots of In-N-Out Burger and riding in a car along highways that are wide and clean and surprisingly void of potholes. These predictions will be accurate in some respects, but what PJ does not predict is how challenging it will be for him to assimilate with his peers. Navigating the lingo and mannerisms of American teenagers will baffle him for the first several years. It will take time to find his place and finally feel that he belongs.

Many years later, when PJ is a college student reflecting back on his childhood in El Salvador, one thing he will remember and carry with him are the moments he and Isaac spent out in the communities with their father. While Pete was chatting with Pastor Victorio and planning medical clinic expansions, PJ and Isaac ran and played to their heart's content. They chopped through foliage with machetes. They strung rope across tree branches and clung to it tightly, swinging their bodies over flowing riverbeds. Like Tarzan. Like kings of the jungle. In those moments, all the danger, the violence, and the claustrophobic feeling of being confined within the walls of their *plazuela*, day after day, faded into distant memory. In those moments, the world revealed itself to PJ and Isaac as one of magic. And freedom. And infinite possibility.

For 10-year-old Isaac, moving to California will mean discovering his love for water polo and for surfing. In 2012, he will compete in the Junior Olympic National Water Polo Championship and in high school he will play on the varsity water polo team. Isaac will thrive living only steps away from the beach and enjoying an active, Southern California lifestyle. But like his brother PJ, Isaac will wrestle with the cultural differences.

In El Salvador, the people Isaac met while working in the communities with his dad were always welcoming and genuine. In Southern California, Isaac will find some marked differences. People there will be distracted and competitive and often wanting more. More money, more fame, more opportunities. As Isaac matures from a 10-year-old to a high school student, he will find himself longing for the simplicity of personal relationships he experienced with the Salvadorans.

Pete will long for this too. So much so that he will continue to fly back to El Salvador for the next decade of his life. Even after his job with ENLACE is complete, Pete will return to visit friends and to check in on the progress of the beach house/missionary retreat center he and Mike Peterson are developing together in Punta Mango. The two friends and business partners will transform a thorny mound of dirt into an oasis of bungalows that can sleep up to sixteen people.

After contributing to the cost of grading the land and installing electricity, Pete will be past his ability to invest. Mike will take over from there, building a full kitchen, seven bathrooms, and a *rancho* with a thatched roof and brightly woven hammocks strung around the perimeter. Adjacent to the *rancho*, Mike will add an infinity pool, yoga platforms, ping pong tables, and a half-pipe.

By 2016, there will be new missionary families staying at Villa Mango every month, many of whom will find rest, solace, and community throughout their time there. Just as Pete and Mike prayed that they would.

The morning the DeSotos left El Salvador, all six of them woke up to an inky sky still filled with stars. Their flight back to LAX departed at 7:30 a.m., which meant that no one really slept the night before. Pete and Dara had been tossing and turning most of the night. When their alarm buzzed, it sent a jolt of emotions through them both. There was excitement mixed with fear and a bit of melancholy—on Pete's end.

Dara was filled with wonder as she tucked her final toiletries into the front pouch of her suitcase. She had imagined this day so many times since moving to El Salvador, and here it was. Actually happening.

Hannah, Issac, PJ, and Kaya filed into the backseat of the car in slow motion. Their eyes blurry and their brains stuck in sleepy limbo, as the car made its journey through the dark highway leading to the airport.

The DeSoto family made their way through the airport check-in line, carrying the same twenty-seven bags they had arrived with five years prior. Their possessions had altered slightly over the years. Kaya was no longer in diapers, and all of the children's clothing had gotten larger and now took up more space. But other than that, they had acquired little in the way of physical possessions.

On board the plane, Pete started reflecting on all he had learned during his time in El Salvador. He thought about his posture now, versus when he had come to El Salvador. It felt like another lifetime ago. Pete held his life more loosely now. And although it hurt to leave, he knew it was the right decision for his family.

He knew this partially because he had chosen to play an April Fool's joke on PJ and Isaac several months earlier.

"I have some news," Pete had told them, gathering the boys together in the living room. "Your mom and I have decided not to move back to California after all."

PJ and Isaac exchanged glances. Their brows furrowed, first in shock and then in major disappointment.

Pete waited for several seconds. He allowed his words to sink in and listened as PJ spat an angry "*Why?*" in his direction. Then Pete's mouth broke into a smile.

"April Fools!" he shouted.

Man were the boys ever pissed off at him.

Hannah and Kaya were too young to care much, but PJ and Isaac most definitely had thoughts about their future. Pete respected his son's wishes and knew he was making the right decision. For them and especially for Dara who sat beside him on the plane. Pete squeezed Dara's hand and she squeezed his back, leaning her head back against the seat and smiling.

After the plane took off, Pete grabbed the journal from his carry-on bag. This is what he wrote:

After our first few months of living in El Salvador, I had a powerful encounter with Jesus during one of my devotional times. I was sitting out on the patio. It had rained the night before. The cool of the morning was being replaced by the warm sun lighting up the green foliage. The beauty of El Salvador was palpable.

I opened my Bible and read a bit in Psalms. Maybe some in Isaiah and Jeremiah. I honestly don't remember what I read, but I do remember my prayer. I began to pray that God would give me a voice. His voice. In the world.

I didn't really know what I was praying or why. It just kinda came upon me. The passages in the old testament where poets and prophets call out on behalf of the disenfranchised jumped off the pages that morning. Over and over I read calls for people to remember those that society leaves behind.

I had been in El Salvador long enough to meet countless people who seemed to not have a voice. Whose stories were not being told. Instead, many of the people I met in the campo *of El Salvador were herded into the masses of people known as the "third world."*

Sure, anecdotal stories made their way back to the US. But, more often than not, they seemed to be motivated by fundraising efforts, or the need to assure donors that their money was being used well: "Jose's life was a mess until organization X moved in, and now his life is forever changed . . ." Or, "Juanita is widowed with twenty-four children and spends eight hours a day walking to get water at the river. Please send money to build a well now."

But these stories never seemed to be told in the voice of the people featured in them. These people were talked about, rather than doing the talking. So often when they did talk, they merely said what they thought the donors of the north wanted them to say.

But some of the most powerful conversations I ever had with Salvadorans were when the campesinos *would start talking about the latest* futbol *match, or about their family members who were en route to* Los Estados Unidos *illegally to find work, or about their frustrations with politics.*

During the World Cup one year, I had been working on a project in a rural town and noticed most the local guys were absent one afternoon, while most us gringos were doing all the work. I walked into one man's corn fields and saw the longest extension cord I'd ever seen. I followed the chord to its end and found three men sitting under tall corn stalks watching a World Cup game on a tiny black and white TV with an antenna. They were taking a break, finding pleasure like I do when I camp out for the weekend to watch the Master's Golf Tournament, or stream surf contests on my computer.

That's when I realized how alike we all were. Although there appears to be many barriers and differences between me and the people of El Salvador, we are much more alike than not. The mother in El Salvador's poor, rural town wants a good life for her children just as much as I do. The father wants to work in a dignified way that provides for his family, in the same way I long to.

It didn't take long after that for me to lose my motivation to "help" the poor people in El Salvador, once I found that these people were not poor. I was not rich. The complex gap between us was less about socioeconomic status than it was about history, wars, bad policy, greed, and some unexplainable fate that allowed me to grow up in San Diego, California with great parents, great education, and plenty of opportunity. While others grew up in desperate towns plagued by war, violence, and a level of scarcity I had never witnessed.

When I spoke with these Salvadorans, I often felt guilty. But they didn't seem jealous. They were not waiting for their lives to be "fixed." They were not waiting for some great hope from El Norte *to do it.*

They were usually determined to work hard until their death and to do their very best. They were resigned to the fact that opportunities in El Salvador were scarce. They grew furious when talking about the war and the violence and the loss. Many cried over the loved one's they had lost. Yes, they often carried a deep sadness and somewhat hopeless view of their country's future.

But, seconds later they could talk about the futbol *rivalry between Barcelona and Real Madrid with passion. They could debate ferociously about the best way to make* pupusas, *the best cheeses to use. It was when the conversation had nothing to do with their state of poverty, their need for resources, or their desire for me to help that their voices came through the strongest.*

It was when I simply asked questions, and chose to listen.

CHAPTER 22

"The Savior"

El Salvador, 2011-2017

And what becomes of El Salvador?

Before we delve into that question, let's pause for a moment.

Imagine, if you would, that *you* are a pastor in Los Abelines, El Salvador.

Yes, you.

Come on. Try it.

You are a pastor in a remote village going about your regular business when you notice a young man from your church approaching you one afternoon. He is in his mid-twenties and you have known him since he was a child. In fact, you recently baptized him, after an intensely dark period of his life. You were there only months ago when this man confessed a belief in Jesus and asked the Holy Spirit to come into his life. A moment that never fails to bring a smile to your lips.

You watch this young man approach and note that he is not smiling today. His eyes look troubled and his mannerisms anxious.

He tells you he needs to confess something. To release himself from its forceful grip.

You nod and brace yourself for what may come. Except there is no preparation for what he says to you next.

"Do you remember?" he asks, "The day the gringo was shot?"

"Yes," you say. And you remember it well.

You remember the "gringo" named Peter DeSoto whom you have since continued to work with over the past near decade. You remember visiting Pete in the hospital with his four children curled up next to him on the hospital bed. You remember the tears in his wife Dara's eyes and the shame that set over your entire village after it happened.

Everyone who lived there felt responsible in some way. Because they weren't able to prevent it. Because history has a way of repeating itself, and history has taught the Salvadorans that some of the most undeserving people are the ones who end up bloody and dismembered on the side of the road.

Pete getting shot wasn't seen as a mere accident or temporary setback for the village of Abelines, it was seen as a mockery of the hopeful future they had dared to dream of and take baby steps toward.

"I shot him," this young man before you mumbles, staring numbly at the floor.

The walls around you begin to expand and contract as you absorb this information. This confession, which is now yours to bear.

What would you do, reader, if this were you?

If you knew Pete, if you knew the gunman, if you now knew the full reality of something you had long wondered about? Would you keep it to yourself because you were supposed to? You are a pastor, after all, and the practice of confession is a sacred act of trust.

But here is the conundrum you are faced with as you see the man in front of you: Forgiveness is crucial.

As a pastor you can forgive this man and tell him so. You can remind him that God also forgives him, but what if the person he most needs forgiveness from is Pete? What if Pete might benefit from face-to-face forgiveness of this man, as well?

The thought is obnoxious in its persistence. It is loud, boisterous, distracting, like a pesky neighbor that continues to knock at your door, despite your best efforts to pretend you are not home.

It is a risky proposition. It could backfire. Badly.

But . . . you know the character of Peter DeSoto and you know that he is not a vengeful man. There are many other men you wouldn't dare share this with, as they might do something drastic and stupid in response. But Pete is not that man, so you begin by telling someone at ENLACE. Just one person you tell. And that person tells someone who tells someone who tells Pete.

Pete's response is that he wants to meet the gunman face-to-face. He books a ticket to El Salvador, and before you know what is happening, you find yourself on a caravan—with Pete and Dara and an

American girl who is writing a book about Pete getting shot, and her husband who is taking photos of the experience—and the whole lot of you are heading, unannounced, toward the gunman's home.

Los Abelines, November 2015

Rose colored dust stirred up into a cloud as the tires of two large pickup trucks pulled into the driveway of an adobe compound. At least a dozen children lived in this compound and were playing barefoot in the dust. Their tiny feet came to a stop and they watched with curiosity as a pastor they recognized emerged from one of the pickup trucks, followed by a group of gringos, several other strangers, and Isidro.

The children recognized Isidro, as he worked for ENLACE and was often visiting Los Abelines. Isidro made his way toward the front door of one of the adobe houses. The outside walls were peeling and the exterior color matched that of the rose/orange dust. An awning made of corrugated metal hung from the front of the home, and underneath the awning was a collection of makeshift seats. An old wooden bench, a plastic patio chair, a rusty bucket overturned.

Isidro greeted the children who stepped back shyly, their bright t-shirts juxtaposed against the clay facade.

A young man, the father of three of these children, emerged from inside. He wore a striped green polo shirt and camouflage pants. His hair was cut short and the faint traces of a mustache decorated his upper lip. He took a seat on top of the rusty bucket, and urged Pete and Isidro to sit with him. Pete sat in the plastic chair, Isidro took the bench, and everyone else stood around. Watching from the sidelines in awkward silence.

The pastor who had brought them all there looked to the ground and made a stealth-like exit to the other side of the compound. Giving Pete and the young man, the alleged gunman, space to talk. The gunman, however, had no clue what was going on or who any of these people were. This was an average Monday in November, and no one had told him there would be visitors.

The gunman's wife stepped into the doorway and surveyed the group of strangers in her front yard. Her dark hair was pulled back into a messy ponytail at the nape of her neck. Her youngest son was propped up on her hip. A naked baby, save for the diaper wrapped around his bottom.

The conversation was bland at first. Introductions. Small talk. Isidro made vague references to Pete and all the fond memories he had of working in Abelines.

Finally, Isidro addressed the man in the striped green shirt and asked, "Can we talk about the accident that happened here eight years ago?"

"The accident?" he asked.

"Yes," Isidro pressed. "When the gringo from *El Norte* was shot."

The man's left foot began to jiggle. He unclasped his hands which had been laying in his lap and began fidgeting with his fingers.

"I've heard a lot about it," he said, "but I wasn't in Abelines the day it happened."

The man's wife took a step backward and disappeared through the dark doorway into her home.

A skinny black dog walked over to the man and nudged a wet nose along his knee. The man ignored the dog.

"So you know nothing about it?" Isidro asked.

"I know that people came to my house several days after the shooting and accused me of doing it," the man said. "But it couldn't have been me. Where would I have gotten a weapon like that?"

The man's eyes darted back and forth. His foot continued to jiggle at a rapid pace.

Pete leaned forward to console him."Look, we're not here to harm you or wish you any ill will."

The man glanced in Pete's direction, perhaps registering the sound of his voice. Perhaps, feeling as though he were speaking to a ghost. With a faint scar across his neck and a hoarse whisper.

The man's dark eyes flitted from Pete to the other side of the yard. He began to clasp and unclasp his hands.

The skinny black dog reappeared. This time carrying an empty chips wrapper in his mouth. The dog cocked his head, looked up at Pete, and then walked away.

The man continued with his alibi. He talked about his car. His car had been parked really far from the scene of the crime, and so it couldn't have been him. He wasn't in Abelines that day and he has people to testify that it's true. And besides, why would he have wanted to harm an entire car full of strangers?

Isidro let the man speak until it was clear he was finished.

"Would it be alright if we all pray together?" Isidro asked.

The man nodded.

His wife stepped out of the house and motioned for all four of their children to join them. The children had stopped listening to these adult conversations long ago and continued scampering around the yard in bare feet. They came forward when called by their mother. Isidro motioned everyone into a big circle underneath the metal awning. Pete and Dara stood on one side of Isidro, and the alleged gunman stood on the other side with his wife and kids.

They bowed their heads, placed light arms around each others' shoulders, and Isidro said a beautiful prayer of forgiveness. He praised God for His glory and said that there were no hard feelings or bad intentions toward anyone who was involved with the shooting, either directly or indirectly.

At the end of the prayer, the man's eyes were red with tears.

Pete shook his hand. Then he, Dara, and the rest of the gringos climbed back into the pickup truck. Ready for the long, bumpy journey out of Abelines.

In 2012, El Salvador's rival gangs, MS-13 and Barrio 18, signed a historic truce. The country's murder rates dropped by nearly forty percent and politicians viewed it as a massive success. But after 18 months, the situation started to disintegrate. The truce had been developed and overseen by imprisoned gang lords, who over time, had less control over their factions from behind bars. And their factions were having difficulty maintaining peace on the streets.

By 2014, violence was once again rampant and the truce was considered null and void. In desperation, the Salvadoran government tried to crack down even harder. They placed gang members back into maximum security prisons. The gangs responded by retaliating against the police and security guards. By 2015, the gangs and the Salvadoran police force were in a full fledged war with one another.

The gangs were determined to assert their control, resulting in a whopping seventy percent murder increase from the year before. In 2015, there were 104 homicides per 100,000 people, which led national publications from *Newsweek* to the *Washington Post* to label El Salvador the "Homicide Capital of the World."

Salvadorans began fleeing their country in record numbers. In the span of only two months, a reported 10,500 children were found crossing the Mexico-US border—without their parents—in the fall of 2015. The vast majority of these kids were from El Salvador, Guatemala, and Honduras.

The parents themselves had been leaving for decades. Many migrated illegally into the United States in order to make money and send it back to support their children. These payments are called remittances. A 2016 study by the Inter-American Development Bank found that 1 out of every 5 Salvadorans received remittances from family members living abroad. For many, these remittances helped fund their basic survival needs, like food, rent, and clothing. In 2015, remittance payments totaled over $3.5 million, making the Salvadoran economy increasingly dependent upon them.

In the wake of pandemic violence, suffering economy, and mass emigration, hope for the country of El Salvador seems elusive, at best. Hope, for a country whose name means "The Savior" and bears a direct reference to Jesus Christ.

According to AJ Sherrill, pastor of Mars Hill Bible Church, the key to finding hope in the most desolate situations is in learning how to distinguish it from sentimental optimism.

In a sermon titled "Becoming Human: Isaiah 11:1-10," Sherrill stated:

"Hope has a capacity for tension and unresolved longings, while optimism needs and feeds off immediacy." He defined optimism as a "disempowered longing" because it relies only on the self and nothing more. Hope, Sherrill explained, is an empowered longing because it rests not on the will, but on the power of the Holy Spirit.

"This doesn't always make hoping easier," Sherrill continued, "but it does mean that our hope is grounded in a greater story than the self. A greater story than the present moment. This is why narrative theology is so important. It gives us a greater story to sink into when all of life seems to collapse and fade around us."

To explore this concept further, we turn once again to Pete. And his journal. After traveling to El Salvador in January of 2017—exactly ten years after he was shot—Pete wrote this:

> *What if hope lies not in curbing gang violence once and for all, but in the fact that there are men like Pastor Victorio who, instead of leaving El Salvador, are choosing to stay? Victorio and his nineteen kids, who are now the next generation fighting the good fight on their own, but with the example of their father who has shown them it can be done.*
>
> *It lies in men like Pastor Pablo Fernandez, Marlena's father, who could be living anywhere at this point. After being kidnapped by the death squad, he was granted asylum in Canada and could have easily stayed. Instead, he chose to go back to El Salvador and fight for peace in the country he loved so much. And through that choice, seeds of hope are sprouting up as he rehabilitates MS-13 gang members.*
>
> *Granted, not everyone can be pastors and not everyone can start nonprofits. Nor do they need to. That's not even the point. People like Pablo's daughter, Marlena Fernandez, are making just as much of an impact simply by raising their kids there and choosing to make El Salvador home. Violence may be happening all around Marlena, but she continues to stay. Whether it's surrender, or it's survival, these are examples of people who get up and live one day at a time. They remain in a situation where there really isn't a perceivable resolution and they demonstrate that they are the hope.*
>
> *In my own journey of trying to understand how to approach poverty and nonprofit work, I've found that there's this good, but almost dangerous pursuit of identifying the ultimate answer. Let's fix*

poverty! Let's find the number one solution! *But what if there is no ultimate answer? There may or may not ever be a solution for the gang issue. It is getting worse every day, but it is also getting better. It's a strange dynamic of both realities happening simultaneously. And that's hard to stomach. But that is life. That is the kingdom narrative in a nutshell.*

So what do we do? How do we deal with this dynamic?

We get up, we draw a circle around our lives, and we identify all the things we can control and the things we can't. We work on what we have control of and everything we don't, we give back to God. Trusting Him with the outcome.

In nonprofit work, this doesn't take you off the hook from making sure that certain strategies you implement are actually working, but you can take the monkey off your shoulders and finally say, "I can't fix poverty. There is so much out of my control." But, if I'm Marlena, or Victorio, or Pablo, I can raise my family and love the people in my life one day at a time. And that alone is pretty powerful.

The story of Jesus really starts making sense when you see that He didn't go after the external stuff, He went after the internal stuff. Because He knew that if people change from the inside, outer change will follow all around them. If people change in their hearts, love and justice will become a byproduct.

One, final example can be found precisely where we began this narrative. In the village of Los Abelines.

The same day Pete went to meet the alleged gunman in November 2015, he also went to visit his old friend, Pastor Victorio Paz. Victorio was quite busy that afternoon. Preparing for an inter-church assembly to take place in his front yard.

Row upon row of plastic chairs were being set up to face the front of his house. A house that nowadays had electricity and running water. Outside Victorio's front door, stood a microphone, a keyboard, and dual speakers to project the sermon and the worship music into the crowd of people who were arriving by the truckload and filling the plastic chairs.

Pete watched in amazement as one truck after the next slowly rolled in. The bed of each truck was crammed with over a dozen people, huddled together, grabbing onto each other and onto the raised grip bars that created a barrier around the entire truck bed. Their bodies moved together in a wave of colorful t-shirts as the truck bounced over each rock in the dusty road. When the truck stopped, they all jumped out and took their seats. The women on one side and the men on the other. Abelines was a traditional, conservative community where all the women and girls wore skirts. Some women even wore lace veils on their heads, as was customary in their faith denomination.

When ENLACE first started working in Abelines, they worked only with Pastor Victorio's church. In 2015, they were working with a dozen different churches, most all of whom were gathering in Victorio's front yard to worship and to celebrate. These churches had spent the last decade collaborating. Making tiny strides toward rebuilding their communities through planting gardens, building medical clinics, repairing roads and bridges after massive rainstorms.

As AJ Sherrill stated in his 2016 Advent sermon:

> This is the time for the church to contend for the image of God in ALL people. This is the time for the church to stand for the voiceless, the poor, the marginalized, the refugee. If there has ever been a time for the need of the church—which much of society has relegated as obsolete—it is now.
>
> A church who listens well. A church who loves radically. A church who gives generously. A church who hopes courageously. A church who sees spiritually and welcomes and provides a resting place for the least and the lost and the left outs of the world. And when we do that, we begin to rehearse a kind of future that we believe all of history is headed toward. This is our narrative theology. This is the vision of hope . . . and it carries a potential power that can bring peace to the entire land. But here's the thing: Optimism and sentimentalism are not going to get it done. It's going to have to be grounded in the Holy Spirit.

As Pete had many times over the years, he recalled his first visit to Abelines in 2003. He remembered the scorpion crawling across the floor of the leaking church. The children with swollen bellies, whose parents were so filled with shame they could not look him in the eye.

Pete surveyed Victorio's front yard twelve years later and what he saw were people with their heads held high. Yes, many still only had a third grade education. Their main form of work was agriculture, and there was still much work to be done. But they were smiling. They were carrying hope in their hearts. And that hope made all of the difference.

ACKNOWLEDGMENTS

Pete and Dara DeSoto:

Special thanks to our parents, John and Lucia DeSoto, and Daniel and Debbie Aicklen. We have no doubt improved your prayer lives with our adventures and have always felt your love and covering. Thanks to our four children, PJ, Isaac, Hannah, and Kaya, for never loosing the spark in your eyes or the skip in your step. This is your story as much as it is ours.

Thank you Christy and Paul from the deepest parts of our hearts. Thank you for walking this journey with us and documenting a season of our lives with integrity, honor and grace. We love you both. And Jesus . . . Thank you for pursuing our hearts ever since the dawn of time. You provide peace and hope when we walk through valleys that are darker than we can imagine.

Thanks to Jaime and Rebecca Huff for being in our corner since the halls of Vanguard University. Thanks to my (Pete's) brother Matthew, sister-in-law Karen, and nephews AJ, Samuel, and Lucas for covering us in prayer and venturing out on your own journeys with Jesus. Thanks to Mike Goldstone for always pointing me (Pete) to the feet and arms of our Savior. To Mira Mesa First Assembly, you taught me (Pete) what church should feel like: home.

Thank you Cindi Sue for teaching me (Dara) what grace looks like and what love feels like. Thank you Ron Bueno for following your heart and calling for the "crazy pastors" of El Salvador. Mike and Brittany Peterson, thank you for sharing and building the dream with us in Punta Mango. Thank you Matt Forrey for your help with the video that promoted our book in its infancy. Thank you Kent and Lisa Davis for your generosity. Thanks to every one of you that gave to the Kickstarter campaign. We are deeply blessed by each person that has been a part of this story.

Christy Krumm Richard:

Whenever I pick up a new book, I read the acknowledgments page first. I love the tiny window it reveals into the mysterious process of bringing any book to life. Unlike a theater production where it obviously requires a whole cast and crew to orchestrate, a book appears from the outside to be a solitary venture. And in many ways it is. But ultimately, writing a book also takes a village.

My village includes the following people: My husband Paul, who not only proofread the entire manuscript and traveled alongside me to El Salvador, but also listened and walked with me for two whole years of learning what it actually meant to be writer. Your friendship, patience (and Stephen King-like adherence to deleting adverbs) has meant the entire world.

To my parents, Conrad and Leslie Krumm, thanks for supporting every last one of my hair brained schemes. Whether it's teaching in France, moving to New York, or making a risky career change so that I could write a book, you guys have always been my biggest fans. Thank you, from the bottom of my heart.

Kate Watson, you have championed this book from the beginning and I couldn't have asked for a better editor, friend and storytelling midwife. This book is no doubt better because of you. Claire Bidwell Smith, I will always be grateful for your awesome feedback and insight into the publishing industry and the whole book proposal process. And of course, Jenna Birch! From our time as newbie freelancers at YourTango until now — thanks for every email and ounce of encouragement along the way.

Thanks to the crew at Epiphany Space for hosting the best Write-A-Thons ever. Where else can an LA writer find creative community, brainstorming sessions, and grilled cheese sandwiches that magically appear at lunch time?

Special thanks to Claire Townsend for opening up your Brooklyn studio apartment so that I could work on this book for an entire month. That time and space was the biggest blessing — and a dream come true. Thanks to my fifth grade teacher, Mr. Young, who was the first person to tell me that my writing would one day be published. I've always held onto that. And you were right.

Thank you to my brother, Brian C. Krümm, for designing the beautiful map of El Salvador at the beginning of this book. Thanks again to Matt Forrey for filming a fantastic book trailer—the crowning jewel of our Kickstarter campaign. Thanks to Kent and Lisa Davis for your incredible generosity. And thank you to Every. Single. One. of our Kickstarter donors. We truly could not have done this without you.

Thanks to Renee Rojas for translating a pivotal moment in the story from Spanish to English. Thank you to all the friends, family, and coworkers of the DeSoto's for allowing me to interview you and welcoming me into your lives. Speaking of which, Pete and Dara DeSoto, it has been the biggest honor. Thank you for trusting me with your story. Thank you for your friendship and honesty and bravery throughout this entire journey.

And to Jesus, the ultimate storyteller. What can I do except give thanks? You carried me through every rough spot. You strengthened me, encouraged me, and showed me your love. This book is for you.

NOTES

This book was crafted from loads of research and interviews conducted over the course of two years. I began interviewing Pete and Dara DeSoto in April 2015. They also gave me access to their personal journals and blogs. In November 2015, we took a research trip to El Salvador made possible through our Kickstarter funding.

In El Salvador, I got to meet and interview the following people and I am so thankful to each and every one of them: Frederick (Fritz) McGough, Absalon Rivas, Walter and Carla Bolanos, Lidia Castro, Pastor Miguel Durán, Pastor Victorio Paz, Mike and Brittney Peterson, and Paco Gonzalez.

Over the next year and a half, I was thrilled to get to speak with the following people as research for the story: Ron Bueno, David and Jenny McGee, Miguel Tomas Castro, Scott Anderson, Sarah Cramer, Brian Howard, John and Lucia DeSoto, Dan and Debbie Aiklen, Cindi Lombardo, PJ DeSoto, Isaac DeSoto, and Lori Margaret,whose first-hand account of the shooting was indispensable.

Psalm 64 & Psalm 116: A Mashup

These are the verses used from each Psalm, listed in the order they are presented on the page: Psalm 64:4, 64:6, 116:1, 116:10, 116:5, 64:9 (*New Living Translation*)

INTRODUCTION

Amy Poehler, *Yes Please* (New York: Dey St., 2014).

PART ONE: SURRENDER

Chapter 1: The Road to Abelines

For a basic overview of El Salvador's history, I consulted: "El Salvador: History," *Lonely Planet,* accessed May 8, 2017, www.lonelyplanet.com/el-salvador/history.

Mark Danner's epic article originally published in *The New Yorker*, but currently shown in full on his personal website, was also insanely helpful in learning about the Morazán region: Mark Danner, "The Truth of El Mozote," *The New Yorker*. December 6, 1993, www.markdanner.com/articles/the-truth-of-el-mozote.

Lastly, I learned about Radio Venceramos and the impact it had on the Salvadoran people through this film: *Innocent Voices (Voces Inocentes)*, directed by Luis Mandoki (2004; Los Angeles: Lawrence Bender Productions, 2008), DVD.

Chapter 2: Earthquakes

The nickname "El Valle de las Hamacas" was first told to me in an interview with Lori Margaret, and it was verified here: *Encyclopaedia Britannica,* "San Salvador," www.britannica.com/place/San-Salvador.

I was able to learn more about the Pipil by reading this novel: Sandra Benitez, *Bitter Grounds* (New York: Hyperion, 1997).

I learned facts and statistics about El Salvador's geological structure and the 2001 earthquakes from these two sources: "Another Deadly Quake Strikes El Salvador," *CNN,* February 13, 2001, http://edition.cnn.com/2001/fyi/news/02/13/salvador.quake/index.ht ml;Julian Bommer and Belén Benito, et al, "El Salvador Earthquakes of January and February 2001: Context, Characteristics, and Implications for Seismic Risk," *Laboratoire de Géologie de l'Ecole Normale Supérieure,* November 20, 2001, www.geologie.ens.fr/~madariag/Papers/El%20Salvador%20Earthquake s.PDF.

Chapter 3: College Sweethearts

John 13:7 (*New International Version).*

Chapter 4: Meet the Lombardos

"About Casa de Fruta," *CASA de FRUTA,* accessed May 8, 2017, www.casadefruta.com/about/index.php.

Chapter 6: La Matanza (The Massacre)

Much of this chapter was based on Mark Danner's article in *The New Yorker* (See Chapter 1 notes).

For further information, I consulted: "The Cold War Timeline," *History on the Net*, accessed May 8, 2017, www.historyonthenet.com/the-cold-war-timeline-2/; Shayda Sabet, "US Foreign Policy in Latin America: An Ideological Perspective," *E-International Relations Students*, accessed May 8, 2017, www.e-ir.info/2013/06/14/us-foreign-policy-in-latin-america/.

Ronald Reagan. Ronald Reagan, "Address to the Nation on United States Policy in Central America," *Reagan Library*, May 9, 1984, accessed May 8, 2017, https://reaganlibrary.archives.gov/archives/speeches/1984/50984h.htm

Chapter 7: The Car Accident

Matt Redman, "Blessed Be Your Name," *Where Angels Fear to Tread* (East Sussex, UK: Survivor Records, 2002).

Luke 18:22, paraphrased (*New International Version*).

PART TWO: RISK

Chapter 8: Culture Shock

For facts and further information on the numerous natural disasters El Salvador experienced in 2005, I found several news reports:

Hurricane Adrian. NBC News, "Storm Floods, Slides Feared in Central America: Adrian Downgraded, But Region Still Getting Heavy Rain," May 20, 2005, www.nbcnews.com/id/7896963/ns/weather-weather_news/t/storm-floods-slides-feared-central-america/#.WQuNoNIrLIU.

Santa Ana volcano erruption. NASA Earth Observatory, "Eruption of Santa Ana (llamatepec) Volcano," October 2, 2005, https://earthobservatory.nasa.gov/NaturalHazards/view.php?id=15654.

Hurricane Stan. Centro de Intercambio y Solidaridad,"Analysis of Tropical Storm Stan in El Salvador," *ReliefWeb*, November 16, 2005, accessed May 8, 2017, http://reliefweb.int/report/el-salvador/analysis-tropical-storm-stan-el-salvador.

Chapter 9: Innocent Voices

In addition to watching the film *Innocent Voices (Voces Inocentes)* [see Chapter 1 notes], I consulted World Bank's in-depth study on child soldiers in El Salvador:Beth Verhey, "The Demobilization and Reintegration of Child Soldiers: El Salvador Case Study," World Bank, 2001, http://siteresources.worldbank.org/INTCPR/882274-1111741856717/20626759/elsalvadorcasefinalwannex.pdf.

James LeMoyne, "Salvadorans Stream Into U.S., Fleeing Poverty and Civil War," *New York Times,* April 13, 1987, www.nytimes.com/1987/04/13/world/salvadorans-stream-into-us-fleeing-poverty-and-civil-war.html?pagewanted=all.

To research El Salvador's gangs, I consulted the following sources:

Barrio 18. Sophie Pinchetti, "Tattooed Terror: El Salvador's Mara 18 Gang," *The Other: Home of Subcultures & Style Documentary,* May 2014, www.the-other.info/2014/street-gangs-el-salvador-mara-18.; **MS-13.** "MS13," *InSight Crime,* last modified March 9, 2017, www.insightcrime.org/el-salvador-organized-crime-news/mara-salvatrucha-ms-13-profile;

Geoffrey Ramsey, "Tracing the Roots of El Salvador's Mara Salvatrucha," *InSight Crime,* August 31, 2012, www.insightcrime.org/news-analysis/history-mara-salvatrucha-el-salvador.

Reginald Denny. Madison Gray, "The LA Riots: 15 Years After Rodney King, Key Figures: Reginald Denny," *TIME,* April 2007, http://content.time.com/time/specials/2007/la_riot/article/0,28804,16 14117_1614084_1614511,00.html.

Chapter 10: Spanish Lessons

Liberation Theology. "Latin American Bishop's Conference Medellín (1968)," *Liberation Theology in Nicaragua,* accessed May 8, 2017, https://liberationtheology.voices.wooster.edu/documents/document-3/.

Oscar Romero. Scott Wright, *Oscar Romero and the Communion of the Saints* (New York: Orbis Books, 2012).

Death Squads. David Kirsch, "Death Squads in El Salvador: A Pattern of U.S. Complicity," *Covert Action Quarterly,* Summer (1990), www.whale.to/b/kirsch.html.

Children were displaced. Sergio Arauz, "El Faro: The Network That Exported El Salvador's Children of War," *Unfinished Sentences,* October 28, 2014, https://unfinishedsentences.org/the-network-that-exported-el-salvadors-children-of-war/.

PART THREE: TRAUMA

Chapter 11: Is Something Wrong With Us?

Mosquito. "Aedes aegypti," *Dengue Virus Net,* accessed May 8,2017, www.denguevirusnet.com/aedes-aegypti.html.

Dengue. Mike Paddock, "Dengue Fever: Symptoms, Treatments, and Prevention," *Medical News Today,* September 25, 2015, www.medicalnewstoday.com/articles/179471.php.

Chapter 12: The Shooting

After interviewing Absalon Rivas and discovering that he was listening to Dream Theater when Pete was shot, I researched the band in the following places: *Guitar World Magazine,* "100 Greatest Guitar Albums of All Time," Future US, Inc., October 2006, updated July 31, 2006, www.progarchives.com/forum/forum_posts.asp?TID=26724; "Metropolis Pt. 2, Scenes From a Memory," *The Metal Archives* (blog), updated October 8, 2016, www.metal-ar-chives.com/reviews/Dream_Theater/Metropolis_Pt._2%3A_Scenes_from_a_Memory/1374/.

Psalm 52:8 (*New King James Version*)

John MacArthur, footnote in *The MacArthur Study Bible* (Nashville: Thomas Nelson, 1997), 790.

Chapter 13: Ciudad Barrios

Ronald Reagan. (See Chapter 6 notes.)

After interviewing Carla Bolanos, I did further research on the Walton International Scholarship program: "Creating a Visionary Opportunity," Walton International Scholarship Program, accessed May 8, 2017, www.wispweb.org/about.html; Associated Press, "The Forbes 400: Walton Tops List of Wealthiest Americans," *Los Angeles Times,* October 15, 1985, http://articles.latimes.com/1985-10-15/business/fi-16339_1_billionaires.

BBC News. Henry Mance, "Gangs Rule in El Salvador Jails," *BBC News,* July 12, 2009, http://news.bbc.co.uk/2/hi/americas/8119089.stm.

As usual, *InSight Crime* was a tremendous help in learning about the culture and history of MS-13, especially their experience inside the Ciudad Barrios prison. This article comprised the majority of my research: Roberto Valencia, "How El Salvador Handed Its Prisons to the Mara Street Gangs," *InSight Crime,* September 3, 2014, www.insightcrime.org/news-analysis/how-el-salvador-handed-its-prisons-to-the-gangs.

The tale of Colonel Monterrosa was written from the following sources: Danner, "El Mozote" (see Chapter 1 notes); John W Lamperti, "The Trojan Horse," Dartmouth Math Home, accessed May 8, 2017, https://math.dartmouth.edu/~lamperti/Trojan_Horse.html.

Chapter 14: Diagnóstico

5.4 magnitude earthquake. Associated Press, "Moderate Earthquake Strikes El Salvador," *Washington Post,* January 18, 2007, www.washingtonpost.com/wp-dyn/content/article/2007/01/18/AR2007011802238.html.

Chapter 15: Who Did This?

All quotes and paraphrases in this chapter are from: Joan Didion, *Salvador* (New York: Simon & Schuster, 1983).

Chapter 16: Home From the Hospital

All lyrics in this chapter are from: Pearl Jam, "Alive," *Ten* (Seattle, WA: Rick Parashar, 1991).

PART FOUR: SURRENDER

Chapter 17: Project Milagro

Brené Brown, *Daring Greatly: How the Courage to Be Vulnerable Transforms the Way We Live* (New York: Avery, 2012).

Significant dates and details for this chapter were obtained from the following source: "Project Milagro Retrospective 2004-2010," *Project Milagro: Bringing Hope & Fresh Water to 10,000 People*, accessed May 8, 2017, www.projectmilagro.com/project-milagro-retrospective-2004-2010/.

Chapter 18: Gethsemane

Thousand Steps Beach. "Beaches - Thousand Steps Beach," *Discover Laguna*, accessed May 8, 2017, www.discoverlaguna.com/beaches/1000steps.htm.

John Wayne Beach House. "5-Night Stay in John Wayne's Former Laguna Beach Cottage, Owned By Award-Winning IMAX Filmmaker, Greg MacGillivray," *Charity Buzz,* accessed May 8, 2017, www.charitybuzz.com/catalog_items/5-night-stay-in-john-waynes-former-laguna-beach-cottage-365813.

A Thief in the Night, directed by Donald W. Thompson (1973; Des Moines: Mark IV Pictures Incorporated, 2004), DVD.

Matt. 26:39 *(New Living Translation)*.

Matt. 26:41 *(New International Version)*.

Luke 22:42 *(New International Version)*.

For further research on the meaning of Jesus' prayer in the Garden of Gethsemane, I consulted: Tim Haile, "Did Jesus *Desire* to Escape the Cross?" *Bible Banner*, accessed May 8, 2017, www.biblebanner.com/ga_art/cuppass.htm.

Matt. 16:23 *(New International Version)*.

I John 4:8; 4:16 *(New International Version)*.

Chapter 19: Antigua

Chicken Bus. Kaushik, "Chicken Buses of Guatemala," *Amusing Planet*, October 14, 2012, www.amusingplanet.com/2012/10/chicken-buses-of-guatemala.html.

Alphy's Soda Pop Club. Jennifer Juniper Stratford, "He, Himself, and He," *Vice*, May 11, 2012, www.vice.com/en_us/article/him-himself-and-he-0000193-v19n4.

Corey Feldman, *Coreyography: A Memoir* (New York: St. Martin's Press, 2013).

Chapter 20: Punta Mango

Surfing Punta Mango. "The Wave at Punta Mango," *Rancho Mango*, accessed May 8, 2017, www.ranchomango.com/punta-mango.html.

$50 boat ride. "Surfing Boat Trips El Salvador," *La Tortuga Verde*, accessed May 8, 2017, http://latortugaverde.com/surfing-boat-trips-el-salvador/.

Bacon-A-Fair. Nancy Luna and Jaryd Lucero, "OC Fair: Big, Bacon-Wrapped Foods on Tap," *The Orange County Register*, July 13, 2012, www.ocregister.com/2012/07/13/oc-fair-big-bacon-wrapped-foods-on-tap/.

Chapter 21: Saying Goodbye

"Hate Cancer, Love the Cure." Kristi McCann, "Legacies of Love From Jenny McGee," *Como Living*, January 30, 2014, http://comolivingmag.com/2014/01/30/legacies-of-love/.

Junior Olympic National Water Polo Championship. Hannah DeSoto, "Kids on Sports: Water Polo Brothers Bring DeSoto Family Pride," *Sun Newspapers*, August 9, 2012, www.sunnews.org/sports/kids-on-sports-water-polo-brothers-bring-desoto-family-pride/.

Beach house/missionary retreat. "Welcome," *Villa Punta Mango*, accessed May 8, 2017, www.villapuntamango.com/#villaintro.

Chapter 22: "The Savior"

This last chapter came together as I consulted many news articles regarding the gang truce and gang violence in El Salvador. Here are the three main sources I used: Keegan Hamilton and Alan Hernandez, "El Salvador's Gangs offered a Truce — And the Government Declared War," *Vice News*, March 31, 2016, https://news.vice.com/article/el-salvador-gangs-offered-a-truce-the-government-declared-war.; Alberto Arce, "El Salvador Throws Out Gang Truce and Officials Who Put It in Place," *New York Times*, November 16, 2016, www.nytimes.com/2016/05/21/world/americas/el-salvador-throws-out-gang-truce-and-officials-who-put-it-in-place.html?_r=0; Joshua Partlow, "Why El Salvador Became the Hemisphere's Murder Capital," *Washington Post*, January 5, 2016, www.washingtonpost.com/news/worldviews/wp/2016/01/05/why-el-salvador-became-the-hemispheres-murder-capital/?utm_term=.344e6ad6ce91.

Children crossing US-Mexico border. Jerry Markon and Joshua Partlow, "Unaccompanied Children Crossing Border in Greater Numbers Again, Raising Fears of New Migrant Crisis," *Washington Post*, December 16, 2015, www.washingtonpost.com/news/federal-eye/wp/2015/12/16/unaccompanied-children-crossing-southern-border-in-greater-numbers-again-raising-fears-of-new-migrant-crisis/?utm_term=.2d03a2b0e875.

Remittances. Lukas Keller and Rebecca Rouse, "Remittance Recipients in El Salvador: A Socioeconomic Profile," *Inter-American Development Bank*, September 2016, https://publications.iadb.org/bitstream/handle/11319/7868/Remittance-Recipients-in-El-Salvador-A-Socioeconomic-Profile.pdf?sequence=4.

All quotes and paraphrases in this chapter are from this sermon: AJ Sherrill, *Becoming Human: Isaiah 11:1-10,* podcast audio, Mars Hill Bible Church.https://marshill.org/shop/becoming-human-isaiah-111-10-aj-sherrill/.

ABOUT THE AUTHOR

Christy Krumm Richard is a writer, dreamer, teacher, and storyteller. She has a master's degree in American Literature from California State University, Long Beach. Her work has appeared in *RELEVANT*, *Woman's Day*, *Los Angeles Magazine*, and various other online publications. Christy lives with her husband in Long Beach, California where she can be found biking through the streets and frequenting local coffee shops. This is her first book.